RENNEWART IN
WOLFRAM'S 'WILLEHALM'

ANGLICA GERMANICA SERIES 2

Editors: LEONARD FORSTER, E. L. STAHL *and* A. T. HATTO

RENNEWART IN WOLFRAM'S 'WILLEHALM'

A STUDY OF WOLFRAM VON ESCHENBACH AND HIS SOURCES

CARL LOFMARK

*Head of the Department of German,
St David's College, Lampeter*

CAMBRIDGE

AT THE UNIVERSITY PRESS

1972

Published by the Syndics of the Cambridge University Press
Bentley House, 200 Euston Road, London NW1 2DB
American Branch: 32 East 57th Street, New York, N.Y.10022

© Cambridge University Press 1972

Library of Congress Catalogue Card Number: 70–179161

ISBN: 0 521 08444 X

Printed in Great Britain
at the University Printing House, Cambridge
(Brooke Crutchley, University Printer)

CONTENTS

v

CONTENTS

PREFACE

I owe a great debt of gratitude to Professor A. T. Hatto, who has always taken a lively interest in this study and read the typescript as it was produced. His comments have helped me considerably and many of his suggestions have been adopted without special acknowledgment. In many cases, however, I have gone my own way, and Professor Hatto cannot to any extent be held responsible for opinions or errors found in this book.

Much of this work is based on an M.A. thesis entitled 'The Rennewart Action in Wolfram's *Willehalm*', which I submitted to the University of London in 1964. Naturally I owe a great deal to the supervisor of that thesis, Professor Frederick Norman.

I am grateful to my wife for helping in many ways, and particularly for her advice on historical problems in chapter 1. I also wish to thank the trustees of the Pantyfedwen Fund of St David's College, Lampeter, for a grant towards publication costs.

C. L.

ABBREVIATIONS

AfdA	Anzeiger für deutsches Altertum
Al.	Aliscans
Archiv	Archiv für das Studium der neueren Sprachen und Literaturen
BBSIA	Bulletin bibliographique de la Société Internationale Arthurienne
B Loq	La Bataille Loquifer
BMZ	G. Benecke, *Mittelhochdeutsches Wörterbuch.* Ausgearbeitet von W. Müller und F. Zarnke, Leipzig 1854–61.
BRABLB	Boletín de la Real Academia de Buenas Letras de Barcelona
Chev Viv	La Chevalerie Vivien
Ch W	La Chançun de Willame
DVJS	Deutsche Vierteljahrsschrift für Literaturwissenschaft und Geistesgeschichte
D Wb	J. and W. Grimm, *Deutsches Wörterbuch,* Leipzig 1854–1961
Enf Viv	Les Enfances Vivien
Euph	Euphorion
GLL	German Life and Letters
GRM	Germanisch-romanische Monatsschrift
JEGP	Journal of English and Germanic Philology
MLN	Modern Language Notes
MLR	Modern Language Review
Mod Phil	Modern Philology
Parz	Parzival
PBB	Beiträge zur Geschichte der deutschen Sprache und Literatur (Tübingen)
PMLA	Publications of the Modern Language Association of America
PSQ	Philologische Studien und Quellen

R	La Chançun de Willame, lines 1981–3554
Rol	Das Rolandslied
SATF	Société des Anciens Textes Français
Stor Nerb	Storie Nerbonesi
Tit	Titurel
Tr	Tristan
W	La Chançun de Willame, lines 1–1980
Wh.	Willehalm
WSB	Österreichische Akademie der Wissenschaften, *Sitzungsberichte*, philosophisch-historische Klasse (Vienna)
ZfdA	Zeitschrift für deutsches Altertum und deutsche Literatur
ZfdP	Zeitschrift für deutsche Philologie
ZfrP	Zeitschrift für romanische Philologie

I · THE ORIGIN OF RENNEWART

It is impossible to do justice to the achievement of a Middle High German narrative poet without first looking at his sources. It is true that any work of art demands to be studied and appreciated for its own sake and not that of its antecedents. But a mediaevalist must consider realistically the known circumstances of mediaeval literature; otherwise he wilfully exposes himself to a completely irrelevant modern subjectivity and his interpretation will tell us more about modern tastes and prejudices than the mediaeval poem. The task of the scholar is not to speculate on what an old poem might possibly 'mean' to us, nor primarily to appreciate and make aesthetic value judgements, but to discover truth and to understand: he must explore and explain the literature of a distant past and describe the intellectual and emotional life which that literature expresses, however foreign it may be to modern taste and experience. The conventions within which the poet worked and his poem took its shape are of the highest consequence. For the mediaeval German narrative poet the most important of these conventions was the derivation of his poem's substance from an authoritative given source, and so a strict comparison of his work with that source offers the most objective and reliable information that is available to us: by studying what the German poet has preserved and where he differs from his source or shifts its emphasis we can gain insight into his own tendencies, his outlook, his intention and his method of working. The German poem cannot be treated as an independent work of art,[1] because it is not independent; its nature and content are to a

---

[1] Critics anxious to treat mediaeval poems as works of art have lately been inclined to regard historical considerations as misleading or irrelevant, to rule out the question of the poet's intention (the 'intentional fallacy'), to ignore information derived from extraneous sources and claim that a great work of art is an internally consistent and self-sufficient organism. Interpretation therefore becomes a detailed description of internal structure. This approach is explained by D. G. Mowatt, 'Studies Towards an Interpretation of the Nibelungenlied', GLL 14 (1961), pp. 257–70; 'Language, Literature and

large extent conditioned by an existing tradition and dependent on the content of a French source, which gave our poet at the very least the outline of the action and a basis for his interpretation of it. This historical study of sources does not preclude treatment of the poem as a particular and unique work of art; it is an essential prerequisite for an interpretation which is based on a study of the poem within its own tradition rather than on such anachronisms as the standards of modern aesthetic theory or literary insights of the Freudian school. German poets very seldom invented new tales; they translated and adapted old ones for a new audience and they accepted the generally recognised limitations imposed on them by their responsibility towards the tale they were telling. That tale was not theirs to alter; only the telling of it was their own. Their work has been compared with that of the portrait painter, who creates his own work of art and yet is bound to express what he sees in a given original.[1] And so, if we wish to understand a poet's art and recognise his personal achievement,

---

Middle High German', *Seminar* 1 (1965), pp. 69–87; H. Sacker, 'The Message of the "Nibelungenlied" and the Business of the Literary Critic', MLR 58 (1963), pp. 225–7. It has been applied to the *Chançun de Willame* by H. S. Robertson, *La Chançun de Willame: A Critical Study*, Chapel Hill 1966. The easy disregard for sources which this method encourages is nowadays common. Its main weaknesses are the assumption that 'greatness' depends on internal consistency (it is strange to choose of all poems the *Nibelungenlied* and the *Chançun de Willame* to demonstrate this) and the notion that great works of art, which 'transcend' their cultural and historical environment, may best be treated as independent of that environment, while we know that they are in fact very largely shaped by their place and function in a tradition and by the trained skill and intentions of the men who made them. Since in the case of mediaeval literature the cultural context is especially dominant and especially unlike that of modern literature, such considerations are particularly relevant for the mediaevalist; when he is able to recognise constraints and conventions which affected the poet's work he is not entitled to ignore them. Some background information is indispensable: even the most modern of critics must use his basic knowledge of the field and his grammar and dictionary cannot be based exclusively on the poem he is reading; but since such knowledge must be used, we may as well take full advantage of all the available information that might illuminate our poem, from whatever source it comes. It is arbitrary to ignore the poem's background and history and to regard the study of literary texts as a mere branch of linguistics (cf. Mowatt, *Seminar* 1, p. 87: 'Literary criticism is part of linguistics, but with the emphasis on the analysis of very complex utterances, whose durability demands an explanation'; cf. p. 84: 'a linguistic question, like all questions of interpretation'). In fact, the uniqueness of a great poem will stand out not when it is treated in isolation but when it is set against the background of the culture to which it belongs.

[1] J. Fourquet, *Erec, Iwein (Bibliothèque de Philologie Germanique*, vol. 5), Paris 1944, p. 22.

we must first know the French tale he was given to adapt and which he acknowledged as the authority that he was obliged to follow.

In his *Parzival* Wolfram has almost certainly contradicted his main source, Chrétien's *Contes del Graal*, and has added new matter of his own invention; nevertheless, he never questions the principle that he is obliged to follow his source closely and his insistence that he has in fact rendered faithfully the authentic version of the tale as told by Kyot shows that he, too, felt bound to accept that principle. In *Willehalm* the source is followed from the beginning to the end and generally spoken of with respect. From the outset we are told truthfully what the source is, that Landgraf Hermann supplied it, and that it is known to the audience (Wh. 3, 8–11; 7, 23–28); if Wolfram were to deviate seriously from his source in *Willehalm* the audience might notice it and the document could be produced, unlike Kyot's tale of Parzival, which was known only to Wolfram and only by hearing.[1] Whereas Wolfram had attacked the true source of *Parzival* (Parz. 827, 1–4), he praises this source with enthusiasm:

> Wh. 4, 30 unsanfte mac genôzen
> diutscher rede decheine
> dirre diech nu meine,
> ir letze und ir beginnen.
> swer werdekeit wil minnen,
> der lat dise âventiure
> in sînem hûs ze fiure:
> diu vert hie mit den gesten.
> Franzoyser die besten
> hânt ir des die volge lân,
> daz süezer rede wart nie getân
> mit wirde und ouch mit wârheit.
> underswanc noch underreit
> gevalschte dise rede nie:
> des jehent si dort, nu hœrt se ouch hie.
> diz mære ist wâr, doch wunderlîch.

In *Willehalm* Wolfram is committed not only by the general principle that every narrative poet must follow his source, as he

---

[1] Parz. 23, 2; 357, 18; 628, 18; 638, 20; 668, 20; 760, 20; 785, 24; 799, 18; 805, 4.

had claimed to do in *Parʒival*, but by his own specification of a written source known to his patron and audience and by his expression of confidence in that source.

The source to which Wolfram is committed is the Old French *Bataille d'Aliscans*, a *chanson de geste* of the late twelfth century, but if we wish to see clearly what Wolfram owes to his sources we must also consider other related *chansons de geste* from which he may have derived material and which may have been known, in outline at least, to his audience. The study of these sources is particularly important in the case of Rennewart, since Wolfram has paid special attention to him and has considerably transformed what he learned about him from the *chansons de geste*. The Renne-wart action creates special difficulties for our understanding of Wolfram's *Willehalm*. Towards the end of the poem Rennewart gains in prominence at Willehalm's expense and Wolfram seems to have difficulty in subordinating the account of Rennewart's career to that of Willehalm's war, which has hitherto been the main action. Rennewart threatens to eclipse Willehalm as the avenger of Vivianz and the hero of the second battle, and his fate arouses so much interest that it becomes impossible for Wolfram to use the moment of triumph after the second battle as a climax and conclusion to the whole work. One important question still remains and demands an answer – what happened to Rennewart? It has been argued that it was the impossibility of fitting Rennewart into the scheme of *Willehalm* that compelled Wolfram to abandon his work when it was almost completed and leave it a fragment.[1] We shall be able to recognise the difficulties which the Rennewart action set before Wolfram and see how he tackled them only when we have traced the history of the Renne-wart action in the *chansons de geste* and tried to establish the true origin and nature of this material.

[1] J. Bumke, *Wolframs Willehalm*, Heidelberg 1959, pp. 53–5.

RAINOUART IN THE EARLY 'CHANSONS DE GESTE'

Wolfram's Rennewart is derived from the Rainouart of the *chansons de geste* of the cycle of Guillaume d'Orange.[1] He plays a large part in Wolfram's immediate source, the *Bataille d'Aliscans* (hereafter referred to as *Aliscans*), and the earliest record of him is in the *Chançun de Willame*, which is the earliest epic of the cycle of Guillaume. Rainouart is never the hero of an epic except in the poems of the *geste Rainouart*, all of which are later than Wolfram's source; in the early *chansons* he is always subordinated to Guillaume and, for all his prominence, he is never more than a contributor to the Guillaume action.

The Guillaume action can be traced back to historical events, though our knowledge of the stages of development from history to epic literature is sketchy. William, Count of Toulouse, was defeated at Villedaigne in 793 by Hishām, son of Abd-al-rahmān I; after this he fought the Saracens continuously, took Barcelona in 803 and founded a monastery at Gellone (804) which he entered as a monk in 806 and where he died in 812 with a reputation for sanctity. After his death the Church remembered him as a saint. In a document of 804 donating land to Gellone he mentions a wife Vuitburgh,[2] who is probably the Guibourc of the epics, and the monasteries of Aniane and Gellone preserve several documents concerning his life.[3] Guillaume is mentioned as a warrior by

---

[1] All the *chansons de geste* belong to one or other of three cycles, the *Geste du Roi* (Charlemagne cycle), the *Geste de Garin de Montglane* (Guillaume cycle) and the *Geste de Doon de Mayence* (cycle of rebel barons). This was recognised already by the *jongleurs*, cf. *Girart de Vienne* (by Bertrand de Bar-sur-Aube, about 1200; ed. F. Yeandle, New York 1930), lines 1448ff, and *Doön de Mayence* (ed. M. Pey, *Les Anciens Poètes de la France*, vol. 2, Paris 1859), p. 1:

> Bien sceivent li plusor, n'en sui pas en doutanche,
> Qu'il n'eut que iii gestes u réaume de Franche:
> Si fu la premeraine de Pepin et de l'ange,
> L'autre apres, de Garin de Monglane la franche,
> Et la tierche si fu de Doön de Maience,
> i chevalier vaillant et de grant sapience.

[2] '...uxores meas Vuitburgh et Cunigunde.' This document is edited by Ch. Revillout, 'Étude historique et littéraire sur l'ouvrage latin intitulé Vie de Saint Guillaume', in *Publications de la Société Archéologique de Montpellier*, 1876.

[3] (i) *Gallia christiana*, vol. vi, col. 730–807.
(ii) *Gallia christiana*, vol. vi, col. 580–601.

Ermoldus Nigellus in his *Carmina in honorem Hludouici Pii*, dated 827, which also refers to popular songs about him.[1] The *Fragment de la Haye* (probably between 980 and 1030) gives an account of him reminiscent of the *chansons de geste* and represents a stage when his legend had been written down in Latin verse.[2] The *Nota Emilianense*,[3] which is certainly earlier than 1075, mentions Guillaume and Bertrand (*Ghigelmo alcorbitanas* and *bertlane*), and the *Diplôme de Saint-Yrieix*,[4] dated 1090, purports to be signed by heroes of the Guillaume *geste*; thus both bear witness to knowledge of Guillaume in the late eleventh century. The *Historia Ecclesiastica* (1131–41) of Ordericus Vitalis mentions a song about Guillaume produced by *jongleurs* (*vulgo canitur de eo a joculatoribus cantilena*).[5] Further information concerning his heroic tradition can be found in the *Vita Sancti Wilhelmi*,[6] but

(iii) *Vita Benedicti, abbatis Anianensis et Indensis, auctore Ardone*, published in *Monumenta Germaniae historica*, Scriptores, vol. xv, p. 192.

(iv) *Chronicon Anianense*, published in *Monumenta Germaniae historica*, Scriptores, vol. i, p. 308.

Cf. also J. Bédier, *Les Légendes Épiques*, Paris 1926, vol. i, pp. 115–17, 124–32.

[1] Published in Migne, *Patrologia Latina*, vol. 105, saec. ix, cols. 569–640. The reference to Guillaume in col. 593.

[2] Published by H. Suchier, *Les Narbonnais*, vol. II, SATF, Paris 1898, pp. 167–92. Cf. C. Samaran, 'Sur la date du Fragment de la Haye', *Romania* 58 (1932), pp. 190–205. The copyist has transcribed Latin hexameters into prose, probably as an exercise. For further information see F. Lot, 'Études sur les légendes épiques françaises', *Romania* 53 (1927), p. 446f; J. Bédier, *La Chanson de Roland Commentée*, Paris 1927, p. 61f; E. R. Curtius, 'Über die altfranzösische Epik', ZfrP 64 (1944), p. 262; M. de Riquer, *Los Cantares de Gesta Franceses*, Madrid 1952, p. 151, and the review by D. McMillan in *Romania* 75 (1954), pp. 255–62; J. Frappier, *Les Chansons de Geste du cycle de Guillaume d'Orange*, vol. 1, Paris 1955, pp. 71–6; P. Aebischer, 'Le Fragment de la Haye', ZfrP 73 (1957), pp. 21–37; W. Buhr, *Studien zur Stellung des Wilhelmsliedes innerhalb der ältesten altfranzösischen Epen*, diss. Hamburg 1963, p. 33.

[3] A brief account of the battle of Roncevaux in bad Latin, discovered at Madrid in 1953. It mentions Guillaume and Bertrand among the twelve peers, who are all nephews of Charlemagne. Edited by Dámaso Alonso, 'La primitiva épica francesca a la luz de una Nota Emilianense', *Revista de Filología Española* 37 (1953), pp. 1–94, also published separately, *Consejo superior de investigaciones científicas, Instituto Miguel de Cervantes*, Madrid 1954. Cf. Frappier, pp. 77–9; P. Le Gentil, *La Chanson de Roland*, Paris 1955, p. 64.

[4] This is a forgery which claims to be a diploma of Charlemagne. The monks who constructed it signed themselves *Guillelmus Curbinasus, Bertrannus validissimus, Otgerus palatinus* and *Rolgerius Cornualtis*. See Lot, p. 466, note 1.

[5] See Bédier, pp. 129–32.

[6] *Vita Sancti Wilhelmi*, origin Gellone, published in *Acta Sanctorum ordinis Sancti Benedicti*, saec. iv, vol. 1, p. 72, and in *Acta Sanctorum Bollandiana*, vol. vi, p. 798. Date about 1125.

this is probably later than our earliest epic, the *Chançun de Willame*. There have been several studies of the history of the Guillaume *geste*, tracing it from the facts of Guillaume's life through the testimonies of all these documents to the heroic poems of the eleventh and twelfth centuries.[1] In all the stages of development which precede the *Chançun de Willame* there is no mention of Rainouart. We cannot therefore say with certainty whether he had originally played too small a part in the matter of Guillaume to be mentioned in these brief clerical accounts of it or whether he was introduced after it had been formed, either as a new invention or after having had a history of his own independent of Guillaume. The only way we can hope to answer these important questions is by looking at the *Chançun de Willame* itself and noting whether the matter relating to Rainouart is an integral part of that poem or whether it shows evidence of an extraneous source and of adaptation to suit a new context.

The *Chançun de Willame*[2] is preserved only in one manuscript (Brit. Mus. Additional 38663), which was discovered in England in 1901. It is by far the oldest poem of the Guillaume cycle. Most Romanists are agreed that it was composed about the beginning of the twelfth century,[3] and Suchier dates the first part of it about 1080.[4] The close similarity to the *Chanson de Roland* in language, style and even motifs, suggests a similar period of composition, and the tradition found in the *Chançun de Willame* is regularly

---

[1] F. Lot, J. Bédier, J. Frappier (see above, p. 6, note 2); L. Clarus, *Herzog Wilhelm von Aquitanien, ein Grosser der Welt, ein Heiliger der Kirche, und ein Held der Sage und Dichtung*, Münster 1865; P. Becker, *Die altfranzösische Wilhelmsage und ihre Beziehung zu Wilhelm dem Heiligen*, Halle a.d.S. 1896, and 'Das Werden der Wilhelm- und Aimerigeste', *Abhandlungen der phil.-hist. Klasse der Sächsischen Akademie der Wissenschaften*, 44, 1, Leipzig 1939.

[2] The text of the manuscript was printed without commentary in 200 copies by the Chiswick Press in 1903. It has since been edited by H. Suchier, *La Chançun de Guillelme*, Halle a.d.S. 1911 (lines 1–1980 only); E. S. Tyler, *La Chançun de Willame*, New York 1919; D. McMillan, *La Chanson de Guillaume*, SATF, 2 vols., Paris 1949–50, and N. V. Iseley, *La Chançun de Willame*, Chapel Hill 1961. All my quotations and line references are from McMillan's edition.

[3] Bédier, p. 346; Lot, p. 453; Becker, p. 24; Buhr, p. 19f; Frappier, pp. 152–6 (who demonstrates that the later datings proposed by S. Hofer and D. McMillan are untenable); cf. P. Meyer, *Romania* 32 (1903), p. 598.

[4] Suchier, *La Chançun de Guillelme*, p. xxx.

older than that of the *Chevalerie Vivien*, *Aliscans* or *Foucon de Candie*.[1] As in the earliest clerical records, Guillaume is still called 'Willame al corb nes', 'Guillaume with the bent nose' (cf. 'alcorbitanas' in the *Nota Emilianense*; 'Curbinasus' in the *Diplôme de Saint-Yrieix*), whereas all the other epics call him 'Guillaume au cort nes', 'Guillaume with the short nose'; at the time when French final stops became silent between consonants the form *al corb nes* could no longer be distinguished phonemically from *al cort nes*, and so the author of *Couronnement de Louis* invented the story of Guillaume's battle against Corsolt to explain why the nose was short (see p. 20, note 4), and it remained short from then on. The *Chançun de Willame* is thus the only epic to have the original form. Its probable date is about 1120. In the *Chançun de Willame* Rainouart is an important figure and he plays the decisive part in the final victory at l'Archamp. Its content may be summarised thus:

The Saracens under Deramed invade France by sea; Tedbalt de Beürges and Vivien, being immediately threatened, prepare for the defence. Tedbalt and his nephew Esturmi, both full of wine, advise against telling Willame of the invasion, lest his intervention rob them of the credit for the valiant deeds which they intend to do in the battle; when they recover sobriety next morning and see the land covered with Saracens they are terrified and when battle is imminent they depart in great haste, leaving Vivien to defend France alone. During their flight Tedbalt insults his liege man Girard, cousin to Vivien, and so Girard knocks him from his horse, takes horse and armour from him, and returns to help Vivien. Outnumbered, Vivien sends Girard to ask for help from Willame and dies in battle. Willame and Girard return with 30,000 men, but all, including Girard, are killed, and Willame returns to Barcelona to fetch 30,000 more men, whom Guibourc has meanwhile collected. The French are defeated once more, but Willame is saved by his little nephew Gui, a child who had persuaded Guibourc to release him from her tutelage so that he could find his way to l'Archamp and help Willame. They kill Deramed and put the rest of the Saracens to flight; thus Willame and Gui alone win the battle where the French armies had failed.

Willame finds Vivien dying and receives his confession. The Saracens take Gui prisoner. Willame, the only surviving Christian, escapes from the Saracens and returns to Orange, where Guibourc admits him after he has proved his identity by freeing some prisoners from the Saracens and showing

[1] Frappier, pp. 150–60.

his nose. Willame goes to Louis and through the intervention of his parents he gets imperial assistance. From the kitchen comes Reneward al tinel, who demonstrates his strength by killing the chief cook and is allowed to join Willame's new army. He runs to Orange, where Guibourc equips him for battle. On his way to the battlefield he meets the cowards, whom Willame has dismissed, and compels them to return. Thanks to Reneward the Christians win the final battle of l'Archamp and the Saracens flee. At the victory feast Reneward is forgotten, so he determines to treat the French as cruelly as he has treated the Saracens; he sends greetings to Guibourc and a challenge to Willame and kills each Frenchman who crosses his path. Willame shows great fear and humility, but only Guibourc's intervention can persuade Reneward to spare Willame and accept wealth, fiefs and a wife. Finally Reneward learns that Guibourc is his sister.

It has been argued, notably by Suchier,[1] that this *Chançun de Willame* is a fairly late fusion (about 1120) of two distinct earlier epics, a *Chançun de Vivien*, source of lines 1–1980, and a *Chançun de Rainouart*, source of lines 1981–3554 (line 1981 is marked in the above synopsis by the beginning of a new paragraph). The problem of the unity of the *Chançun de Willame* is the key to the origin of Rainouart: if Rainouart always belonged to the matter of Guillaume, then we should be able to demonstrate the unity of the *Chançun de Willame*; if, however, the *Chançun de Willame* was put together from two distinct sources, one of which contained all the Rainouart material, then we should expect that Rainouart was once independent of Guillaume's legend.[2]

The unity of the *Chançun de Willame* was defended energetically by Bédier in his sub-chapter *L'enseignement de la Chanson de Guillaume* (pp. 346–57); his argument is that the discovery of the *Chançun de Willame*, which tells roughly the same story as

---

[1] Suchier, 'Vivien', ZfrP 29 (1905), p. 642f, hence his separate edition of lines 1–1980. He also believed that its first part was derived from a lost Vivien epic (*ibid*, pp. 641–82; cf. note 2).

[2] It is possible that the first part of the *Chançun de Willame* is itself composite; the matter of Gui certainly has the appearance of an intrusive accretion which turns a moving tragedy into a comic victory. In the introduction to his edition of lines 1–1980 Suchier himself distinguishes a 'Vivienlied' (lines 1–938) from the remainder, including the intervention of Guillaume and of Gui, which he believes was invented later (*La Chançun de Guillelme*, pp. lvi–lix). This problem, however, does not affect our enquiry into the independence of Rainouart.

Aliscans, proves that the main elements of *Aliscans* had belonged together in one epic poem soon after 1100 and thus discredits the earlier theory that *Aliscans* was a composite work that had grown out of the merging of several distinct heroic legends or lays. This view has more recently been supported and elaborated by Adler[1] with arguments about the mediaeval aesthetic sense. He shows that the mixture of the sublime with the grotesque or comic was acceptable and that comic characters could play their part in serious works (he quotes Thersites in the *Iliad*). In the *Chanson d'Antioche* the Tafurs (see pp. 28ff), who in many ways resemble Rainouart, fight side by side with the French Christian knights, and the first part of the *Chançun de Willame* (i.e. lines 1–1980, hereafter W) includes the comedy of Tedbalt de Beürges and the comic picture of Guillaume sitting astride Gui's tiny horse. There are other examples of the heroic cook in mediaeval litera- ture,[2] which makes Rainouart's origin in the kitchen of Louis less improbable. Particularly important for Adler is the complete religious sense of the epic as a whole: Vivien is a failure, since he breaks his vow; Guillaume is a failure, since he returns to Orange defeated and is therefore not recognised by his wife, who had believed that his *lignage* preferred to die in battle rather than flee from the field; and so 'the proud champion of the proudest *lignage* is finally offered the services of Rainouart, "de la cuisine al rei...un bacheler" (l. 2948).' Guillaume begins as husband to a Saracen convert, in the middle he is confessor to a Christian knight (Vivien), and at the end he is godfather to a Saracen. All this seems to argue meaning and symmetry in the construction of the *Chançun de Willame* as one complete epic poem and to prove that 'la Chanson de Guillaume est en même temps une chanson de Rainouart.'[3]

These arguments are clearly open to objection. The dis-

---

[1] A. Adler, 'Rainouart and the composition of the Chanson de Guillaume', Mod. Phil. 49 (1951–2), pp. 160–71.

[2] Following E. R. Curtius, *Europäische Literatur und Lateinisches Mittelalter*, Bern–Munich 1963⁴, p. 432f, Adler quotes Nabuzardan, Nebuchadnezzar's cook in *L'Ystore Job* (based on Pierre de Blois, 13th century) and a certain Harcheritus (Adler misquotes 'Harcherius') quoted by Ordericus Vitalis about 1140.

[3] Bédier, p. 347; quoted by Adler, p. 160.

covery of the *Chançun de Willame*, upon which Bédier's view is based, certainly proves that Rainouart had served the Guillaume action long before the composition of *Aliscans* and therefore much earlier than some scholars had believed, but it can prove nothing about the formative period earlier than the *Chançun de Willame*. Bédier shows that many of the early *chansons* could not be fully appreciated unless the audience knew the content of other *chansons* of the cycle, which suggests that the main pattern of events which underlies the Guillaume cycle had already become fixed when the early *chansons* were composed; but he does not show, and could not show, that any knowledge of Rainouart was necessary for the full appreciation of W or of any other early *chanson*. The Guillaume action makes better sense without Rainouart than with him. We therefore have no reason to believe that Rainouart had been a part of the matter of Guillaume for long before the *Chançun de Willame*.

Adler's demonstration that the mixture of serious and comic elements in one work was possible falls a long way short of proving the original unity of the *Chançun de Willame*; it merely prevents us from excluding on principle all comic elements from its antecedents. It is in any case doubtful whether his conclusions, based mainly upon clerical Latin evidence taken from Curtius, can be fairly applied to the earliest *chansons de geste*, particularly since the *Roland* and *Gormont et Isembard* do not contain such comic episodes. The *Chanson d'Antioche* (see below, pp. 28ff), which Adler quotes, is not much earlier than the *Chançun de Willame*; we know very well that a character like Rainouart could appear in heroic literature after 1100, for the *Chançun de Willame* itself is proof. To prove its unity of composition we should need to know whether such things were possible in vernacular literature during the centuries before the *Chançun de Willame*, when its narrative substance was being formed, but we know far too little about vernacular heroic literature in those centuries to make judgements about its aesthetic principles. Against Adler's argument, based on a few Latin examples, that the heroic cook is a *topos* in mediaeval literature (*coquus miles insignis*)[1] one might quote the notoriously unheroic Rumolt of the *Nibelungenlied* (which is truly mediaeval and based on vernacular heroic sources) and argue that a cook, like anybody else, might be heroic or otherwise; in the Eddic *Atlamál* the coward Hjalli is Attila's cook. Since cooks neither produced nor controlled heroic literature, there was no reason why they particularly should be glorified in it. Adler's religious interpretation of the complete poem is perhaps ingenious, but improbable in a poet who never conceals his total hostility to the Saracens and appears to see no religious problem at all. Even if we accept this interpretation it will not prove that Rainouart belongs to the Guillaume *geste*, for it could be the work of the author of our *Chançun de Willame*; the exercise of knitting together the dissimilar traditions of Guillaume and Rainouart would compel him to seek an overall plan and create some impression of unity. As regards the symmetry which Adler finds, even if we grant it was the poet's work and not the scholar's, it will apply perfectly well to the second part alone (lines 1981–3554, hereafter: R): in R Guillaume is at first husband to a Saracen convert, then confessor to Vivien and finally godfather to Rainouart, and only R tells of Vivien's vow and of Rainouart's success where Guillaume had failed. We do not have to read the first part (lines 1–1980, hereafter: W) for the sake of this symmetry, and so it proves nothing about the unity of the poem. In his concern to reconcile the comic elements in R with the heroic ethos of W Adler has left unexplained the more important fact that Rainouart is the effective hero throughout R while Guillaume quickly loses his prominence. Such a complete and abrupt change of hero in a tale derived from the life and legend of one man, whose story is treated elsewhere in a *Vita*, should be accounted for in an article that hopes to prove the unity of the poem's composition. While Bédier and Adler find essential unity in the *Chançun de Willame*, other scholars[2] point to its internal contradictions and the appa-

---

[1] Curtius, *loc. cit.*, whom Adler cites in support of this *topos*, makes no such claim and quotes, apart from Rabelais, only Rainouart, Harcheritus and Nabuzardan.

[2] R. Weeks, 'The Newly Discovered Chançun de Willame', Mod. Phil. 3 (1905), pp. 211–34; Suchier, 'Vivien', p. 642f; F. Rechnitz, *Prolegomena und erster Teil einer*

rent join at line 1981 and conclude that the actions of Guillaume and Rainouart were hitherto separate; they have indeed been more successfully merged in *Aliscans* than they had been nearly a century earlier in the *Chançun de Willame*, but still not well enough to prevent the detection of the two parts by scholars long before the *Chançun de Willame* was discovered.

There are striking inconsistencies in the *Chançun de Willame* between the lines before and after 1981. At the very end of the battle of l'Archamp, when Desramé has been killed by young Gui and the Saracens have fled to their ships, Guillaume jubilantly pronounces Gui his heir and the note of victory sounds:

> Ch W 1978   Apres ma mort ten tote ma herité.
> Lores fu mecresdi.
> Ore out vencu sa bataille Willame.

This is the end of W. In the very next line Guillaume is riding again:

> Ch W 1981   Li quons Willame chevalche par le champ,
> Tut est irez e plein de maltalant.

Soon he is fighting the Saracens again (though they had all fled, lines 1855–60) and Gui, who had lately been invincible, is taken prisoner and forgotten (he is last mentioned as an active hero at 1962ff). Guillaume finds Vivien alive under an olive by a stream (1988–92), though his corpse had several days earlier in a previous battle been left by the Saracens near a pathway where the Christians should not find it (927f). Guillaume had set out for the battle from Barcelona, where he had left Guibourc (932f), but he returns to Guibourc at Orange (2055).[1] He attacks and kills Alderufe (2096–2209), although this particular Saracen has already been

---

kritischen Ausgabe der Chanson de Guillaume, Bonn 1909; P. Studer, 'La Chançun de Rainouart, Material for a Critical Edition', MLR 15 (1920), pp. 41–8; McMillan, *La Chanson de Guillaume*, vol. 2, pp. 127–31; Frappier, pp. 141–8; Buhr, p. 20; M. Delbouille, in *La Technique Littéraire des Chansons de Geste*, Liège 1959, p. 341.

[1] The existence of two different traditions is charmingly illustrated in manuscript D of the *Chevalerie Vivien*, where Vivien seeks a messenger

> D, 857   Qui m'en alast a Guillelme al cort nes,
> A Bargelune u li quens est remeis,
> Ou a Orange, ne sai dire louquel.

killed by Vivien (376, 637–42). Guibourc recalls having given to Gui arms taken from famous warriors, including her former husband (2358–62), whereas at 1541–52 she had given him tiny arms to suit his size.

A careful study of the *Chançun de Willame* by Mme. Wathelet-Willem[1] has detected differences between W and R in style, lexis and word usage which by virtue of their generally subconscious origin must suggest two different authors. For example, to express sadness W often uses *croler le chief*, while R prefers *suspirer*. W refers more often than R to the place and time of the events, it has a greater variety of epithets, its imagery is far more imaginative and varied and it has many references to animals and hunting (e.g. the image of a hunted boar defending itself is used six times in W but never in R). It uses *lignage* where R has *parenté* and *glut* where R has *leccher*. *Lignage* is important only in W; Rainouart is outside the *lignage* of Montglane. When mentioning numbers of troops W expresses thousands in multiples of five, while R has 3,000, 4,000 and 7,000. In W the Christians are *Franc, Franceis, Norman*, while in R there are also *Aleman, Bretun, Flamenc* and *Roman*, i.e. men from outside France proper. R also uses different terms for the Saracens, and only R uses words of Saracen origin (e.g. *almançur, amirail, amurafle, besanz*). In W only six Saracens are named (disregarding the interpolation 1704–28), while R names 27 Saracens, 25 of whom are unimportant. In W the only Saracen god mentioned is *Mahom*, while in R the Saracens also worship *Antechrist, Apolicant, Apolin, Asturat, Bagot, Belzebut, Finement, Macabeu, Tartarun* and *Tervagant*. W has many Christian heroes and only one Saracen of note (Desramé), while R has only one really prominent Christian, who is himself of Saracen origin, and any number of Saracens. In W the Saracens throw their weapons; in R they strike with them.[2] Humour is used in W almost exclusively in the

---

[1] J. Wathelet-Willem, 'La Chançun de Willame, Le problème de l'unité du MS British add. 38663', *Le Moyen Âge* 58 (1952), pp. 363–77.

[2] Towards the end of the eleventh century the lance became heavier and was used as a thrusting weapon instead of being thrown, cf. D. Ross, 'L'originalité de "Turoldus": le maniement de la lance', *Cahiers de Civilisation Médiévale* 6 (1963), pp. 127–38 (refer-

Tedbalt episode, with the purpose of stressing Vivien's danger and courage by providing a foil; in R there is any amount of farcical humour which serves no serious purpose. Religion is more important in W than in R. These are only the most striking of the differences noted by Wathelet-Willem; there are many others. To these we may add Suchier's observations on assonance and other formal differences: *Vivien* assonates in W with *–ie* and in R with *–an*, and W distinguishes between assonances in *–en* and *–an*, which in R assonate together. The *laisses* are longer in R. *Aymeri* appears regularly in R as *Naymeri*. W is far more indebted than R to the *Chanson de Roland*. It is significant that the prologue anticipates only the events of W: it mentions Desramé's attack, the death of Vivien, Guillaume's intervention and the death of Desramé, but it does not mention Guillaume's journey to Laon, the second battle with the strangely revived Saracens or the activities of Rainouart. Different characters appear in W and R; only Guillaume and Guibourc appear frequently in both and Guillaume is far less prominent in R. The characterisation in R is less careful and detailed;[1] its main character, Rainouart, amounts to little more than a personification of strength and ignorance. Lines 1981–2645 can readily be understood as a summary of an omitted introduction to R.[2] All this evidence, strongly supported by the absence of such marked internal contradictions within W, indicates clearly that the *Chançun de Willame* is not a unity and the matter of W and R were once separate.

Since we know that our version of the *Chançun de Willame* is not the archetype,[3] we must assume that the substance of R was

---

ring to lance tactics in the *Chanson de Roland*) and R. C. Smail, *Crusading Warfare*, Cambridge 1956, p. 113, note 1. The use of the lance as a thrusting weapon in R accords well with its later date.

[1] J. Schuwerack, 'Charakteristik der Personen in der altfranzösischen Chançun de Guillelme', *Romanistische Arbeiten* 1, Halle a.d.S. 1913, pp. 130f.

[2] Schuwerack, p. 130, note 1.

[3] See R. Weeks, 'The Newly Discovered Chançun de Willame', Mod. Phil. 2 (1904), pp. 1–16. p. 6: 'Ch W is the result of a number of blendings and remaniements, the traces of which are perfectly visible to unprejudiced eyes.' The poem as preserved on the manuscript is in poor condition, the lines often having too many or too few syllables (cf. McMillan, vol. 2, pp. 44–5, who says that 43% of the lines are metrically

added to that of W in one of its ancestors and put back the date of our independent Rainouart source to a period earlier than our version of the *Chançun de Willame*. The narrative of R as we have it does not make complete sense on its own and so it can never have existed as a *chanson* in its own right. Consequently, there must have been a Rainouart tradition prior to the *Chançun de Willame* on which that poem could draw.[1]

Having thus decided that the *Chançun de Willame* is a composite work, we have to face one major question: if R is derived from material which was once independent of the Guillaume *geste*, why does it include an account of some events which have been narrated in W and clearly belong to the matter of Guillaume rather than that of Rainouart. R recalls Vivien's death and only R has Guillaume's rides to Orange and to Laon and the portrait of Guibourc as the valiant defender of Orange who lets no man enter unchallenged. The answer to this probably lies in the history of the Rainouart matter before the composition of the *Chançun de Willame*. The merging of Guillaume and Rainouart matter to form one epic could not be effected by simply placing two dissimilar tales side by side. It is likely that the common background of war against the Saracens led to the introduction of references to Guillaume within the still independent Rainouart tradition. A few points of contact could stimulate the desire for more and cause poets to attempt to bring the two traditions into a consistent relationship with each other. In this way, Guillaume material probably appeared in the matter of Rainouart before the join. The characters and episodes might develop differently in the two traditions, and some episodes might become regularly attached to the one rather than the other – thus Guibourc's defence of Orange,

wrong), assonances change in the middle of sentences, the geography is confused and contradictory (which suggests several copyings in England) and there are two accounts of Willame's expedition to relieve Vivien, sufficiently different to have been placed side by side by a remanieur.

[1] The view of Becker, pp. 82–9, that Jendeus de Brie invented the Rainouart action to lengthen his poem of *Aliscans* and the poet of the *Chançun de Willame* added its substance to W from memory, has found no support in scholarship.

the confession of Vivien and the ride to Laon were regularly narrated with the Rainouart rather than the Guillaume material. Guibourc herself may have been introduced to the Rainouart matter quite soon, for she is very prominent there and has a distinctly more active, self-reliant and warlike character in R and the later *geste Rainouart* than elsewhere. Not until this process had become fairly advanced and the two traditions similar and related to each other could a *jongleur* take the decisive step of joining them and narrating both traditions together as one epic.[1] We have noted that the beginning of R, lines 1981–2647, forms a résumé of the action of W according to a different tradition from W; we may conclude that the Rainouart matter had come to need some of the action of W to form its own introduction and the *jongleur* who compiled the composite *Chançun de Willame* failed to eliminate the discrepancies between W as narrated in the first part of his new poem and the version of the same events as they appeared at the beginning of R.

We may now regard the Rainouart material as different in origin from the rest of the *Chançun de Willame*. It is not likely that Rainouart had been closely linked to the Guillaume cycle very long before the composition of the *Chançun de Willame*, because the contradictions and absurdities resultant from his introduction had not yet been resolved. It is unlikely that he could ever have played a minor part within the Guillaume *geste*, and remained for that reason unmentioned in all earlier records of the *geste*, because his unusual physical strength and brutality and the quite extraordinary feats which are peculiar to him make it difficult for him to be a minor character – wherever he appears he is always the dominant character and refuses to be subordinated. And so his complete absence from all the historical and literary records of the Guillaume action prior to the *Chançun de Willame* suggests he had been recently introduced. Since it appears that

---

[1] It is likely that the two main sources of the *Nibelungenlied* were assimilated to each other in this way before they were joined together, and that the *Ältere Not* had an introduction giving briefly the history of Siegfried and Brunhild, cf. *Das Nibelungenlied* ed. Bartsch/De Boor, Wiesbaden 1956, p. xxxi–xxxii; A. T. Hatto, *The Nibelungenlied*, Harmondsworth 1965, p. 393.

Rainouart had a different origin from the rest of the Guillaume cycle, it now remains to consider what his origin may have been. It is to this problem that the rest of this chapter must be devoted.

POSSIBLE HISTORICAL SOURCES

The demonstrated independence of R, the second part of the *Chançun de Willame*, definitely argues an independent source. To trace the origin of the Rainouart action we must consider the nature of this source and look more closely at Suchier's theory of a lost *Chançun de Rainouart*.

The narrative of R could never have been an independent epic, for it is not intelligible without reference to a more complete narrative.[1] Particularly the first 700 lines, which, as we have noted, are probably a summary serving as a link with Guillaume's action, are so full of contradictions and omissions as to make their existence as the introduction to an independent epic unthinkable; Rychner writes (p. 30): 'la première partie de R n'offre que les restes mutilés d'un recit plus complet, correspondant à Aliscans'. The researches of Becker and Rychner show that *Aliscans* often follows an older tradition than R; this led Becker to believe that the *Chançun de Willame* was an adaptation, based on inaccurate memory, of *Chevalerie Vivien* and *Aliscans*, an idea which has since been generally discarded as quite untenable.[2] But although *Aliscans* cannot be the source of R, it remains firmly established that the *Chançun de Willame* is not the source of *Aliscans*. This is why Suchier put forward his theory of a lost *Chançun de Rainouart* as the source of the Rainouart action in both *Chançun de Willame* and *Aliscans*.[3] Frappier (pp. 141–8;

---

[1] See J. Rychner, 'Sur la Chanson de Guillaume', *Romania* 76 (1955), pp. 28–38.

[2] Becker, pp. 81–9; for the objections to this view see Frappier, p. 206. It is not likely that a poet who knew *Aliscans* would create unnecessary internal contradictions which that poem had resolved, that he would omit all reference to Aelis, or that his version would be written in genuinely more archaic French than its source.

[3] Suchier, 'Vivien', ZfrP 29 (1905), p. 642f. In the same year a similar hypothesis (a lost *Chanson de Rainouart* as source of *Bataille Loquifer* and the other poems of the *geste Rainouart*) was put forward by J. Runeberg, *Études sur la Geste Rainouart*, diss. Helsinki, 1905, pp. 152f, 163. G. Rolin, in his edition of *Aliscans* (1894) had already

203–7) follows Suchier in deriving R from the *Chançun de Rai-nouart*, which he assumes is later than the source of W, and accounts for the differences between R and *Aliscans* and for the *Chançun de Willame* poet's attempts to link W and R. His position, which is now generally accepted (cf. the enthusiastic support of Riquer in his French edition, p. 149), may be illustrated thus:

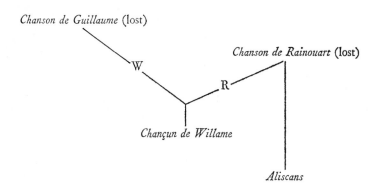

Thus, the *Chançun de Rainouart* is likely to resemble *Aliscans* in some respects, rather than the older *Chançun de Willame*. We expect it to be a fuller account, in which the unintelligible allusions of R made better and more complete sense, and to include the events leading up to the battles, in which Guillaume sets out from Orange, not Barcelona. We need to know how Guillaume became involved in the first, unsuccessful battle, so there must be some reference to Vivien's lone struggle, his vow and his death. The *Chançun de Rainouart* must thus contain some events which are included in W; we have seen above (p. 16) how this may have come about, and we should not regard these events as part of the Rainouart legend, but as necessary accretion to a nucleus, which is the more detailed part concerning Rainouart himself. The ultimate origin of the Rainouart action lies in the history of this nucleus before it was recorded in epic form.

The origin of all three cycles of old French heroic epic is to be

assumed this distinction by constructing a stemma for the *Rennewartepos* quite inde-pendently of that of the *Wilhelmslied* in *Aliscans* (p. lxiv).

found in historical events, which gave rise to heroic lays, or perhaps legends, and were eventually given epic form. De Boor writes: 'Die Chanson de geste...ist...im Kern historische Wirklichkeit, deren heroischen Kampfesernst kein Rankenwerk der Phantasie ersticken kann.'[1] History is usually the ultimate source of heroic literature,[2] though the literary tradition will alter events and interpret and evaluate them in its own way, and mythological or invented elements may be introduced in the course of time. Mediaeval historians have used Germanic heroic lays as source material and expressed confidence in the historical truth of the events they record;[3] this indicates at least that this kind of literature was once expected to be based on true history. Knowing that all three cycles of French heroic literature also began with historical events, we may expect the origin of an independent heroic tradition to be historical, though the rule need not apply always and everywhere. As a rule, a heroic poem which is not derived from historical events will prove to be secondary and developed to serve a tradition that *is* historical in origin, as the tale of Corsolt was invented to solve a problem that had arisen in the tradition of Guillaume, which *is* historical.[4] And so, having

---

[1] H. de Boor, *Geschichte der deutschen Literatur*, vol. 2, *Die höfische Literatur*, 4th edition, Munich 1960, p. 114, cf. vol. 1, p. 241 (on the *Chanson de Roland*). Cf. also P. Rajna, *Le origini dell'epopea francese*, 2nd edition, Florence 1956, p. 380; I. Siciliano, *Les Origines des Chansons de Geste*, Paris 1951, p. 45.

[2] Cf. O. Höfler, 'Deutsche Heldensage', *Von deutscher Art in Sprache und Dichtung*, 2 (1941), pp. 73–98; also *idem*, 'Die Anonymität des Nibelungenliedes', DVJS 29 (1955), pp. 167–213, especially pp. 209–13. Cf. Runeberg, p. 162: 'L'épopée, c'est l'histoire nationale des temps naifs.' Tacitus tells us that the Germanic peoples used nothing but traditional songs to record their history: 'Celebrant carminibus antiquis, quod unum apud illos memoriae et annalium genus est....', *Germania*, 2, 3.

[3] Cassiodorus and Jordanes (*Getica* XXXIV) follow Gothic heroic lays (cf. O. Höfler, 'Die Anonymität des Nibelungenliedes', DVJS 29 (1955), p. 173). Snorri Sturluson bases his history of the kings of Norway upon heroic lays, freely admitting that the poets may have been biased, hoping to flatter the kings they served, but Snorri considers it impossible that a poet would dare to invent deeds and happenings that had never taken place, for the contemporary audience at least would know that the king was being flattered with empty lies, and that would be scorn, not praise (Snorri's Prologue to *Heimskringla*).

[4] Guillaume goes to Rome to rescue the Christians from the formidable Saracen giant Corsolt; after a long battle he kills the giant but first loses the tip of his nose in the encounter. Returning to France, he says his nose has been shortened, but his fame will be the longer for it. The tale is told in the *Couronnement de Louis* (where it has probably

found Rainouart's origin to be independent of Guillaume, we must decide whether he is a secondary, non-historical addition to the Guillaume matter or whether he once had an independent tradition of his own, which may have found expression in Suchier's *Chançun de Rainouart*. To do this we must look for historical events which could have given rise to Rainouart's own tradition, which, at first independent, became merged with the matter of Guillaume when the *Chançun de Rainouart* was joined with the *Chançun de Vivien* to produce the composite *Chançun de Willame* which we know.

Monica Barnett derives *La Bataille Loquifer*, a poem about Rainouart which continues the narrative of *Aliscans* and leads into the *geste Rainouart* (a series of poems dealing with the fantastic exploits of Rainouart after the battle of l'Archamp), from the history of the Normans in Sicily, and she traces Rainouart himself to this source in the introduction to her edition of that epic, which is the earliest of the poems about Rainouart.[1] The first manuscript of this poem was stolen by the Norman king William II of Sicily after the death of its author, Jendeus de Brie, who had made a fortune with it in Sicily. Contemporary descriptions of the frightening appearance and uncouth behaviour of such Norman leaders as Bohemund and Tancred are reminiscent of Rainouart, and the Normans were noted for such cruelty and courage as Rainouart exhibits. The tradition of Rainouart's illegitimacy would be acceptable among the Normans.[2] Their wives occasion-

---

been interpolated); there is a reference to it in *Aliscans* (4071ff), where a Saracen called Isorés has taken the place of Corsolt. It became necessary for some such tale to be invented when Guillaume's epithet *al corb nes* became *au cort nez* as a result of phonological changes in the language (see p. 8). A similar case, where a tale was invented to account for a false but popular etymology, occurs in the history of the Irish hero Cúchulainn, whose name originally meant 'hero of Culann' but was widely assumed to mean 'Culann's dog', because the more common meaning of *cú* is 'dog'. Cuchulainn as a boy visited the smith Culann and was attacked by his fierce watchdog, which he killed with his bare hands; moved by Culann's grief at losing his dog, the boy acted as Culann's watchdog himself until a new dog had grown up to take his place.

[1] M. Barnett, *La Bataille Loquifer*, Ph.D. thesis, London 1959. Cf. also Gaston Paris, 'La Sicile dans la littérature française du moyen âge', *Romania* 5 (1876), p. 110f.

[2] *Moniage Rainouart* fol. 297 col. c, fol. 319 col. d; *Aliscans* 6407b.

ally helped them in battle, as Guibourc helps Guillaume against Tiebaut (B Loq 2752–800 *et passim*). *La Bataille Loquifer* describes ships as having towers and carrying small boats (B Loq 297f, 351f, 382–7), as Norman ships of the period did. When in difficulties, Rainouart invokes Saint Julian, a favourite Norman saint. Much of the fighting in *La Bataille Loquifer* is at sea, and Guillaume and Rainouart are prevented by a storm from coming to the aid of Guibourc against Tiebaut; Sicily was notorious for its storms. Palermo is mentioned in *La Bataille Loquifer* and the later part of *Aliscans*, where Rainouart appears (B Loq, *passim*; Al. 3260, 6373a). There are records of Saracens having used axes and clubs during the Sicilian wars, a potential source for Rainouart's club.[1] Saracens in Sicily held important positions in the state in the service of Norman kings, as the Saracen Rainouart is found among the Christians. All these features suggest that Rainouart could fit into the eventful uneasy period in which the Normans conquered Sicily from the Saracens, 1061 to 1091.

Barnett then finds historical sources for three of the characters of the Rainouart *geste*. A possible historical Desramé, Abd-al-rahmān, son of Hābib ibn Abu Ubaida, had fought in Sicily in 747.[2] The Saracen Borel, who with his sons is killed by Rainouart in the *Chançun de Willame* and *Aliscans*, may correspond to a certain Burielle or Borel who, with his sons, was a source of trouble to the Normans in Sicily during the second half of the eleventh century. Rainouart himself is traced to Roger de Hauteville, one of the Norman conquerors who became King of Sicily and was distinguished for his valour. Roger had three wives, of whom the second was named Eremburg and the third Adelaide; these names resemble those of Rainouart's two wives, Ermentrud and

---

[1] I use the term 'club' for convenience, but the early French *chansons* seem to understand by *tinel* a wooden yoke with iron bands, used for carrying containers of wine or water; Rainouart would naturally use this in the kitchen, since his main duty is to carry water for the cooks (cf. below, p. 78), but when provoked he might employ it as a club. When this *tinel* is broken and replaced (for battle) by an ordinary club, this also is called *tinel* (among other things), and the word serves in the *geste Rainouart* to describe any club. See J. Wathelet-Willem, 'Quelle est l'Origine du tinel de Rainouart?', BRABLB 31 (1965–6), pp. 355–64.

[2] He distinguished himself when his father attacked the Greeks in Sicily in 739–40 and won victories there on his own account in 747–8, cf. Barnett, p. lxxx.

Aelis.[1] Further, the Sicilian Norman royal house was linked to that of Provence (where the Guillaume legend came from) through the marriage of Mathilde, the daughter of Robert Guiscard, to Aymeri of Narbonne, and it appears that the Guillaume matter was already current among the Sicilian Normans in the late eleventh century, since Bohemund claimed to be descended from Guillaume.[2] There is a further correspondence in *La Bataille Loquifer* when Rainouart, lost at sea after killing Clarion, is rescued and brought to Porpaillart by a marquis of Montferrent; Ordericus Vitalis mentions in about 1090 a certain Boniface de Vasto, Marquis of Montferrat, who is uncle to Roger's wife Adelaide.

These three identifications, however, are all open to objection, and the source proposed for Desramé is quite surprising. The adventures of a cavalry leader who fought the Greeks in Sicily in 747–8 are most unlikely to have created a heroic tradition among the Normans, who arrived in Sicily three centuries later. The Saracen leader Desramé already belonged to the matter of Guillaume and he is Guillaume's principal enemy in the first part of the *Chançun de Willame*; although the historical enemy of Guillaume was not Abd-al-rahmān but Hishām, it was not doubted prior to Barnett that Desramé represented the Moorish ruler Abd-al-rahmān I.[3] Abd-al-rahmān was by no means an uncommon name; another Abd-al-rahmān who played an important part in the battles with the Christians in Spain and Southern France, the background of the Guillaume epics, was Abd-al-rahmān al-Ghafiqi, Governor of Andalusia, who defeated the Christians at Arles and was killed at Poitiers in 732. Five Umayyad kings of Spain called Abd-al-rahmān ruled at Cordoba, like the Desramé

---

[1] In the *Chançun de Willame* and *Aliscans* ms. M he marries Ermentrut; in all other *Aliscans* mss and in the *geste Rainouart* he marries Aelis. Barnett claims that *Adelais* (nominative form of *Adelaide*) was pronounced *Aëlis* in Sicily, but I have been unable to confirm this.

[2] Barnett, p. lxxvi, quotes *Chronicon Faventinum, Muratori Rerum Ital. SS*, Bologna 1936–9, vol. 28, part 1, p. 14: 'Abuiamons, qui de semine Guillelmi de Derenga ab omnibus extimabatur.'

[3] Cf. Rolin, pp. xxxii–xxxviii; D. Scheludko, 'Über das Wilhelmlied', *Zeitschrift für französische Sprache und Literatur* 50 (1927), pp. 1–38.

of the epics, between 755 and 1024; two of these were particularly powerful. The famous name may have become a generic term to refer to the strong Moorish king, as the name of Caesar is used for other emperors (cf. German *Kaiser*, Slavonic *Czar*) and that of Charlemagne is used in Slavonic languages for any king (Russian король, Polish *król*).[1] Perhaps Wolfram's reference to the author of *Aliscans* as 'Cristjâns' (Wh. 125, 20) is another example of a famous particular name being used generically and applied to the author of *any* French source. Abd-al-rahmān would be the natural name to attach to a strong Saracen king, and so there is nothing to prevent us from deriving Desramé from all five of the Umayyad kings. Lot (p. 249f) has shown how a number of historical Guillaumes became merged in the creation of the Guillaume of the epics. Epic tradition also merged Pepin, father of Charlemagne, with Pepin, father of Charles Martel, and Louis, son of Charlemagne, absorbs all the other Louis.[2] The epic tends to forget different characters of the same name, as the poet of *Doon de Mayence* (p. 201, l. 6650ff) found it necessary to point out:

> Segnurs, vous savés bien, et je en suis tous fis,
> Que plusors Kalles ot (chà arrier) à Paris,
> A Nerbonne la grant ot plusors Aymeris,
> Et à Orenge rot maint Guillaume marchis,
> Et si rot maint Doön à Maience jadis.

Thus the nature of the growth of the heroic epic makes the Moorish kings of Spain more plausible than the Sicilian adventurer as source for Desramé. The prominence of Desramé in the *geste Rainouart* may best be attributed to its late date, for comparison

---

[1] Cf. also Lithuanian *valdimieras*, king, from St. Vladimir of Kiev, who conquered all Russia and introduced Orthodox Christianity there after his own conversion; Croat *bān*, governor, from Bajan, leader of the Avars (died 603); perhaps Kazikumuk (a Caucasian language) *shamkhala*, king, from Shah-Baala, the name of the first Muslim khans of Daghestan (but the *Encyclopaedia of Islam*, under *Daghestan*, supports another etymology). The name of the Hethittite king Labangash also became a title. The source of such words is always a *foreign* king's name: король was used in Old Russian to refer to the Swedish, Polish, Lithuanian or Hungarian king and never applied to a Russian ruler. See V. Kiparsky, *Die gemeinslawischen Lehnwörter aus dem Germanischen*, Helsinki 1934, pp. 240–3. Caesar, however, was used as a title in Rome.

[2] Cf. W. Comfort, 'The character types in the Old French Chansons de Geste', PMLA 21 (1906), p. 284.

of the *Chançun de Willame* with *Aliscans* will show how Desramé becomes more and more important in the Guillaume cycle.

The identification of the epic Borel with the Borel or Burielle of Sicilian history is also dubious. We know nothing about this historical Borel except that he fought the Normans at some time after their first attack on Sicily in 1061. The Borel of the cycle of Guillaume appears first in the *Fragment de la Haye*, which can be dated with reasonable certainty between 980 and 1030; the *Fragment* is an exercise based on a lost Latin poem in hexameters, and in it Borel is already completely integrated into the Guillaume action: Borel and his sons fight with Wibelinus and his father. In the epics Guibelins (Wolfram's Gibelîn) is mentioned only as a supporter of Guillaume fighting in his army: the killing of Borel is presumably the heroic deed which created his reputation. The epic Borel must therefore be much older than Norman Sicily, and he, like Desramé, must have been introduced into the *geste Rainouart* from the *geste Guillaume*.[1]

King Roger I of Sicily is unlikely as the source of Rainouart. He was certainly not a Saracen who had risen from low beginnings (such as employment as a cook), and his death in 1101 was much too recent for the historical facts about him to be forgotten or grossly distorted when the second part of the *Chançun de Willame* was composed (this could hardly be much later than 1120), let alone its antecedents. The chronological confusion that places Rainouart beside Guillaume and Aymeri as well as the poor condition of our only manuscript of the *Chançun de Willame*, suggests that the Rainouart action is much older than Roger I. It certainly appears to be fully developed by his time. There is no need to derive Rainouart's Ermentrut from Roger's Eremburg (since *irmin* and *trūt* are both common in Germanic names) or Aelis from Adelaide, and if the latter became legendary, it is more probably as queen of Jerusalem than as Roger's wife. All these

---

[1] The possibility that the Sicilian Borel did enter the *geste Rainouart* but was later merged with the Borel of the *geste Guillaume* is improbable: it requires that two different Saracens, both called Borel and having a large number of sons, were independently adopted by the heroic literatures of foreign and hostile peoples. The same improbability applies to the two Desramés.

events are in any case much too recent to have created the legend of Rainouart.

It is also far from certain that Rainouart's background is Sicilian and Norman. The maritime features and the constant war against the Saracens can be supplied equally well by the Arelate, where the Guillaume legends arose. Rainouart himself is certainly born in Spain, and the town of Porpaillart, which is so prominent in the *geste Rainouart*, is generally agreed to be in Spain or the extreme south of France.[1] Palermo is the only Sicilian name in the *Chançun de Willame* and *Bataille Loquifer* and it is only the much later epic *Renier* that really shows knowledge of Sicily. While it is true that Saracens did serve under the Norman kings of Sicily, it is not very likely that this happened while the Normans were conquering Sicily from the long-established Saracen rulers. It was Roger II who first engaged Saracens in state service on a large scale during the twelfth century, and the first Saracen *ammiratus* under the Normans was Abd-al-rahmān al-Nasrani (known as Christodolus), who died about 1131.[2] The phenomenon of a Saracen with a Germanic name might equally well be found in Spain, where Christians and Muslims freely intermarried and where a whole social class, the *muwallads*, consisted of ex-Christians who professed Islam so as to avoid severe taxation;[3] in Cordoba the mother of Abd-al-rahmān III was a Christian. The towers and small boats upon Norman ships were not exclusively Norman; Venetian ships had small boats on board which could be raised and used as towers when need arose,[4] and Genoan ships also had towers, and developed in time into floating fortresses.[5] Robert Guiscard introduced such features to Norman ships in the 1080's. Barnett's claim that Saint Julian was

[1] Most scholars believe Porpaillart is in Spain, but Barnett herself favours Lattes, the port for Montpellier, which she thinks might have been called 'Port Pelliel'; for all relevant literature see M. Barnett, 'Porpaillart in the Cycle of Guillaume d'Orange', MLR 51 (1956), pp. 507–11.

[2] W. Cohn, *Geschichte der normannisch-sizilischen Flotte*, Breslau 1910, pp. 65–8. Cf. also Cohn, *Das Zeitalter der Normannen in Sizilien*, Breslau 1920, pp. 34–7.

[3] P. Hitti, *A History of the Arabs*, London 1958[6], p. 510f.

[4] Cohn, *Geschichte der normannisch-sizilischen Flotte*, p. 56.

[5] E. Heyck, *Genua und seine Marine im Zeitalter der Kreuzzüge*, Innsbruck 1886, p. 60.

a specifically Norman saint is also dubious. There are many saints Julian, but the only one whom Rainouart could be referring to is Saint Julian of Brioude, a native of Vienne who fought in the Roman army and was martyred at Brioude in 304.[1] He was venerated not only in Sicily, but in Provence, particularly at Vienne and Brioude, both prominent towns in the *geste* of Guillaume. It is at Brioude that St. William of Gellone is said to have become a monk and dedicated the rest of his life to the service of St. Julian.[2] In the *Charroi de Nîmes* Guillaume determines to take his men to the saint's church at Brioude (i.e. the church of Saint-Julien-de-Brioude) and in *Le Moniage Guillaume* he enters the monastery at Brioude to dedicate himself to St. Julian. At Brioude the shield of Guillaume and the club of Rainouart were exhibited in the church of St. Julian, a detail referred to in *Le Moniage Guillaume* (I, 93–6), and in that poem Guillaume twice calls upon St. Julian (Mon. Guill. I, 80, 83). The Arsenal manuscript of *Aliscans* (Al. *a*, 7823–8) also tells us that Rainouart's club is at Brioude, where pilgrims to Compostela can see it. St. Julian and Brioude therefore belong to the matter of Guillaume and were established in it before the Normans entered the Mediterranean. Guibourc's taking part in battle can be explained without her being a Norman, for it was quite common for Saracen women in Spain under the Abbasids to take an active part in warfare (cf. Hitti, p. 333). Sichelgaite, the wife of Robert Guiscard, who is Barnett's only example of the Norman wife in battle, was by birth and upbringing a Lombard, not a Norman.[3] If the Saracens used clubs in Sicily, then they probably used them at the same date elsewhere; in any case Rainouart's use of the club is far from unique (cf. pp. 159f), and Guillaume himself uses one in the *Prise d'Orange* (line 826).

---

[1] Consult A. Butler, *The Lives of the Saints*, revised ed., London 1956, under 28 August, and *Enciclopedia Cattolica*, vol. 6 col. 744, under *Giuliano di Brioude*.

[2] 'He obtained the requisite permission from Charlemagne, and then made his way to Brioude in the Auvergne, where he hung up his weapons in the church of St. Julian, after he had laid an offering on the altar' (Butler, *The Lives of the Saints*, vol. 2, 28 May). The same information taken from the *Vita Sancti Wilhelmi* is found in W. Smith and H. Wace, *Dictionary of Christian Biography* (4 vols), London 1877–87, vol. 2, p. 808, under *Guilelmus*. This St. Julian is also the patron saint of Versailles.

[3] Cf. R. Yewdale, *Bohemund I, Prince of Antioch*, Princeton 1924, p. 6.

The conclusive objection to the Sicilian Norman theory is the chronological one. It is quite possible that events in Sicilian Norman history may have made their contribution to the poems of the *geste Rainouart*. Runeberg's *terminus post quem* for *La Bataille Loquifer* is 1147, when the Marquis of Montferrat left for the Second Crusade; this would agree quite well with the use of legendary material derived from events of the late eleventh century. But events of that date are simply too late to be feasible as an *origin* for Rainouart or for the main action concerning him which is developed in the *geste Rainouart*. Even if the events in Sicily are earlier than the *Chançun de Willame*, which is just possible, the time left for them to become known and for this history to develop into legend and epic is far too short to explain the growth of so much Rainouart lore and to account for the considerable differences between these historical facts and Rainouart's epic tradition. For the transformation of history into epic requires time, as the author of an Arab saying recognised:

'Combien de temps faut-il pour que le passé, ce squelette, se couvre d'un manteau d'or?'[1]

Another possible historical influence upon Rainouart is the savage band of poor Christians on the First Crusade known as the Tafurs.[2] Guibert of Nogent gives a brief account of these people at the end of his history of the First Crusade,[3] apparently deriving all his information from the *Chanson d'Antioche*. This epic was probably written in the Holy Land by a crusader between 1098 and 1101;[4] it belongs to the *Cycle de la Croisade*, the only epics that mention the Tafurs. In the *Chanson d'Antioche* there are very large numbers of them; they are poor, badly dressed, barefoot, lean and hungry. Their extreme hunger drives them to eat the

---

[1] Quoted thus in French by Lot, p. 257.

[2] See Adler, pp. 160–71, who includes a detailed comparison of the Tafurs with Rainouart.

[3] Guibertus Novigentis, *Gesta Dei per Francos*, vii, 23 (date 1108). Published in Migne, *Patrologia Latina* 156, saec. xii; cols. 811–12 refer to the Tafurs.

[4] A. Hatim, *Les Poèmes Épiques des Croisades*, Paris 1932, especially p. 235. Hatim's dating of the *Chanson d'Antioche* and his conclusion that it is Guibert's source are regarded as proved by his reviewer John La Monte, *Speculum* 10 (1935), pp. 97–100.

corpses of dead Saracens, a practice stressed by the poet every time they are mentioned, but denied by Guibert of Nogent, who regards it as a pretence to frighten the enemy. Some carry improvised weapons, and their savagery terrifies their Christian allies as much as the Saracens. They live apart from the rest of the army and cannot be controlled by the leaders of the Crusade. Their adviser is Peter the Hermit and they have their own king, whom they call 'li rois Tafur', possibly from Armenian *tahavor* meaning 'king',[1] since there were very many Armenians among the poor of the First Crusade.

It is known that large numbers of badly armed or unarmed poor joined the First Crusade, hoping to earn the promised plenary indulgence. They suffered extreme hardship from famine and from Saracen attacks, particularly after the death of their protector, the papal legate Adhemar,[2] and many may have been attracted to this rough gypsy-like existence as their sole hope of survival. And, as P. Paris observed,[3] it is unlikely that they would have been satisfied during extreme famine with merely pretending to eat human flesh or that such a pretence would serve any practical purpose, and so the account given by the *Chanson d'Antioche* is likely to be in its essentials true.

There are striking similarities between the Tafurs and Rainouart. Like them, he is poor and badly dressed (Ch W 2649), has no arms except an improvised club and is capable of great cruelty. Guillaume is unable to exercise his proper authority over him, but has to beg and bargain with him (e.g. Ch W 2731f; 3397; 3460ff), and with good reason he is feared by the Christians as well as by the Saracens. Such terms as *ribaus* and *diables* are applied liberally to both Rainouart and the Tafurs. Like the Tafurs, he inspires more fear in the Saracens than the Christian leaders can (Ch W 3334–42; cf. Guibert: *magis insolentiam Thafurum, quam*

---

[1] This etymology is proposed by Hatim, *op. cit.* p. 195, and attacked by L. Sumberg, 'The "Tafurs" and the First Crusade', *Mediaeval Studies* (Toronto) 21 (1959), p. 226f. Peter may have come from Amiens rather than Armenia.

[2] W. Porges, 'The Clergy, the Poor, and the non-Combatants of the First Crusade', *Speculum* 21 (1946), pp. 1–23.

[3] In his edition of *Chanson d'Antioche*, vol. 2, p. 8.

nostrorum quodammodo principum vehementiam formidabant). The poor on the First Crusade were cared for, after the death of Adhemar in 1098, by Bishop William of Orange (Porges, pp. 6, 18, 23); we need assume only a little ignorance or imagination on the part of the minstrels back home in France for him to be confused with the William of Orange who cares for Rainouart. Their cannibalism, the most important feature of the Tafurs and the sole reason for their appearance in the *Chanson d'Antioche*, is never found in Rainouart, possibly because it would not become an epic hero, but it might remind us of the scene where he roasts the chief cook on a spit (Al. 4364–403; Wh. 286, 3–22).[1] As the Tafur king makes heroes out of despised paupers, so Rainouart makes heroes out of cowards (Ch W 2975f: *Ices couarʒ que vus ici veeʒ,/Ceste est ma torbe, mun pople, e mun barneʒ*), and as the Tafur king, also a born nobleman who has been reduced to poverty, wins his way back to authority among the paupers, so Rainouart wins his proper fame and power by leadership of the deserters. The French of Outremer, among whom the *Chanson d'Antioche* originated, might understand Peter the Hermit's birth as an Armenian, while to the French of France, who developed the *Chançun de Willame*, he may have seemed a Saracen; for the Armenians lived within the Saracen part of Asia Minor but had resisted the Seljuk invaders and readily supported the crusaders, just as Rainouart, a Saracen by birth and appearance, fights for the Christian cause.

We may reasonably expect that the author of the composite *Chançun de Willame* knew the *Chanson d'Antioche*, since both poems are concerned with war against the Saracens and written very early in the 12th century, our *Chançun de Willame* being generally considered twenty years or so later than the *Chanson d'Antioche*. We may see the influence of the Tafurs in the fact that one of Guillaume's languages is Armenian (Ch W 2171) and in the presence of a heathen called Tabur (Ch W 3171: *Tabur de*

---

[1] Wolfram's remark that the cook was prepared like a sheep (Wh. 286, 12: *der bant in, sam er wære ein schâf*) corresponds to Al. 4373: *Ausi le lieve com s'il fust noviaus nes*, which suggests a roasted child rather than a sheep.

Canaloine; cf. Wh. 435, 19: *Fâbors und Kanlîûn*), who is particularly savage and unarmed (Ch W 3174: *Ne porte arme for le bec e les ungles*) and attacks Rainouart with his teeth.[1] We hear too little of him to know whether he is a cannibal, but Aenrés, a very similar character in *Aliscans*, where Tabur does not occur, is definitely represented as a cannibal (cf. Al. 5824f: *Maint François a mangié et estranglé,/Un mail d'acier porte grant enhanté*). It is therefore likely that the poet of the *Chançun de Willame* saw an affinity between Rainouart and the Tafurs and applied to him features derived from the paupers themselves, their king and Peter the Hermit. But we cannot regard the Tafurs as an ultimate source for Rainouart. Their history is too recent for them to be the origin of an epic tradition which is fully formed by 1120 or soon after, and of two very different characters in that epic who are enemies to each other. The differences between Rainouart and the Tafurs are fundamental ones, while the correspondences can be accounted for. Rainouart is a single character who wins himself an army, while the Tafurs are a community who choose themselves a king and are advised by Peter the Hermit. Rainouart is not lean or underfed but a giant with extraordinary strength and speed and with strong ties to the imperial kitchen. He is not very interested in religion, while the Tafurs are Christian fanatics who despise all Turks. He is essentially armed – *Rainouars al tinel* – while the Tafurs are unarmed[2] or poorly armed, using stones, sticks or clubs (not exclusively clubs)[3] only because they have no other weapons. Rainouart's outstanding characteristics are his size, strength and appetite, his courage and pride, and his love for the kitchen and his trusty *tinel*; those of the Tafurs are their cannibalism and savagery, their poverty (Guibertus stresses their

---

[1] Ch W 3176: *Baie la gule, si l'i quidad tranglutre,/Tut ensement cum une meure pome*; 3186: *Les branz d'asier mangue e runge/Od les denz granz, que Danpnedeu confunde!*

[2] Guibert, *ibid*: '*Nudipedum exercitus, ac vitae genus. – Erat praeterea et aliud quoddam in exercitu illo hominum genus quod nudipes quidem incederet, arma nulla portaret, nullam ipsis prorsus pecuniae quantitatem habere liceret; sed nuditate ac indigentia omnino squalidum, universos praecederet, radicibus herbarum, et vilibus quibusque nascentiis victitaret.*'

[3] *Chanson d'Antioche*, chant VIII, l. 451: *Portent haces danoises et couteaus acerés,/ghisarmes et maçues et pels en son arsés,/Li rois porte une faus dont l'acier est temprés,/qui il en ateindra moult iert mal assenés.*

vow to possess no money, see p. 31, note 2) and their fanatical zeal for the Christian cause. Rainouart is therefore too different from the Tafurs in essentials to be derived from them, though his portrayal in the *Chançun de Willame* may owe a great deal to them and they have probably left their mark on the Guillaume *geste*.[1] The Tafurs may well have stimulated the poet's imagination and led him to give prominence to a comparable character, the language used to describe Rainouart may have carried Tafur associations for poet and audience, and the Tafur precedent may have increased Rainouart's cruelty and account for his being feared as much by the Christians as the Saracens. But this cannot be his origin.

We have now considered the two historical sources which have been postulated for Rainouart and found them both inadequate as sources for the whole Rainouart action or the character of Rainouart, though both may have played some part in the formation of the *geste Rainouart*. Since no other historical hypothesis is now current,[2] we must now consider whether it is likely that what we know of Rainouart could be derived from any historically founded legend.

Since a heroic tradition generally begins as a record, perhaps biased and interpreted, of historical events, the events it records are usually credible as poetically presented history to the society which creates it. It may develop further and further away from consciously recorded history, but this process is slow as long as the society has not yet lost sympathy with the heroic values which inspired the legend.[3] The transition of the Guillaume *geste* from consciously recorded history was not yet quite complete when Wolfram said '*ditz mære ist wâr, doch wunderlîch*' (*Willehalm* 5, 15)

[1] Thus *Charroi de Nîmes* 512: *la pute gent Tafure* (Wh. 74, 4: *Tâfar*, a heathen country); cf. also *Tabur* and *Fâbors*.
[2] Suchier, in *Literarisches Zentralblatt für Deutschland* 57 (1906), col. 1277 (also *La Chançun de Guillelme*, p. lxii), draws attention to some similarities between Rainouart and Havelok the Dane and suggests that both these heroes may be derived from the historical Reginwald of Northumbria (died 921). The evidence for this possibility is very limited and it has since been disregarded by Romanists.
[3] Chadwick, vol. III, p. 762–4.

and showed by his prayers and his direct testimony that he believed in the essential historicity of the story he told.[1]

It is easy to see the actions of Roland or Guillaume as poetic exaggeration of historical fact. One can conceive of their physical strength and courage as the poetic realisation of the power and prestige they really did enjoy as a result of high rank and a striking personality; Richard Cœur-de-Lion was still able to stir popular and poetic imagination thus at the end of the twelfth century. But it is difficult to believe that the core of the Rainouart action could ever have been acceptable as the poetic realisation of history, even in a hypothetical earlier version that was closer to reality. His club cannot be exaggerated from any weapon that a Christian or Saracen could have employed with such success as to earn legendary renown. His extraordinary greed, cruelty and crudity cannot be exaggerated from qualities that characterised a great man and created a heroic tradition. The references to magic[2] and the many supernatural creatures and events in R are difficult to reconcile with a historical origin. The very important motif of his Saracen origin is not supported by his name, which is Germanic, and if there were any historical background to his aversion to the Saracen religion and his willingness to become a soldier of Christ, this natural sympathy in any Saracen important enough to earn fame in battle would certainly have been recorded by the Christians and probably made good use of. If we reduce the Guillaume of the *chansons* to realistic proportions we have a strong Christian leader, living dangerously close to the Saracens and constantly at war with them; his example might well fire the poetic imagination to produce the tales we know where his stature is increased by the poet's enthusiasm. But if we reduce the essential features of Rainouart's character to realistic proportions, we have a lazy,

---

[1] This does not imply that Wolfram thought his source literally true in detail (as we may gather from his occasional polemics against it, see p. 72f), but he did regard the story it told as a true story.

[2] E.g. the portrayal of Guibourc as a magician or wise woman, Al. 4282: *Je cuit Guibors nos veut tos encanter* (Aimers to Guillaume); Al. 4466: *Guibors fut sage de la loi sarrasine*; Al. 184c, 60: *Une suer ai, ne sai en quel regné,/Orable a non, molt est de grant biauté,/Ja n'a si sage de ci qu'en Duresté*; Ch W 2591: *Dame Guiburc fu ne en paisnisme,/Si set maint art e mainte pute guische./Ele conuist herbes, ben set temprer mescines.*

gluttonous drunkard, with no ideals or religious conviction and minimal intelligence, but enough brawn to be a general bully and wield a crude, unorthodox weapon in battle, with which he could scarcely hope to achieve great things. Very poor and inadequately armed, he could never have led men in war, and as a type he would have been too lamentably common to inspire a poetic tradition that might exaggerate his strength and his rank. For these reasons it seems unlikely that a legend of Rainouart could have been produced by historical events, or indeed that any such legend could have been taken seriously as heroic matter at a date when heroic legend and poetry was still expected to represent historical fact – Rainouart could not become a heroic character until the heroic age was over. The conclusion that historical events are unlikely as the ultimate source of the Rainouart action applies only to its genesis. Many of the episodes which the growing action assimilated may quite well have been derived from history – an example of this is the battle of l'Archamp, which becomes an essential part of the Rainouart action. Some details may be older than Rainouart or even older than Guillaume.[1] Perhaps there was a historical source to the episode in which Rainouart, just before catching up with the imperial army, wades across a river and baptises his club. The Rhône, particularly near Arles, had a reputation for being very difficult and dangerous to cross, since it was fast-flowing, carrying logs and rocks with it, and had a bed of mud and sand (Rolin, pp. xliv–xlv). It seems plausible that this scene might recall a heroic deed when someone swam the Rhône with his weapon to join the Christian army. Historical sources like these might be found for episodes which we associate with Rainouart, but they will not do as an ultimate source for the Rainouart action.

Since a historical origin seems improbable, we must now consider whether it is likely that an independent *Chançun de Rainouart* ever existed at all. We expect in a heroic epic a chain of events which are linked to each other by causality and motivation to

---

[1] Cf. Siciliano, *op. cit.*, p. 210: 'Charlemagne historique fait naître sa légende, mais... autour de son nom se rassemblent des fables plus vieux que lui.'

form a consecutive narrative (cf. Bumke, p. 57). Desramé attacks Vivien and defeats him, consequently Guillaume intervenes; Guillaume is also defeated, and so he sends to Louis for help and with a new army he ultimately defeats Desramé. This causal chain links the main events of the *Chançun de Willame* (Bumke, *ibid*). Often there is one particular event in the series which is unusual and provides a focus for interest, such as the invasion by wagon in the *Charroi de Nîmes*, the conquest of the Saracen princess in the *Prise d'Orange*. It would be very difficult, if not impossible, to conceive of an epic poem which did not have such a consecutive narrative constructed out of a chain of events. Consequently, if the events to do with Rainouart ever formed a *Chançun de Rainouart*, an epic narrative which was originally independent of Guillaume, then it should be possible to relate those events to each other in such a chain of causes and motives.

We learn from the *Chançun de Willame* and *Aliscans* of Rainouart's escape or theft from Desramé and his youth in Louis' kitchen, followed by his participation in the battle of l'Archamp. There is no obvious reason for his departure from Saracen lands and his coming to France; the existence of two different explanations – according to one, he feels instinctively hostile to the Saracen gods (*Enfances Vivien* 4774–863), in other poems he is stolen by merchants (*Chançun de Willame* 3508–36; Al. 3258–60, 6373a–75) – suggests that these may be late inventions designed to explain how the Saracen giant came to be in the Christian army. Why he wishes to kill his own kinsmen is also not clear. There is no action for Rainouart in the imperial kitchen; Wolfram's tale of his companionship with Alyze as a child and his growing love for her does not occur in the French poems: he simply *is* in the kitchen until Guillaume comes along. His brutal treatment of the cooks also contributes nothing to the action but only illustrates his character by showing his strength and temper. We are entitled to ask whether he has been behaving thus all the time he has been at Laon, and if so where Louis recruits his cooks from and why the king should suffer such conduct from one he keeps so low. The account of his youth is linked to his part in the battle only by

Guillaume and Guillaume's war, which naturally cannot have formed part of an independent *Chançun de Rainouart*. But without Guillaume we cannot see how he comes to take part in the battle at all, for it would be out of character for Louis to send him. In the battle, too, there is no action to knit Rainouart's deeds together; he simply keeps hitting people with his club, most of them unimportant people whom he despatches up to ten at a time. The motif of his freeing the counts, which Wolfram uses so effectively to give direction to his actions, is far less prominent in the *Chançun de Willame* and cannot have appeared in a *Chançun de Rainouart* since it is part of the Guillaume tradition.[1] Suchier suggested that the function for which Rainouart was introduced was to avenge Vivien[2] but this could not have been his *original* function (i.e. in a *Chançun de Rainouart*) and it is peculiarly improbable, since Vivien was formerly avenged by Bertrand, and it is unlikely that an outsider would be introduced specifically to perform a noble deed that has long since belonged to a well-known hero of Guillaume's own family. The battle cannot be the unusual event which created a legend for Rainouart and linked the several episodes, because it belongs to the Guillaume *geste*, for which it did fulfil that function; it is in any case quite inadequate as a motivator for Rainouart's character and background or as a link with his life in the kitchen. Everything we know about Rainouart illustrates his character and personality – he is obviously strong, violent and excitable to an extraordinary degree – but he is never associated with any chain of actions and events.

Since the interest of Rainouart is not in a developing action but in the figure of Rainouart himself, it may appear that the Rainouart action has not grown out of a historical sequence of events but out of a character, which was a nucleus, attracting events and characters from the Guillaume *geste* to itself and generating further episodes of its own. But Rainouart's outstanding charac-

---

[1] Haucebier, who captures and imprisons the counts, is probably the Habirudar, who according to Ermoldus Nigellus (line 372) is killed by Guillaume. In *Foucon de Candie* the task falls to Foucon. This therefore seems to belong to the Guillaume rather than the Rainouart matter.

[2] Suchier, *La Chançun de Guillelme*, pp. lxv–lxvii.

teristic is clearly his strength, and it is a commonplace for warriors to be strong. The prospective legendary hero should be characterised by a more unusual feature if he is to be remembered for it – Guillaume's nose contributed more to his lasting heroic tradition than his strength did – and to provide the basis for an epic he must interest for what he does and suffers rather than what he is: it is the consecutive series of events that gives an epic that essential narrative thread which leads from a beginning to a satisfying end. To be the hero of an epic Rainouart needs more than a character – he needs to be active, and he needs a background for his activities; since that background is always supplied for him by the *geste* of Guillaume, in particular Guillaume's war, it seems likely that Rainouart became an epic hero only when he was introduced to the Guillaume *geste*.

Though it is impossible to prove that a hypothetical work never existed, that conclusion does now appear inescapable in the case of Suchier's *Chançun de Rainouart* (i.e. an independent Rainouart epic earlier than any known epic other than, possibly, the *Roland*), since no historical events are known which might have given rise to a heroic legend of Rainouart agreeing with our earliest records of him, and since those records themselves seem particularly difficult to derive from any historical facts and do not contain a chain of consecutive events that might be causally linked to form a Rainouart action and later expanded into epic form. Instead, Rainouart appears to have taken his action from the Guillaume *geste* and it is only for the character himself that we need to seek an independent source. For, although the Guillaume *geste* supplies a background for his activities, it is clear that Rainouart himself is an intruder there, as we have seen from the history of the *Chançun de Willame*. Rainouart is not needed before or after the great battle, and in it he is a *deus ex machina* who is introduced in order to defeat an otherwise invincible enemy (for it is out of the question that Louis could succeed where Vivien and Guillaume have failed).[1] Because Rainouart is

---

[1] It seems likely that, at earlier dates, first Guillaume and then Gui had become attached to the tale of Vivien's heroic death in much the same way, cf. p. 9, note 2.

an outsider, the account of his history prior to the battle does not easily fit into *Aliscans* (it has to be told between inverted commas) and does not occur at all in the *Chançun de Willame* – it may have been invented later than the *Chançun de Willame* to satisfy curiosity about this new and unusual character. After the battle he is at once forgotten by the French, and it was unfortunate for the authors of the *Chançun de Willame*, *Aliscans* and *Willehalm* that he could not remain forgotten: he had stimulated too much interest and his story required a proper end, and so he had to be reintroduced and sent away with gifts. Given a suitable background, Rainouart's character thus becomes engaged with a sequence of events and can generate an action, and so we must seek not an original Rainouart action but the origin of the character and the characteristic motifs that are particularly associated with Rainouart.

THE FAIRY TALE

Having looked in vain for a convincing origin of Rainouart in historical and heroic literature, we must now consider the possibility of a source for Rainouart's character and the motifs especially associated with him in popular literature. Rainouart is generally to be found in the company of supernatural creatures, in fact all his enemies other than those taken from the Guillaume action are monsters and giants (Aenré, Agrapart, Crucados, Flohart, Grishart, Loquifer, Walegrape). Such creatures are indeed found in heroic literature, but they can generally be shown to have found their way there from myths and folk-tales; in popular literature such characters, whose interest depends upon extraordinary qualities or feats of strength and not on their place in a historic chain of events, are the order of the day. While Guillaume and all his family live, like Roland and Charlemagne, in a recognisable world of remembered history among human heroes, Rainouart lacks a definite historical setting and lives among creatures of fantasy, among whom his own closest relatives are not the least fantastic, and he appears to belong to their world rather than to that of Guillaume. We must therefore examine the possibility that Rainouart came, together with such characters as these, from a folk-tale and was introduced with them to the matter of Guillaume, where he found a position in history and a share in important events.

A. H. Krappe[1] suggested that the *geste Rainouart* may be derived from fairy tales of the types *Der starke Hans* and *Bärensohn*. Krappe's method is not very satisfactory – he finds ten characteristics which Rainouart shares with the fairy tale hero without considering whether these are important and original features of Rainouart (he leans far too heavily on the *Enfances Vivien* and *Aliscans*, which are rather late epics of the cycle), and so some of his ten points are probably not representative of the oldest Rainouart tradition.[2] Nevertheless, Krappe's parallels are very striking and give us cause to consider his suggested origin of Rainouart seriously. To decide the question fairly we must use our oldest source of information on Rainouart and compare *all* his characteristic features with those most commonly found in the fairy tale. We therefore have to compare the fairy tale hero with the Rainouart of the *Chançun de Willame*, which is our oldest and our most archaic source.

The *Chançun de Willame* gives us a full and clear picture of Rainouart. He is extraordinarily strong and a giant.[3] He carries a club, which he calls his *tinel* (see p. 22, note 1) and for which he has a deep affection; he refuses to employ any other weapon, except in one episode when he uses the sword his sister gave him. He hates horses.[4] He is young and has had to live in exile

---

[1] A. H. Krappe, 'The Origin of the Geste Rainouart', *Neuphilologische Mitteilungen* 24 (1923), pp. 1–10.

[2] For example, his third point, 'at an early age he illtreats his teacher', occurs only in the *Enfances Vivien* (4818–63) and *La Bataille Loquifer* (2903–7), both of them late and unreliable sources for Rainouart lore, and his ninth point, that Rainouart kills his brother, is suspect because it is uncommon in the fairy tales and absent from the *Chançun de Willame*; Walegrape in *Aliscans* is his half-brother (Al. 6407b: *Ains, voir, ta mere ne resembla la moie*; cf. *Moniage Rainouart* fol. 297 col. c; fol. 319 col. d).

[3] The word is not used in the *Chançun de Willame* but there are many references to his size and that of his club which show that he is a giant (e.g. 2650–2; 2713; 2758) and he easily lifts part of the roof of a building (3413).

[4] Ch W 2840: *Suʒ ciel n'ad rien qui tant hace cun cheval*; cf. Ch W 2668, 2836: *Ne sur cheval ne quer jo ja munter*.

since early childhood,[1] but he remembers his beautiful sister and loves her intensely.[2] He is poor and goes barefoot, and he suffers constantly from pranks and practical jokes. He is aggressive, cruel and short-tempered,[3] and he longs for battle. He has a remarkable appetite and loves the kitchen; when offered a bed in the knights' quarters he refuses, preferring to sleep in the kitchen, and during the battle he dreams nostalgically of the king's kitchen ('C'est sa manière à lui de regretter *douce France*' – Frappier, p. 223).[4] He sleeps late, often in the kitchen (thus he misses the departure of Guillaume's army). He is clumsy and stupid: he cannot learn to kill Saracens without crushing their horses, and his vain attempts to thrust with his club are repeated until we yawn at his incapacity to understand. He supports the Christians, though of Saracen origin, but he is not deeply religious. He is of royal ancestry and finally marries a lady of royal rank. The royal ancestry, however, may have been invented when he was introduced to courtly literature, for it is evident in the *Chançun de Willame* that he is in the process of being made courtly: he speaks courteously when addressing Guibourc, and Willame insists he is well-behaved (e.g. *Chançun de Willame* 2819f) and recognises his noble birth (3163), though his behaviour at every moment contradicts this and shows him to be anything but a gentleman. If we disregard these superficial courtly features the essential picture is of a young, brutal, stupid Saracen giant with a giant's appetite, armed with a club and helping the Christians, rewarded at last by marriage to a princess. The test of Krappe's fairy tales as the origin of Rainouart is whether this picture can be derived from them.

[1] Ch W 3145: *un chevaler, un fort, un fier, un iofne,/un aloseȝ*. His moustaches and beard are just beginning to appear (2688, 2880).

[2] At the end it is only his love for Guibourc that prevents him from reverting to heathendom, killing Guillaume and conquering France.

[3] This is essential to the comedy when the cooks play tricks on him; it also works against Guillaume when Rainouart is not invited to the victory feast. In *Aliscans* the French fear his sudden anger so much that they cross themselves when he displays his strength (4745) and when he becomes violent they are instantly as silent as though holy mass had begun (2905–6).

[4] His thoughts of food during the battle are doubtless derived from Gui. All Guillaume's *lignage* have enormous appetites, cf. E. R. Curtius, 'Über die altfranzösische Epik', ZfrP 64 (1944), p. 291: 'Die Komik des *Archamp* (W) speist sich zum grössten Teil aus der rabelaisisch anmutenden Gefrässigkeit der Wilhelmssippe (1056ff; 1427ff).'

The two fairy tales concerned, *Der starke Hans* and *Bärensohn,* are found merged in practically every variant, because the bear is known for his strength and so the bear's son is a strong man. It is therefore very difficult to distinguish between them, and such distinction is unimportant in the present context, but generally we assume that the feats of strength belong to the type *Der starke Hans* while the animal background, the escapades in the house stocked with food, the battle with the demon and the rescuing of the princesses belong to *Bärensohn.* Many motifs occur in both tales. In Grimm's *Kinder- und Hausmärchen* the type *Der starke Hans* is represented by two tales, *Der junge Riese* (number 90) and *Der starke Hans* (number 166) and *Bärensohn* by *Dat Erdmännekin* (number 91). It is no easy matter to list the characteristics and motifs of these tales, since they are known in hundreds of variants, each slightly different from all the others, but Friedrich Panzer published a study of the 202 *Bärensohn* and 54 *Der starke Hans* variants he knew (he later added a brief survey of 19 further *Bärensohn* tales which he discovered in the course of his researches). Using the features which occur most commonly in Panzer's variants and seemed to him fundamental it is possible to construct the essential outline of the two types.

Bärensohn. One of the hero's parents, generally his father, is a bear (occasionally another animal or a robber), who has captured his mother and taken her to his cave, which he has sealed with a rock. He has made her his wife and she has borne him a son, who often shows some feature of the bear (e.g. bear's ears, claws, ugliness, great size).[1] In childhood the hero shows his strength, generally by moving the rock which blocks the entrance to the cave, and then escapes with his mother into the world; sometimes he kills his animal father and takes his mother back to her former husband. Anecdotes about his childhood (introduced from *Der*

---

[1] In variant 153 the father is a tramp, but the hero has bear's ears, which indicates an earlier version in which the father was a bear. In variant 49 he is not fathered by a bear but his name is Björnöre (bear's ears). In variants 65 and 69, where there is no bear, his name is Jean de l'Ours, and in variants 26 and 51 (with no bear) he is called Hans Bär or Bärensohn. There are also variants in which the bear has been completely eliminated.

starke Hans) illustrate his enormous strength and appetite.[1] Often he is a lazy child and will do no work; if he goes to school he is a poor scholar and kills the other pupils or the teacher. When he finds work, his pay is to administer one blow to his employer (which he seldom does); the job is usually to collect wood, and he comes back with uprooted trees. If employed by a smith he hammers the anvil into the ground. He soon creates such havoc that his employer tries to kill him, usually by some kind of trick, and on failing sends demons, wild animals, and sometimes the devil himself to kill him. He acquires a club, either an enormous iron one from the smithy or a whole tree trunk, and this is his only weapon; the first club made is usually too light and has to be replaced by a bigger and heavier one. Setting out with his club, he meets two giants, whom he overcomes in feats of strength, and they become his companions. They come to an empty house which is well stocked with food and lodge there. Each day two of them go out and one stays behind to cook the dinner; at midday a dwarf or demon comes and attacks the cook. He defeats each of them in turn until he meets the hero, from whom he narrowly escapes. By his flight the defeated demon reveals a hole in the earth beneath which he keeps three princesses prisoner, and the other giants let the hero down by rope. He finds the princesses guarded by wild animals or dragons, which he kills. The climax of these adventures is his battle with the demon himself, in which his club usually proves inadequate and he finally kills the demon with a sword found in the underworld or given him by the princesses. The companions pull up the three princesses by rope, then either keep the rope or throw it down, leaving the hero below; they force the princesses to swear to tell the king they are the rescuers. After further adventures the hero escapes from the underworld, often with the help of an eagle, goes to the king's palace and punishes or pardons the companions. He wins the hand of the youngest of the princesses, often with the help of a

[1] In variant 71 he does not stop eating for seven years; in variants 89 and 202 he eats a whole ox at one sitting when he is a week old; in a Tartar variant (195) he eats two camels before a gargantuan dinner. Panzer cites numerous examples of such prodigies of appetite, pp. 32 and 51f.

talisman from the underworld, and (perhaps after further adventures) marries her.

Der starke Hans. This is a loose collection of episodes rather than a coherent tale, and it is generally used in *Bärensohn* as a source for illustrative episodes (in return it usually includes features derived from *Bärensohn*). The essential features are these. The hero is very often fathered or suckled by a bear. He is a lazy boy and eats prodigiously (there are numerous episodes to illustrate his laziness and his appetite). He grows fast and shows extraordinary strength early in life. His parents send him away because they cannot satisfy his appetite, and he arms himself with a heavy club. People frequently mock him and play tricks on him, and he takes violent revenge. He finds work (at a smithy or collecting wood) and his employer (fearing the blow which Hans may one day claim as his pay) sends him on dangerous missions in the hope of killing him. Generally he is sent first into the woods, where wild animals attack him, but he overcomes them; in many variants he is made to join the army but proves invulnerable. Sometimes the employer sends him down a well and drops a millstone on him, sends him to a mill possessed of demons, or sends him to hell to get money from the devil, but Hans returns successfully from all the missions and the employer is not able to kill him.

In many important and fundamental respects this hero resembles Rainouart. He is young, strong, and a giant with a giant's appetite. He carries a heavy club and no other weapon. He sleeps late. He is obliged to live away from his proper home from early childhood. He suffers not only exile in youth, but also poverty, and he is generally despised (at least until he shows his strength). He is unintelligent and suffers constantly from tricks that are played on him. He fights against all kinds of giants and monsters. In his most dangerous battle his club breaks and he has to use a sword (often given him by a princess). His adventures are crowned with success and he finally marries a princess.

Certainly there are differences. There is no smith or forester, no apprenticeship and no dragon in Rainouart lore – in these respects Siegfried is nearer to Bärensohn – but the smith and the dragon are absent from many variants, and there are many tales of Bärensohn that never mention the bear (cf. p. 41, note 1). The apprenticeship to a smith or a forester may be a secondary motif in the fairy tale, since its function is apparently to explain how the hero comes by his club: in the smithy variants the club is of iron, and in the wood-gathering variants it is usually of wood). The tale provides no source for Rainouart's beloved sister, his cruelty and aggressiveness and his love for war, but these may have come together with the aristocratic background when he was introduced into the heroic literature of a military aristocracy.

Some features of Rainouart which we do not find in the fairy tale could be derived from more important characteristics which he does share with Bärensohn. Rainouart's love for the kitchen might easily be derived from his great appetite, a feature shared by Bärensohn. His love for his club and his hatred of horses may be derived from his carrying a club as his only weapon, as Bärensohn does, and having no use for horses since he is too strong for them (Bärensohn sometimes kills the horse or carries it home together with its cart because it is too weak to pull the load of wood he has collected). In variants of the fairy tale we can find Bärensohn loving his club and sleeping with it (Panzer, p. 43, variant 166) becoming a cook in the royal kitchen (p. 39, var. 52, 147) and quarrelling with the other cooks (p. 113, var. 147), joining the king's army (p. 61, var. st. H. 7, 12, 17, 19, 20, 31, 32, 41, 51, 52, 54) and routing the enemy with his club (p. 61, var. st. H. 19) killing great numbers of heathens, because some of them singe his clothes and beard (p. 54, var. st. H. 16) killing horses (p. 57, var. st. H. 7, 31; by using his club as a whip, var. 7) tossing his club into the air and catching it (p. 41f, var. 78, 136, 143, 151, 158, 163, 167, 183) becoming a knight (p. 61, var. st. H. 20) and being richly rewarded by the king (p. 61, var. st. H. 19, 20).[1] Bärensohn's battles against monsters in the underworld

---

[1] Many of these features of Rainouart doubtless occur in more variants of the tales than I can quote, because I have read only a few variants and Panzer, since he was not looking for these features, mentions them only incidentally.

resemble Rainouart's battles against comparable creatures at l'Archamp. Bärensohn freeing the princesses might be compared with Rainouart liberating the Christian prisoners. Bärensohn's long contests with other giants, who afterwards become his companions, are perhaps comparable to Rainouart's long battle in *Aliscans* against Baudins, whom he ultimately wins as his companion. The thrashing of the cooks by the demon in *Bärensohn* is reminiscent of similar scenes in the *Chançun de Willame*; the transfer of this violence from the demon to the hero himself is easily understood, since Hans on the third day turns the tables on the demon, treating him as he treated the cooks, and the demon is altogether absent from Rainouart matter; here too the tale offers parallels in detail to the *Chançun de Willame*, for example the cooks are tied up (p. 82f, var. 40, 192, 194) thrown against the wall (var. 38, 78) or thrown into their own fire (var. 81). The treachery of Bärensohn's companions after the demon and the monsters have been killed and the princesses freed is reminiscent of the ingratitude of Guillaume and the French to Rainouart after the battle. Like Bärensohn, Rainouart is hostile to his father. The hero's introduction into heroic literature would easily account for his acquisition of military qualities, such as aggressiveness, cruelty and a longing for war, for the aristocratic background in place of peasantry, and for the elimination of dragons and demons and substitution of a more realistic historical background. If Panzer is right in deriving Siegfried and Beowulf also from tales of this type, then they too will show how the animal father is forgotten and military standards are introduced when the hero enters heroic literature; Krappe also suggests (p. 10) that the replacement of the animal father by the pagan king could be a stage in the transition from fairy tale to epic. Similarly, the traditional apprenticeship of Bärensohn might have been changed into menial labour in the king's kitchen as a means of linking Rainouart to the Guillaume cycle.

The fullness of this evidence for a fairy tale origin, together with the lack of reliable evidence for a historical origin and the absence of a coherent Rainouart action in the earliest literature that mentions him must encourage us to believe that the double fairy tale *Bärensohn–Der starke Hans* is in fact the source of the fundamental features of Rainouart. That belief will be strengthened by ample evidence, much of it quoted by Panzer, that fairy tale heroes of this type have elsewhere found their way into heroic literature and played an important part there.[1] Whether or not we accept Panzer's source for Siegfried and Beowulf, we can hardly fail to recognise Bärensohn in the Bjarki of the *Hrolfssaga kraka*, and he is no less recognisable in a Samurai tale quoted by Hatto.[2] Such parallels demonstrate that this type of hero can and does become engaged with a particular sequence of historical events and, having found a part to play in them, may become a hero in the literature of the nobility. That process may be helped by the fact that *Der starke Hans* is a particularly loose collection of episodes, lacking a framework of its own to hold the adventures together (most fairy tales have at least a biographical framework), and is therefore especially liable to become attached to other narratives which can supply such a framework. The namelessness of the hero may also have played its part. Bärensohn has no particular name; in the tales he is simply called 'Hans' or 'The Bear's Son' or 'The Boy with the Club'. This makes it possible for him to adopt the name of a historical or literary character, whose whole personality he may then threaten to usurp; there are variants in which he is called 'Roland' (st. H. 51 and 52) and even 'Marko Kraljević' (var. 158), such is the proximity of Bärensohn to heroic tradition. In this way he may have taken the perfectly ordinary name of a real man called Rainouart (for such a name belongs to the real world rather than the world of the fairy

---

[1] Cf. Panzer, p. 229: 'Es ist oben schon andeutungsweise gesagt worden, dass in der Chronik des Gargantua, in den Sagen von Thor und Herakles Elemente des Märchens vom starken Hans sich deutlich genug wiederfinden; ich könnte hinzufügen, dass es mit seinem ganzen Aufbau etwa auch in der Finnbogasaga oder in der Erzählung der Kalewala von Kullerwo wiederbegegnet.'

[2] A. T. Hatto, 'Archery and Chivalry, A Noble Prejudice', MLR 35 (1940), p. 51, note 1. In the army of Oguri Sukeshige there is a strong man called Shoji who uses a whole tree as his weapon and crushes man and horse together with blows from above, like those of Rainouart; he plays a major part in ensuring Oguri Sukeshige's victory. On the origin of Bjarki in *Hrolfssaga kraka* see L. Mackensen, *Handwörterbuch des deutschen Märchens*, Berlin 1934–40, under *Bärensohn*.

tale) and replaced completely the person himself, about whom nothing whatever is known.[1]

This gives us a reasonably credible picture of the way Rainouart and the matter associated with him came into existence. The hero of the tales of *Bärensohn* and *Der starke Hans* is a young, strong, good-natured giant with an animal father; he carries a club and has an enormous appetite. He is of interest for his strength and his escapes from innumerable attempts to kill him, which result in his ultimate victory over his tormentors. In such a form the tale is very old and is known in all parts of Europe and Asia.[2]

During the centuries when Christendom was threatened by the Saracens an episode was invented in which this hero fought the Saracens; at first this was only one of his adventures, but, being topical, it became popular and created a new tradition. The consequent development of a warlike side to his nature made him more aggressive and cruel, and since the new episode required the fairy tale setting to be changed for the realistic background of war in Spain, the animal father became the Saracen king and was called Desramé, the standard name for Saracen kings. The hero, too, acquired a name, perhaps taken from some historical antagonist of the Saracens. His becoming a warrior also accounts for his social rise from peasantry to aristocracy, while the way he is treated at court and his own consistent pattern of behaviour still show that he properly belongs to the lower social class.

---

[1] Rainouart's name is Germanic; this is not unusual for a Saracen in literature, cf. 'Gormont', 'Tiedbalt d'Arrabe', in *Parzival* 'Îsenhart', in *Kudrun* 'Sîvrit von Môrlant'. It is a compound of *ragin* (power, greatness) and *ward* (defence, defender). Many names constructed with these elements, including countless variants of *Raginward*, may be found in Förstemann's *Altdeutsches Namenbuch*, cf. also W. Schlaug, *Studien zu den altsächsischen Personennamen des 11. und 12. Jahrhunderts* (*Lunder Germanistische Forschungen* 30), Lund 1955, pp. 141, 239f; O. von Feilitzen, *The Preconquest Personal Names of Doomsday Book*, Uppsala 1937, p. 346f; A. Dauzat, *Les Noms de Famille en France*, Paris 1945, p. 84. It has always been a common name throughout Western and Northern Europe, cf. Norse 'Ragnar', 'Rǫgnvald', English 'Reginald', and such French forms as 'Renard', 'Rainouart', 'Renault'. I have studied the history of this name and its variants in my typed M.A. thesis (*The Rennewart Action in Wolfram's Willehalm*, London 1964, pp. 345–9), hoping to discover clues as to the provenance of Rainouart, but this line of enquiry proved inconclusive.

[2] Panzer, pp. 3–14. The great majority of Panzer's variants are Indo-European.

This type of tale became more topical and attractive to the nobility with the rise of *chansons de geste*, and its similarity to the *chansons de la croisade* could not be overlooked. His affinity to the Tafurs in those *chansons* was doubtless also noticed, and their cruelty and ability to terrify friend and foe affected his character. Being similar to the *chansons de la croisade*, the tale of Rainouart could now be suitable entertainment for an audience of knights; if his earlier history had belonged only to the lower stratum, he was now no different from the heroes of the new, fashionable art form, the *chansons de geste*. A *jongleur* could now sing of him at court in epic verse, finding a suitable introduction in an earlier version of lines 1–1980 of the *Chançun de Willame*, which also told of war against Desramé and the Saracens. The paucity of heroic action in connection with Rainouart could be overcome by imitating motifs found in W and using its milieu as a background for Rainouart's activities: thus the flight of the cowards from the second battle in R seems to be a copy of a similar flight in W of Tedbalt de Beürges with Esturmi and all the cowards from the first battle, who also tear down their flag for fear of being recognised (*Chançun de Willame* 252–78; 328–30). Guillaume's battle with Alderufe in R (2096–209) is an obvious copy of his battle with Desramé in W (1919–63), and the name Alderufe is taken from W (637). Rainouart's 'retreat' to fetch his club may be related to Vivien's vow never to retreat under any circumstances. In particular, Rainouart takes over the rôle of the Gui of W (cf. Frappier, p. 231): Gui, a small child left behind by the French army but privately armed by Guibourc, meets the cowards fleeing from the first battle and attacks them, goes on to arrive late on the battlefield and rescues Guillaume from certain defeat through his quite incredible prowess; like Rainouart, he is related to Guibourc, he dreams of food during the battle, and finally kills Desramé, puts all the Saracens to flight, and leaves Guillaume by comparison so sadly in the shade that Guillaume marvels greatly and makes Gui his heir. The author of R quickly gets rid of Gui before introducing Rainouart and never mentions him again, while Rainouart takes over the greater part of Gui's action.

When the career of Rainouart, thus constructed, became a part of heroic epic tradition, the magic elements began to be reduced to mere exaggeration and the new background supplied some realism. As a hero of the nobility, Rainouart had to become more courtly and be a knight, finally a Christian knight. We see him acquiring courtly qualities in the *Chançun de Willame*, but such qualities do not deeply affect his behaviour prior to Wolfram's version of the story: in the *chansons de geste* we are often told he is chivalrous and polite but we always observe the very opposite in his conduct, though in the later redaction of *Aliscans* he is considered a fit husband for the king's daughter. With such a redaction as his source, Wolfram has made of him a serious and morally responsible young man, whom he can compare with his own Parzival.

II · WOLFRAM'S TREATMENT OF HIS SOURCE

WOLFRAM'S VERSION OF 'ALISCANS'

Wolfram's source was a version of the *Bataille d'Aliscans*,[1] a *chanson de geste* of over 8,000 lines, written about 1185. Several scholars[2] have believed that Wolfram also knew other *chansons* of the Guillaume cycle, because twelve of the thirteen known manuscripts are cyclical (i.e. they contain other *chansons* of the cycle) and because *Willehalm* occasionally alludes to matter found in other *chansons* or agrees in details with other *chansons* against *Aliscans*. S. A. Bacon[3] showed, however, that to explain all these features we should have to assume that Wolfram knew six *chansons* besides *Aliscans*, borrowing a detail or two from each and yet contradicting or showing extraordinary ignorance of all of them in important matters of content,[4] and Bumke (pp. 15, 18–34) found it necessary to introduce a new interpretation of the Vivianz action in order to explain the discrepancies between Wolfram and the *Chevalerie Vivien*, which he believes Wolfram knew and used as source material.[5] Furthermore, the cyclical manuscripts generally contain *chansons* of the *geste Rainouart* (*Bataille Loquifer*, *Moniage Rainouart* and *Renier*), which Wolf-

---

[1] I quote always from the Halle edition, *Aliscans, Kritischer Text*, edited by E. Wienbeck, W. Hartnacke and P. Rasch, Halle a.d.S. 1903.

[2] San-Marte, *Über Wolframs von Eschenbach Rittergedicht Wilhelm von Orange und sein Verhältnis zu den altfranzösischen Dichtungen gleichen Inhalts*, Quedlinburg and Leipzig 1871, p. 40; E. Bernhardt, 'Zum *Willehalm* Wolframs von Eschenbach', ZfdP 32 (1900), pp. 36–57; J-M. Minckwitz, *Romania* 32 (1903), p. 318f; Bumke, pp. 13–18.

[3] S. A. Bacon, *The Source of Wolfram's Willehalm* (*Sprache und Dichtung* 4), Tübingen 1910, pp. 39–85, especially p. 84f.

[4] For example, at several points his agreement with a *chanson* called *Guibert d'Andrenas* against *Aliscans* is striking, and yet he clearly does not know that its hero, whom he calls Schilbert von Tandarnas, is Willehalm's brother, and to judge by his initial *T* he had met the place name *Andrenas* only when preceded by *d'*, i.e. as part of the hero's name.

[5] Bumke's attempt to prove that Wolfram knew the *Chevalerie Vivien* is discussed and found inadequate by G. Meissburger, 'Willehalmprobleme', *Archiv* 198 (1961–2), pp. 310–14.

ram shows no sign of having known, and the Venice manuscript (St Mark's, fr. VIII, CIV, 5; henceforth referred to as M), which is the closest to Wolfram and also represents the oldest tradition, is not cyclical; since practically all cyclical manuscripts are late, it is likely that the collection of related *chansons* in single manuscripts had not begun or was not widespread until the 13th century and that Wolfram's source was not cyclical. Similarly, the English manuscripts which preserve the oldest *chansons de geste* (the *Chanson de Roland*, the *Chançun de Willame* and *Gormont et Isembard*) are not cyclical. Several of the important features that Wolfram appears to have taken from other *chansons* occur also in the *Storie Nerbonesi*, an Italian prose compilation by Andrea da Barberino about 1400, and in the *Prose Aliscans* (15th century); J. M. Nassau Noordewier[1] studied these works and came to the conclusion that they are based on a version of *Aliscans* which is different from the one we know and which in many respects resembles Wolfram's *Willehalm*. The *Prose Aliscans* begins with an assurance that it has made no alterations whatever to the *chanson* other than turning it into prose and slightly altering the language.[2] Similarly, the *Kitzinger Bruchstücke*,[3] some fragments of a Middle Low German translation of *Aliscans* which cannot have been copied from Wolfram (cf. Bacon, p. 130f), sometimes agree with Wolfram against all known *Aliscans* manuscripts, and from her study of the relevant passages Bacon concludes that its source was closer to the source of *Willehalm* than any *Aliscans* manuscript known to us today[4]. None of the known *Aliscans*

---

[1] J. M. Nassau Noordewier, *Bijdrage tot de Beoordeeling van den Willehalm*, Delft 1901 (thesis for the degree of *Doktor in de Nederlandsche Letterkunde*, Groningen).

[2] Nassau Noordewier, p. 41, note 2. The *Prose Aliscans* is edited by F. Reuter, *Die Bataille d'Arleschant des altfranzösischen Prosaromans Guillaume d'Orange*, Halle a.d.S. 1911. Reuter gives a summary of the content together with the full critical text. On the *Prose Aliscans* see also J. Weiske, *Die Quellen des altfranzösischen Prosaromans von Guillaume d'Orange*, diss. Halle 1898, especially pp. 63–70.

[3] Edited by K. Roth, *Denkmäler der deutschen Sprache*, Paderborn 1874. See also H. Suchier, 'Über das niederrheinische Bruchstück der Schlacht von Aleschans', *Germanistische Studien* 1 (1872), pp. 134–58.

[4] Bacon, pp. 129–35. It is not uncommon for the translators of a French poem to have used an earlier version than that preserved in France—hence the importance of Hartmann for the *Yvain* text and Pfaffe Konrad for the *Chanson de Roland*; in France the original poems may be superseded by revised versions and then lost. For the same

manuscripts could have been Wolfram's source – the only one which could possibly be old enough (Arsenal 6562; *a*) is very distant from *Willehalm*. When Bacon studied the source of *Willehalm* in detail she concluded, in agreement with Nassau Noordewier, that there is no reason to believe that Wolfram knew any *chanson de geste* other than *Aliscans*, though he may possibly have had 'a slight acquaintance with some other branches of the cycle', which he may have 'picked up here and there by allusion in conversation' (p. 106). It would be quite natural for anyone who had heard something interesting about Wolfram's Guillaume d'Orange to tell Wolfram about it, and it is not impossible that Wolfram had at some time in his career heard one or other of the *chansons* recited. Landgraf Hermann, who provided him with his source, could have given him useful information about the *geste* to which *Aliscans* belonged (cf. Singer, p. 5f). But since Wolfram shares no more than a detail or two with each of the relevant poems and contradicts them all elsewhere, he cannot have used them consciously as sources. His allusions to striking events such as the conquest of Nîmes by wagon (Wh. 298, 14ff; the story is told fully in the *Charroi de Nîmes*) may be ascribed to Wolfram's general knowledge of his subject, and the occasional correspondences in detail are best explained by assuming that his manuscript of *Aliscans* was similar to those used by the other translators.

In independent studies of the *Aliscans* manuscripts, P. Rasch[1] and P. Lorenz[2] both arrived at the conclusion that the Venice manuscript M is the nearest to the archetype; they quote considerable evidence for this view, which has never since been challenged. M is a 14th-century manuscript by an Italian hand, with many mistakes and omissions, but its readings are generally preferable to those of all known French manuscripts and it very

reason, really old poems like the *Chanson de Roland*, the *Chançun de Willame* and *Gormont et Isembard* survived only in England, while in France they were replaced by later poems of the same cycles.

[1] P. Rasch, edition of *Aliscans*, pp. xxx–xlvii.

[2] P. Lorenz, 'Das Handschriftenverhältnis der Chanson de geste "Aliscans"', ZfrP 31 (1907), pp. 385–431.

probably derives from an early manuscript which found its way to Italy before the early version of *Aliscans* was ousted by the longer revised version which we know from the French tradition. In the quest for the source of *Willehalm*, Bacon (pp. 136–66) compared all the *Aliscans* manuscripts and found that M was also the nearest manuscript to Wolfram's source; this conclusion has also stood unchallenged for over half a century. The main observations upon which it rests are these:

Manuscripts MLV preserve a shorter version of *Aliscans* in which *laisses* 122–65, which were not in the original (see Rasch, pp. xxx–xlvii) and record Rainouart's battles with the sons of Borrel, Agrapart, Walegrape, Grishart and Flohart, do not occur; Wolfram never mentions any of the events or persons that occur in these *laisses*. Only the shorter version (MLVde; 'de' copy from both versions) contains *laisse* 121a, which records the name of Sinagon's horse, Passelevrier (Al. 121a, 11), though the relevant line is missing in M; Wolfram knows the name of Synagûn's horse (Wh. 368, 22: *Passilivrier*). The *Prose Aliscans*, *Storie Nerbonesi* and the *Kitzinger Bruchstücke* also follow the shorter version, but the author of the *Kitzinger Bruchstücke* adds a summary of the *laisses* 122–65, which apparently he knew but did not find in his source. Wolfram's source clearly followed the shorter and older version.

   The comparisons of the *Aliscans* manuscripts with *Willehalm* have shown that Wolfram agrees with M in many more cases than with other manuscripts (for detailed examples see Bacon, pp. 147–57); it is particularly striking that Wolfram's personal and place names most resemble the forms found in M. Lines missing from M sometimes correspond to omissions in *Willehalm* or passages where Wolfram is independent of the source (e.g. Wh. 288, 10–17, Al. 4392–5, M omits 4393a and Wolfram omits the three names in that line, giving Rennewart ten brothers instead of thirteen; Wh. 91, 27–92, 1, Al. 1643–43d, M omits 1643c, making the passage unintelligible, and Wolfram is quite independent. M and Wolfram omit Al. 4339 and 4369). Only M distinguishes between Baudus d'Aumarie, son of Aiquin, and Baudins de Valfondee, cousin to Rainouart, as Wolfram distinguishes Poydwîz and Poydjus. All other manuscripts call both Baudus, using the form Baudin for the oblique case, and mention Aumarie and Valfondee in connection with both; M is itself not completely free from confusion (e.g. Baudus son of Aiquin is 'de Valfondee', Al. 5139, all mss). Wolfram's source may also have confused Maudus de Rames (*e*: *Baudus*), leader of Desramé's fifth army, with Baudus d'Aumarie, giving *Poydwîz von Raabs*. Türheim's *Rennewart* calls Baudins '*Baldewîn von Falfundê*', which does not seem to be derived from

Wolfram's '*Poydjus von Vriende,*' but from the French form, and most resembles the form of M: '*Baudins de Valfondee*'. Bacon finds 22 instances where Wolfram seems to agree with other manuscripts against M or has material which M omits, but these do not favour any particular manuscript and may be put down to the patent carelessness of the M scribe, who cannot have understood what he was copying (and for that reason is unlikely to have introduced any alterations other than meaningless errors which are easily recognised). M has possibly preserved an archaic feature in giving Guillaume the battle-cry *Orenge!* rather than the French royal cry *Monjoie!*, to which he was not really entitled (cf. Singer, p. 49f). A more important difference between M and Wolfram is that Rainouart in M (as in the *Chançun de Willame*) marries Ermentrut, though he loves Aalis, while in *Willehalm* he seems destined to marry Alyze, as in the other *Aliscans* manuscripts. It seems that the source of M is older than Wolfram's source, since in M the elimination of Ermentrut is only beginning, and in *Willehalm* it is complete. Wolfram's source thus resembles the sources of *Prose Aliscans* and *Storie Nerbonesi*, where Ermentrut has been eliminated but the revision with the expanded Rainouart action has not been introduced.

An interesting by-product of these *Aliscans* studies, which also supports M, is a theory attributed by Bacon (p. 147) to Saltzmann concerning the origin of Mîle, Willehalm's sister's son, who does not occur in *Aliscans*. Al. 32ff reads in M:

> un espiel porta par molt ruiste fieror.
> Lo jorn a mort maint fil de vavasor
> et a Guillaume le fil de sa seror.[1]

This refers, of course, to the death of Vivien and many other vassals of Guillaume. But if Wolfram's manuscript had, instead of *maint*, simply *m* or *mil*, these lines would give the impression that *Mil*, the son of a nobleman and of Guillaume's sister, fought valiantly with the sword until he died. Only M will support this theory, since it alone has the essential singular forms *porta* and *a* (Mm), and *fil de* (CM); the others generally have *portent*, *ont* and *maint gentil vavasor*, so that the passage is quite unambiguous. This is a most attractive explanation of the origin of Mîle, since confusion of *m*, *mil* and *maint* is frequent in the *Aliscans* manuscripts[2] and since Wolfram produces other characters through mistaking a word in the source (e.g. Jeschûte, Perc. 670f: *gisoit*; Antikotê, as well as Salatrê, Al. 1171, 32: *Salatré, li rois d'antiquité*; Cordeiz, as well as Amîs, Al. 1779: *Amis de Cordres*; Eskelabôn,

---

[1] Bacon misquotes M as: '*le jor*' and '*sar seror*'; '*le jor*' appears in the Halle edition and is amended, with many other errors, in the review of that edition by R. Weeks, *Romania* 35 (1906), pp. 309–16.

[2] I find '*m.*' or '*mil*' confused with '*maint*' in the variants of lines 1974, 3018, 3023, 3249, 3275a, 4323, 5797, 7430 and 7445c.

Al. 358: *xiii esclavon*; Libilûn, Al. 346: *un neveu Aarofle le blon*; Nöupatrîs, Al. 222: **(un) aupatris*; Brahâne, Al. 5006: *l'aufage brahaigne* (its proper name in *Aliscans* is Liart, Al. 6596d, 1): the places Bailîe, Al. 5076: *en sa baillie*, and Griffâne, Al. 570: *m. paien grifaigne*). Even scholars have been known to make this kind of mistake, as Bumke has entertainingly demonstrated.[1]

For these reasons we may regard M as the best representative, not only of the archetype, but also of the *Aliscans* tradition which Wolfram knew and used. All the editions of *Aliscans* are earlier than the discovery of the importance of M and none of them is really critical. M was not known to Jonckbloet, Guessard and Montaiglon, whose editions are based on 'a'; Rolin's text, which is notoriously unreliable,[2] is also based on 'a', though Rolin knew M and realised it was important. The Halle edition, which is still in general use, was produced as a *Seminararbeit* by three of Suchier's students, each of whom independently edited two or three thousand lines; the stemmata of Wienbeck and Hartnacke both favour 'a' and accord very little importance to M, and Rasch, who first recognised the priority of the MLV redaction, was unable to produce a satisfactory stemma and adopted that of Hartnacke; in any case the lines he edited, Al. 5380–8510 relate for the main part to the final episodes which do not appear in *Willehalm*, so that comparison is only possible for the last part of Book IX, where Wolfram has reorganised his source material so thoroughly that consideration of *Aliscans* manuscripts does not help very much. The work of Lorenz, who clarified the manuscript position,

---

[1] Bumke, 'König Galopp', MLN 76 (1961), pp. 261–3. Lachmann and Leitzmann both made kalopeiz, Wh. 360, 9, into the name of a Saracen king and edited 360, 8f: *aht hundert pusînen/hieʒ blâsen rois Kalopeiʒ*, although all manuscripts have *der kunich* instead of *rois*, and this king appears neither in *Aliscans* nor elsewhere in *Willehalm*.

[2] Rolin's edition is based partly on Wolfram's *Willehalm* and partly on the editor's arbitrary choices from the variants known to him; he produces a stemma but does not follow it. It is designed to justify some of Rolin's controversial opinions (e.g. each *laisse* originally ended with a half-line; many of Vivien's and Rainouart's deeds were originally performed by Guillaume). Its shortcomings were instantly recognised by its reviewers, e.g. P. Becker (ZfrP 19 (1895), pp. 108–18), who after a detailed examination says he would have preferred a text in alexandrines or Provençal. Gaston Paris remarks: 'M. Becker n'a pas de peine à montrer que cette publication bizarre est denuée de toute valeur scientifique,' *Romania* 24 (1895), p. 311. Further reviews, all very unfavourable: H. Suchier, *Literaturblatt für germanische und romanische Philologie* 15 (1894), p. 331f; W. Förster, *Literarisches Zentralblatt für Deutschland*, 1895, cols. 376f; G. Paris, *Romania* 23 (1894), p. 490.

establishing the importance of MLV and particularly of M, did not appear until 1907, and is thus later than all the editions. There is therefore no edition which deserves to be called critical, and no edition of *Aliscans* should be treated as representative of Wolfram's source when it is in contradiction to M, particularly since all editions are based, to a greater or less extent, on 'a', which is very distant from Wolfram.

Willehalm scholarship has generally disregarded the problem of the *Aliscans* manuscripts on the grounds that no known manuscript can be Wolfram's source. Thus Mergell[1] writes:

> Die französische Chanson lebt in Varianten, und es hat sich bis jetzt kein Kriterium dafür gewinnen lassen, dass Wolfram eine der überlieferten Handschriften gekannt habe.

And, rather more cautiously, Bumke:[2]

> ...aus keiner der erhaltenen Hss. ist Wolframs Vorlage sicher zu rekonstruieren.

Both go on, however, to compare *Willehalm* with the Halle text of *Aliscans*, as though that were Wolfram's source, disregarding the knowledge which has long been available concerning the relationship of the *Aliscans* manuscripts to *Willehalm*. This attitude has led to a number of errors. For example, Mergell gives Wolfram credit for creating two different characters out of Baudus[3] and blames *Aliscans* for resurrecting him from the dead[4] despite the fairly clear distinction of Baudus and Baudins (i.e. Poydwiz and Poydjus) in M, and Bumke (pp. 11–55, especially pp. 12–14) discusses at length Wolfram's isolation of his subject-matter from the cycle on the assumption that Wolfram's source must have been cyclical, while M suggests it was not. A great deal of Bumke's work concerning the structure of *Willehalm*, Wolfram's purpose and treatment of the source, and his chapter en-

---

[1] B. Mergell, *Wolfram von Eschenbach und seine französischen Quellen*, 1. Teil, *Wolframs Willehalm*, Münster 1936, p. 2.
[2] Bumke, p. 14, note 14.
[3] Mergell, p. 94: 'Wolfram hat aus dem Namen Baudus zwei Gestalten entwickelt: Poydjus und Poydwiz.' Cf. Rolin, p. lxi.
[4] Mergell, *loc. cit.*: 'Baudus, den Al. kurzerhand wieder von den Toten auferweckt (Al. 5193).'

titled 'Rennewart und der Schluss der Dichtung' (pp. 34–55), follow from the assumption that Wolfram had drastically cut down the Rennewart action and eliminated most of Rennewart's battles in order to subordinate him to Willehalm. But by reference to the *Aliscans* manuscripts and the other translations we can see that Wolfram's source contained very few of the battles he refers to.[1] By using such knowledge as we have about Wolfram's source, we may gain a quite different impression of Wolfram's practice and intentions than has been arrived at by comparing *Willehalm* with the Halle edition.

Although Rolin's ambitious attempt to reconstruct Wolfram's source has been severely criticised, largely because it purports to be a critical edition of *Aliscans*, it is clearly possible to draw some useful conclusions from the comparison with M and with the other translations of *Aliscans* as to the content of Wolfram's source.

It is very probable that Guillaume's banner was blue and gold in the source (Stor. Nerb. II, 513; Wh. 328, 9; 264, 4). The angel probably promised Vivien he would see Guillaume before he died (Prose Al. 369v; Wh. 49, 24–6; 65, 21). Guillaume, not Guibourc, suggested that he should go to Laon for help and leave her to defend Orange in his absence (Prose Al. 378v; Wh. 95, 16–28). At Orleans Guillaume was asked to pay customs duty (Prose Al. 380v; Wh. 112, 22 – 113, 24) and there was some reference to the *commune* (Prose Al. 380v; 394v; Wh. 113, 13).[2] Guillaume did not ride from Orange to Orleans without resting (Al. 2075f; 2082), but the number of days taken was not stipulated

---

[1] In M Rainouart kills Margot, Aenré (M: estele), Borrel, Haucebier, Jambus, Elinant, Malquidant, Samuel, Samul, Salmuant, Golias, Gliboés, Cadour, Tempesté, Jesué, Marados, Bustor, Tenebré, Triboé (M: Gibbe) and Giboé; in *Willehalm* he kills Esserê, Oukidant, Samuel, Samirant, Môrende, Gollîam, Fâbur, Kâtôr, Tampastê, Tedalûn, Malakîn, Gibûê and Kanliûn, and wounds Purrel and Halzebier. In the other *Aliscans* manuscripts (and the Halle text) he also kills Agrapars, Crucados, Walegrape, Grishart, Flohart, Eürés and Gohier; these battles are narrated at great length. Bumke's statement, p. 42, that Wolfram has excluded all the battles of Rainouart after Desramé's flight, presupposes that *Willehalm* is finished; this is a controversial issue, however, cf. pp. 210ff.

[2] The sudden appearance and hostility of the *chastelain* is quite unmotivated in Al. 2081–144.

(Prose Al. 380r; Wh. 112, 3–5). Guillaume sent for Rainouart and spoke to him as soon as Louis had surrendered him (Prose Al. 390v; Wh. 191, 29ff). Guibourc defended Orange by manning the battlements with armed corpses (Stor. Nerb. I, 436; Wh. 111, 15–25). There was a conversation between Guibourc and Desramé during the siege of Orange (Prose Al. 391v; Wh. 215, 10ff). Knights of Burgundy, Brittany, Flanders and Brabant, and perhaps other nations, were present at the banquet at Orange (Prose Al. 396r; Wh. 269, 24–7). Rainouart did not fight with monsters and giants or try to ride his horse back to front (absent from MLV, Stor. Nerb. and Prose Al.). There was an episode which prompted Wolfram's Matribleiz scene, where some of the Saracen dead were honoured, perhaps at Guillaume's prompting as in *Storie Nerbonesi*, where Rainouart's brothers are buried according to the heathen rite (Stor. Nerb. II, 526; Wh. 465, 1–30).

The *Storie Nerbonesi* and *Prose Aliscans* are, like *Willehalm*, far more tolerant towards the Saracens than *Aliscans* is, and when referring to the embalming scene and to the discussion at Orange between Guibourc and Desramé, in which Thibault and Desramé are ready to forgive Guibourc if she will return to them, Nassau Noordewier (pp. 40, 49–52, 54) suggests that the source of *Willehalm* may also have been more sympathetic to the Saracens. But the total lack of sympathy with the Saracens in the *chansons* of the Guillaume cycle, which *Aliscans* generally shares, makes this appear improbable, and while there is no evidence for direct influence from Wolfram upon these late prose versions, we must reckon with the influence of a new religious attitude to heathens in an age which no longer could whole-heartedly embrace the ideals of the crusade and may therefore have required the old *Aliscans* to be suitably adapted. Nevertheless, the correspondences in detail and in expression which Nassau Noordewier quotes can hardly be fortuitous and they seem to indicate that the old *Aliscans* poem had motifs which Wolfram and the prose redactors could revise in the same spirit. There is in *Aliscans* a religious dispute between Guillaume and Aerofles (Al. 1185–228, probably modelled on Guillaume's dispute with Corsolt, *Couronnement de*

Louis 835–53) and Rainouart disputes at length with Baudins; knowing as we do that *Aliscans* is much inclined to repetition (cf. p. 102f), it would not be surprising if an early version contained a similar dispute at Orange. From this Wolfram and the prose redactor could independently produce a conversation at Orange which showed the Saracens sympathetically (*Prose Aliscans* is not so sympathetic as Wolfram and the conversation soon becomes a quarrel), even if the conversation in the common source had been little beyond an exchange of insults. Provided the burial of the heathen dead was mentioned, the German and Italian adaptors, both inclined to treat the Saracens with respect, might independently claim that the rite was performed by courtesy of the Christian victors in Saracen fashion (*secondo il modo barbero, schône nâch ir ê*) in honour of Gyburg or Rennewart (it is no more than Wolfram's heathens had once done for Gahmuret). This seems likely in view of the differences between Wolfram and the prose versions. The conversation in *Prose Aliscans* is concerned mainly with Desramé's paternal love and willingness to forgive, while in *Willehalm* it is primarily a religious dispute, as we might expect knowing Wolfram's especial interest in the religious problems underlying the conflict. In *Storie Nerbonesi* Rainouart's brothers are put into magnificent coffins in his honour,[1] while in *Willehalm* Gyburg's relatives are embalmed to honour her; this is consistent with Wolfram's desire to subordinate the Rennewart action and with the respect for Gyburg he expresses at the beginning of Book IX. These prose redactions cannot show us exactly what Wolfram's source contained, but, since neither they nor Wolfram are given to pure invention of important matter, their agreement with him can show where our *Aliscans* has lost an episode or a motif of substance which belonged to the *Aliscans* tradition which they and Wolfram used.

---

[1] Stor. Nerb. II, 526: *tutti i fratelli di Rinovardo furono soppelliti secondo il modo barbero, messi in ricche sepolture per suo onore.* Cf. Nassau Noordewier, p. 39f; Bacon, pp. 98–100.

The résumé of the Rainouart action follows the *Aliscans* text as represented by M; the reading of M is italicised when it is at variance with all other manuscripts and the reading of the Halle critical text is then given in brackets. The numbers in the left-hand column are those of the *laisses* in *Aliscans*.

74–5. While Guillaume is being entertained by Louis at Laon he sees Rainouart come from the kitchen, his hair clipped and his face blackened with soot by the chief cook. The squires make fun of him and beat him with sticks until he loses his temper and crushes one of them against a pillar: Guillaume asks Louis who Rainouart is and Louis explains that he is a Saracen whom he bought from merchants for a hundred marks but whom he dislikes on account of his size and so he makes him work in the kitchen and will not let him be baptised. It is his job to carry water for the cooks. The cooks seek revenge for their companion and continue to torment Rainouart until he throws four of them violently to the ground. Finding his club burned by the cooks, he breaks it and swears he will make a bigger and stronger one. Guillaume asks for him as a gift and promises to feed him well; Louis is delighted to grant his wish. Louis says that he knows Rainouart is of noble birth and that he has been in the kitchens for seven years (Prose Al. 389 r°: Guillaume asks Rainouart to join his army).

Book IV. While Loys and Willehalm are watching the knights at sport, Rennewart comes across the courtyard carrying water for the cooks. When the knights make him spill the water he returns for more, but when they do it a second time he kills one of them by throwing him against a pillar. Loys apologises to Willehalm for Rennewart's unwonted bad behaviour, and explains that he is made to work in the kitchen despite his noble birth because he refuses to be baptised. Willehalm asks if he may take Rennewart with him, and Loys, after at first refusing, is at last persuaded by Alyze to part with him. Willehalm sends for Rennewart but Rennewart refuses to speak to him until addressed in his own language. Then he tells Willehalm he comes from Mekkâ, but since Mahmet has failed him he has turned to Christ, though refusing to be baptised, and he longs for release from the ignoble life in the kitchen. Willehalm is impressed at his striving for nobility in his present circumstances, tells him that Loys has given him to him, and Rennewart promises to help him in the war. Willehalm sends Rennewart to a

76. As the French troops assemble, Rainouart weeps in the kitchen because he has to stay behind and lead an ignoble existence, though he is of royal blood and should be king of Spain. He comes barefoot to Guillaume, falls on his knees and begs to be taken to Aliscans, basing his plea on his experience as a cook. Guillaume says he could not endure the hardships of war, having been used to plenty of food and sleep, but Rainouart begs for release from the humiliating life of the kitchen, and Guillaume promises he may come. Needing a new club, Rainouart fells a fir-tree and takes it to a smith, who fastens iron bands round it for a fee of 100 sous. (*e* 3379, 22ff: He goes to the kitchen, destroys the cooks' pots and quarrels with the cooks.)

77. The French are terrified to see Rainouart with his club and he warns them that they must leave it alone. Rainouart tells Guillaume he must not delay the march for Orange any longer, and Guillaume calls his army together. At the feast before departure Rainouart gets drunk and falls asleep in the kitchen, and the squires bury his club in a heap of dung. Early next morning the army leaves, escorted by Louis, Queen Blancheflor and Aelis. Rainouart is awakened by the trumpets and runs after the army; when he is wading through a stream the shock of the cold water restores him to his senses and he remembers his club. Guillaume, seeing him turn back for it, rides up to him and accuses

Jew to be equipped with arms, but Rennewart asks for nothing except a beechwood club with steel bands round it, a camel-hair coat and new shoes and trousers. That night the cooks singe his hair and his clothes and Rennewart in anger destroys their pots with his club. Willehalm finds him lamenting next morning and consoles him with the promise of new clothes and a long-overdue haircut, telling him he must be ready early the next morning for the army's departure. The next morning Rennewart oversleeps and finds the army gone; when he catches up, Willehalm asks where his club is. Rennewart thanks him for reminding him and asks Willehalm to wait while he returns for it. Willehalm agrees to wait, and says Rennewart must bring any other soldiers who may have been left behind. Since the cooks have hidden his club he kicks in the doors and kills the chief cook; then he runs back with his club to Willehalm.

When the army reaches Orleans, Loys hands over his command to Willehalm and prepares to turn back. Rennewart takes leave of King Loys, then goes out of doors to Alyze, who begs him to forgive her father for the wrong done to him at Munlêûn and kisses him; Rennewart bows and politely takes leave of her. The army, led by Willehalm, then hastens towards Orange.

him of cowardice; Rainouart explains, refuses Guillaume's offer of
a messenger to fetch it, and returns
to Laon. (78–80 only in *a*.)
81–3. Rainouart forces the squires
to fetch him his club, but they cannot lift it, so he goes and takes it
himself and runs singing from the
stable. He meets the chief cook who
orders him to light the fires and
get on with his work. When he
refuses the cook threatens to light
the fire with his club and calls him
bastard; Rainouart kills him with
the club. The squires ride to Guillaume and complain, but Guillaume refuses to punish Rainouart
and tells them they should not torment him but handle madmen and
drunkards carefully. Guillaume
rides to meet Rainouart, who prepares for a trial joust, but Guillaume assures him that he only
meant to help him carry the club.
The whole army waits impatiently
while Rainouart washes his club in
a stream; Aelis, looking on, falls
in love with him, but her mother
disapproves. Later on, Guillaume
tried to arrange for them to marry,
*but Louis objected and Ermenjart
arranged that he should marry her
niece Ermentrut instead*, then
Rainouart became King of Spain
and ruled at Cordoba. Aelis sends
for Rainouart, embraces him and asks
pardon for any wrong she may have
done him; he readily forgives her.
At the sound of the trumpets he
leaves her to rejoin the army. At
Orleans Louis, the Queen and
Aelis turn back, and the ladies

faint for grief at parting: Guillaume's family return to their
homes and Guillaume presses on
towards Orange.

84–90. Guillaume sees smoke as he
approaches Orange and he leads his
army to the rescue; when Guibourc
sees the army she takes them for
Saracens and faints for fear. The
town is burnt but the Saracens have
withdrawn to build siege engines.
Guibourc will not admit Guillaume until she has seen his nose.
He introduces Rainouart to her and
asks her to take good care of him.
Guillaume's relations arrive with
their armies and a banquet is prepared.

Book V. Orange is besieged, and
Gyburg disputes with Terramêr.
One night the Saracens attack and
burn the town. Willehalm sees the
smoke and comes to the rescue,
but the Saracens have withdrawn.
Gyburg is overcome with joy at
seeing Willehalm. When they enter
Orange, Gyburg asks who Rennewart is and Willehalm explains.
Rennewart goes to the stables to
attend to Volatîn. Willehalm's relatives come to Orange and a feast is
prepared.

91–5. Rainouart attends, bringing
his club, and is seated beside *Aymeri* (Aïmers). The knights make
him drunk and torment him until
he seizes the club and hits a marble
pillar so hard that it smashes into
two pieces. Aïmers says Rainouart
will be a great asset in the battle.
Everyone retires to bed. Having
drunk too much, Rainouart falls
asleep in the kitchen. He is awakened by the chief cook setting fire
to his moustaches; he throws the
cook on to the fire and boasts that
he has dared to kill Guillaume's
cook because he is son of Desramé
and related to many powerful kings.
The cooks complain to Guillaume
and refuse to cook dinner, but
Guillaume laughs and reproves
them for provoking Rainouart; he
sends Guibourc to Rainouart. Gui-

Book VI. Rennewart enters the hall
and leans his club against a pillar.
Since leaving Munlêûn his beard
has started to grow. Rennewart is
introduced to old Heimrîch, who
arranges that he sit at the edge of
the table next to Gyburg, and
Gyburg extends the tablecloth
to reach him, at which he politely
bows. Rennewart eats and drinks
heartily and when some squires
come to interfere with his club, he
warns them, very good-humouredly,
that they must leave it completely
alone. When they knock it over, he
loses his temper and hits a pillar
with it so that sparks fly to the
roof; all the squires run away and
the meal is quickly ended. That
night the squires tease him again,
but Rennewart does them no harm
and finally goes to sleep in the

bourc finds him in the kitchen and offers him fine clothes; he follows her, dragging his club behind him, to her room. When he tells her he has a wise beautiful sister, who is a queen she guesses he may be her brother and wraps her cloak over him. He promises to tell her his lineage after the battle. She arms him and gives him a sword that once belonged to Tiebaut; he finds it too small and throws it down, but Guibourc persuades him to wear it and gives him armour. He is delighted and returns to the kitchen.

96–7. Rainouart eats great quantities of food in the kitchen, then goes to the knights, who try to lift his club. Only Guillaume manages to lift it *chest-high* (a foot off the ground); Rainouart then tosses it from hand to hand in the air. Rainouart tells Guillaume they must hurry to battle, and so Guillaume collects his army and they set off.

Rainouart forgets his club and blames Guillaume for not reminding him, so Guillaume sends Gui back to Orange for it. Gui and Guibourc are unable to lift it, so they have it loaded on to a wagon.

kitchen with his club as his pillow. (An excursus tells how he was bought by merchants and brought to Loys, how he used to play with Alyze and fell in love with her, but was separated from her because he refused to be baptised.) Before dawn, when the cooks begin to prepare the first meal, the chief cook sets fire to Rennewart's beard and Rennewart roasts him over the fire. The cooks disperse and Rennewart laments the damage to his beard and the implicit dishonour to himself and to Alyze and to all his noble family. Willehalm sends Gyburg to the kitchen; she consoles Rennewart, offers him better clothes and wraps him in her cloak. He tells her about his Saracen background and his sister, so that Gyburg thinks he may be her brother. She gives him Synagûn's armour and sword; he thinks the sword is too small for him, but finally decides to wear it; Gyburg then leaves to go to church. A council is held at which the army leaders and Gyburg speak. While a meal is being prepared, the knights try to lift Rennewart's club, but only Willehalm can raise it above his knees, and then Rennewart swings it above his head. After the meal, the army leaves for the battle.

Book VII. Rennewart's interest in the army is so great that he forgets his club again. When Willehalm reminds him he is thoroughly ashamed of himself; Willehalm sympathises with him, and to spare

The whole army waits for Rainouart's club, and when it arrives,
Rainouart seizes it with such delight that the wagon collapses.
That night he sleeps beside the
kitchen fire with the club for his
pillow.
98–106. Rainouart oversleeps and
finds the camp burning and the
army gone. He runs after them, but
has to return when he remembers
his club, which he finds burnt but
stronger. Guillaume comes within
sight of the Saracens and allows
over 10,000 cowards to leave the
army and return to France. On
their way back they meet Rainouart at a bridge in a narrow place
and invite him to join them, but he
attacks them with his club and forces
them to return to the battle. Guillaume grants Rainouart's request
that he may command them. Guillaume divides his army into seven
groups, the first of which is com-
manded by Rainouart. A wounded
messenger tells Desramé that the
Christians have come. Desramé is
armed by kings; he becomes furious
when a Saracen tells him of Rainouart and says that they will all be
destroyed by him. Desramé has his
trumpets blown and divides up his
army.

him the embarrassment of turning
back he sends one of his men back
to Orange to fetch it by wagon
with the rearguard. The next morning Rennewart forgets it again for
the same reason. This time he is
very angry and wonders whether
God is testing him; he runs back
to find it burnt but stronger. Willehalm meanwhile allows the imperial
troops to return to France and
praises the others who stay with
him. On their way back the imperial troops encounter Rennewart
at a narrow spot called Pitît Punt,
and he immediately attacks them so
violently that they recognise him
as God's instrument punishing
them for desertion in the holy war.
A 'wise man' offers Rennewart an
easy life with them in France, seeking the pleasures of *minne* or beer,
which angers Rennewart so much
that he kills many more of them,
and forces them to agree to follow
him into battle. When they reach
Willehalm the army has already
been divided into five groups, and
Willehalm gives Rennewart command of the imperial troops, who
form a sixth group and use his
name as their battle-cry; their flag,
the Cross, which had been put into
a sack, is restored to them. When
Willehalm speaks of rewarding
Rennewart or serving him, Rennewart says there is a secret reward
he hopes to earn by his valour in
the battle. One of the Christians
wounds one of Tybalt's men, who
alerts Terramêr, who fears that
Loys has brought the imperial

army against him, but asserts his own right to rule the Roman Empire as descendant of Pompeius. Terramêr divides up his army and rides into battle.

107–14. Baudus li fils Aiquin kills Gui and Miles; Aïmers (M 5165: *Naymeris*, 5168: *Aimeris*) wounds and pursues Baudus and kills him by *Gorhier's* (Gohier's) tent. Aïmers is surrounded and cries 'Nerbone!', and his father Aymeri and his brothers come to his rescue; Rainouart comes to help Guillaume. Sinagon attacks so fiercely that the Christians almost lose hope of victory; Rainouart prays to Mary for help. He calls his men together and threatens to crush the first man who retreats; they quickly kill large numbers of Saracens. A messenger advises Desramé to withdraw for fear of Rainouart, but *Baudins* (Baudus) silences him. Rainouart comes to the ships and frees first Bertrand, then the other prisoners, throwing their fifty Nubian guards into the sea. The freed French arm themselves with Rainouart's aid, but Rainouart is unable to provide horses, since his club always kills man and horse together at one blow. In this way he kills *Elmant* (Elinant), *Macudant* (Malquidant), Samuël, *Saumul* (Samul), *Samuant* (Salmuant), Morindes (not M), Baufumé and others. Bertrand advises him to thrust with his club, and after a long series of failures, Rainouart learns to unhorse his enemy and provides

Book VIII. When Willehalm's group is attacked by Tybalt and Ehmereiz (Terramer's second group), Rennewart comes to his aid killing men and horses together with his club. Ehmereiz is surrounded but rescued by his men. Synagûn (Terramêr's third group) intervenes and fully engages Willehalm's group. Each of the Christian groups is opposed by a Saracen group; only the sixth (under Rennewart) is getting the better of the enemy. Josweiz (Terramêr's seventh group) comes to the aid of Tybalt, so that Rennewart's army is engaged with two Saracen groups at once (Terramêr's second and seventh groups). Poydwîz von Raabs (Terramêr's eighth group) presses the armies together, though he is hindered by the large stone coffins of the dead of the first battle. Marlanz von Jerikop (Terramêr's ninth group) attacks the Christians' weak points, leading his vassal Gorhant, whose men are armed with clubs. The whole heathen army, driving the Christians back, crosses the Larkant, bringing their gods on wagons. At last, Terramêr himself attacks with massive forces, and the Christians can earn glory not by advancing but by holding their ground.

horses for all, killing *estele* (Estiflé) and others, Rainouart impresses them by killing six or eight Saracens with every blow.
115–21c. Bertrand kills Aiquin and rides to Guillaume to tell him of Rainouart's prowess. Guillaume meets Margot de *occident* (Bocident) but cannot injure him with the sword and flees from him; Rainouart intervenes and crushes Margot and his mare, though Margot was his *uncle* (cousin). Guillaume thanks him. Rainouart rests and the Saracens recover. Rainouart kills his cousin *estele* (Aenré) and declares that he is Desramé's son and will kill his father and his brothers if they will not accept Christianity.

Desramé enters the fray, injures Gaudins, challenges Guillaume and attacks him. Guillaume wounds Desramé, but he is rescued by *1,000* (20,000) Persians. *Guillaume kills five Saracens. Naymer (i.e. Aïmer) kills Chaen and Auchin in front of Guillaume. Rainouart kills 20 Saracens with four blows.* Borrel kills several Christians and is killed by Rainouart. Sinagon riding Passelevrier attacks Bertrand, but they are separated. *Baudins* (Baudus) is equipped by Desramé with a big club and sets out to find Rainouart. Rainouart meets Haucebier, who will not condescend to fight until Rainouart says that Guillaume, whom Haucebier was looking for, is dead. Rainouart kills Haucebier, but the blow breaks his club and

Book IX. Terramêr's army intervenes at the places where the Christians are strongest and advances so fast that the gods are left behind. The Christian groups are broken up by the force of the Saracen attack and the soldiers have to collect around any Christian banner they can reach. Heimrîch kills Cernubilê von Amirafel and Poydwîz von Raabs, and Bernart kills Cliboris von Tananarke. Terramêr kills Milôn von Nivers, one of Rennewart's men, whom Rennewart promptly avenges by killing Fabûr, Samirant, Samûêl, Oukidant and Môrende. Rennewart's army forces Terramêr's first group (led by Halzebier) to withdraw to the ships; Halzebier's group retreats in order, pursued by Rennewart and

Rainouart fights Haucebier's men with his fists until he remembers his sword; he kills Gollias and Gliboés with it and is delighted with its efficiency. Rainouart is surrounded by Saracens, but Guillaume and his family rescue him. The Saracens flee pursued by Rainouart and Guillaume. Rainouart meets his father and threatens to kill him unless he becomes a Christian; Desramé attacks Rainouart but is wounded by him and put to flight; Rainouart kills his brother Jambus. (122–65 not in MLV.)

166–79. Rainouart kills *Gibbe* (Triboé), *Cadoc* (Cador), *Tenebre* (Tempesté) and *malachin* (Samuël, Jesué, Marados, Bustor and Tenebré), marvelling at the efficiency of his sword. He pursues the Saracens and destroys all their ships except one, in which Desramé, Sinagon, *Persague*, *Bargis* and *Tenpeste* (five other kings) escape to *Gories* (Cordres). *Baudins* (Baudus) joins the Saracens who have been left behind and promises to help them. *Baudins* (Baudus) finds Rainouart and challenges him; they try without success to convert each other, and their religious debate is resumed in the intervals during their long battle. Rainouart prays to God at length asking that he may defeat *Baudins* (Baudus) and have him for his companion. Guillaume and his brother come to help, but Rainouart will not let them intervene. Rainouart defeats *Baudins* (Baudus) but spares his life when *Baudins* offers to become a Chris-

some of Willehalm's men. When the Christian prisoners hear the cry 'Munschoye!' they too shout 'Munschoye!' and Rennewart forces the unarmed Nubian guards to set them free. Rennewart provides them with arms by killing Saracens, but is unable to kill his enemy without harming the horse until Berhtram teaches him to unhorse the Saracens by thrusting with his club. Rennewart kills Esserê and provides the freed prisoners with horses, upon which they attack Halzebier, who by now is battle-weary, but kills Hûnas von Sanctes before the others kill him. Oukîn, father of Poydwîz, sees his son's horse Lignmaredî (later to belong to Rennewart) with the saddle empty and laments his son by attacking Willehalm, who kills him. Purrel, with fresh troops, kills many of Rennewart's men until Rennewart severely injures him, but breaks his club in so doing and has to fight on with his fists until Gibelîn reminds him he is wearing a sword. Rennewart finds his sword very efficient, kills Gollîam von Belestigweiz and wounds Gibôez von Cler and forces Terramêr's second group (under Tybalt and Ehmereiz) to withdraw. Bernart kills Ektor, and Ektor's contingent retreats; the remaining Saracens then retreat, though still defending themselves, some to the ships and others to the mountains and swamps. Eight Saracens defend the fleet while the survivors board the ships. Willehalm meets Terramêr and

tian and to let Rainouart have the kingdom of Spain. (Prose Al. 419v: Guillaume finds after the battle that Rainouart is missing and searches high and low for him until he finds him, just after his victory over Bauldus.) Guillaume congratulates Rainouart and the French have a feast on the Saracens' supplies. Rainouart gives *Baudins* (Baudus) leave to return to his country until he has recovered from his injuries. (Stor. Nerb. II 526: the Christians bury their dead, and the bodies of Rainouart's brothers are buried richly in the heathen manner in his honour.) Rainouart rouses the French at midnight to prepare to return to Orange. Guillaume finds Vivien's body and buries it. A poor peasant complains to Rainouart that some Saracens have robbed him and Rainouart goes and kills them and gives the peasant their horses. The peasant, desiring to serve Rainouart, returns with him to Guillaume, whose brothers escort him to Orange. The army rides quickly to Orange; Rainouart is too weary to keep up and is left behind. 180–4. Guibourc prepares a feast for the French and Rainouart is forgotten. He reaches Orange late for the meal and stands outside resenting Guillaume's ingratitude. At last, he returns in tears to Aliscans. On the way he meets some French knights and tells them of Guillaume's ingratitude and of his own intention to raise a Saracen army and attack Guillaume, depose

wounds him. Terramêr's son Kanlîûn comes to his aid but is killed by Rennewart who comes to help Willehalm and kills Gibûê, Malakîn, Kâtor, and Tampastê; Terramêr is badly wounded when he is carried to his ship. Tedalûn kills Gandalûz, one of Rennewart's men, and is killed by Rennewart; Poydjus, though challenged by Rennewart, avoids battle. The Saracens flee, and the Christians collect booty, feast and drink, some of them to excess. The Christian dead are embalmed. Willehalm notices that Rennewart is missing and is overcome with grief, but Bernart insists he hide his grief, which is unbecoming to a military leader in the moment of victory. Willehalm puts Matribleiz in charge of the Saracen prisoners and tells him to collect the Saracen dead and have them embalmed. Finally, he sets Matribleiz free and sends him with the heathen dead to be buried according to their own custom, for love of Gyburg and as a token of respect for Terramêr.

Louis, be crowned at Aix and marry
Aelis. He sends greetings to Guibourc and a challenge to Guillaume. When Guillaume receives
the message he is afraid and sends
twenty knights to apologise to
Rainouart and bring him back.
When he refuses to come, the knights
try to capture him but he quickly
puts them to flight. Hearing of
their failure Guillaume rides to
Aliscans with his brothers, Aymeri
and Guibourc and a hundred
knights. Rainouart repeats his
threats to Guillaume, who is too
frightened to go near him. Guibourc goes up to Rainouart and
reminds him of the occasion when
she took him to her room, armed
him and gave him fine clothes, and
begs him to forgive Guillaume.
Rainouart pardons Guillaume for
love of Guibourc, who tells Guillaume to step forward and thank
Rainouart for his graciousness.
Guillaume falls at Rainouart's feet
and thanks him. They return to
Orange and Rainouart sits between
Guibourc and Guillaume at supper.
184a–89a. At supper Rainouart
tells Guibourc that he is son of
Desramé and how, after a beating,
he killed his tutor Giboé and ran
away with some merchants who
took him to *Galice* (Palerne) and
sold him to Louis, in whose
kitchens he worked for seven
years. (He has long thought
that Guibourc might be his sister.)
Guibourc tells him she is his sister,
and weeping, they kiss. Rainouart
is baptised and dressed in fine

clothes. Guillaume makes Rainouart his seneschal and gives him fine
armour and a horse (called Li
Margaris). *Baudins* (Baudus) comes
back to Rainouart and he and his
men are baptised.
(M ends here. The others continue
as follows:)
Guillaume sends his brothers to
Louis to tell him of the victory
and bring Aelis back. Aelis comes
to Orange and is married to Rainouart, who receives Tortelose and
Porpaillart in feoff from Guillaume and will be king of Spain
one day. Aymeri and his sons return to their countries, and Guibourc exhorts Guillaume to rebuild
Orange. Rainouart and Aelis leave
for Porpaillart.

WOLFRAM'S ADAPTATION

The comparison of *Willehalm* with its source will enable us to
draw reasonable conclusions as to how Wolfram meant his poem
to be understood; in particular it may show what part he intended
the Rennewart action to play in the whole epic and give us a firm
factual basis from which to conjecture as to how he envisaged its
completion. By noting which episodes Wolfram elaborates and
which he shortens, by studying the changes he makes and by
classifying the kinds of detail over which he is often at variance
with his source we shall be able to judge his own attitude to his
subject matter.

It would not be legitimate, however, to assume that when
Wolfram does not differ from his source he necessarily approves
of what he has copied. His freedom to alter what he finds is
severely limited by the convention of a courtly poet's obligation
to follow his source; Wolfram acknowledges this obligation
himself and frequently assures his audience that he is faithful to

the French version.[1] This convention restricted his freedom more in *Willehalm* than it had done in *Parzival*, since this time the source was most probably complete and certainly known to the patron, Landgraf Hermann von Thüringen, and in all probability to the audience as well (cf. 7, 23ff), and so Wolfram can risk being at variance with his source (as distinct from passing quickly over one episode and elaborating another) only when the change is essential and defensible or else when it will not easily be detected. In *Willehalm* (unlike *Parzival*) the details which Wolfram explicitly claims to have derived from his source can often, though not always, be found there (cf. Bacon, pp. 13–39, especially p. 38f). Even when he considers the source to be in error he will often render faithfully what it says. When describing Willehalm's dress as he rides from Orange to Munleun Wolfram tells us truthfully what the source contains (Al. 2343f) but declares it wrong:

> 125, 20 Cristjâns ein alten tymît
> im hât ze Munlêûn an gelegt,
> dâ mit er sîne tumpheit regt,
> swer sprichet sô nâch wâne.
> er nam dem Persâne
> Arofel, der vor im lac tôt,
> daz friwendîn friwende nie gebôt
> sô spæher zimierde vlîz;
> wan die der künec Feirafîz
> von Secundilln durch minne enpfienc:
> diu kost für alle koste gienc.

In this case one may well agree with Vogt (p. 298), who condemns Wolfram's objection to his source as 'schulmeisterlich', because Wolfram's insistence that Willehalm is wearing Arofel's fine armour has destroyed an impressive contrast between the poorly-clad hero at the king's gates (Al. 2343: *si a vestu i mavais siglaton*) and the luxury of the king and his courtiers and guests at their festival. But here Wolfram was able to justify his disagreement with the source, and the amendment might forestall any objection to his tale's consistency on this count, and so he argues his

---

[1] Cf. Bacon, pp. 13–39, where 36 assurances of this kind are studied. Wolfram emphatically acknowledges his obligation to follow the source in *Parzival* (15, 10ff; 338, 17ff).

case. More often, however, Wolfram will render his source faithfully, as he is obliged to do, but dissociate himself from it by expressing disapproval. When Margot von Pozzidant rides a mare into battle (Al. 5712: *N'ot pas destrier, ains cevauce jument*; M: *ciualce une jument*), Wolfram translates faithfully (395, 7: *ein jumenten rîten,/dar ûf er wolde strîten*), but since Christian chivalry considered it improper to use a mare as a war-horse,[1] he adds a critical comment:

> 395, 12   der orse muoter man niht wil
> sô hie ze lande zieren:
> wir kunnen de ors punieren.

The displeasing detail is preserved, although it runs counter to Wolfram's more sympathetic portrayal of the Saracen nobility, and Margot is one of the few Saracens whom Wolfram does not praise (though Margot's men are praised enthusiastically). In the case of Desramé, who in *Aliscans* also rides a mare, Wolfram evades this problem, perhaps quite innocently, by reading *la brahaigne* as the name of the horse without considering the sex which such a name implies.[2] Wolfram preserves the report that Margot's men have green horn for skin and moo like cows (Al. 72–93, 5724; Wh. 35, 3–17; 395, 23–6), although it does not accord with his own desire for realism. Wolfram accepts and develops his source's representation of Gyburg as a good warrior who boldly defends her husband's castle, although he had in *Parzival* outspokenly condemned any woman who wore armour (Parz. 409, 12ff: *swâ harnaschrâmec wirt ein wîp,/diu hât ir rehts vergezzen,/sol man ir kiusche mezzen*); such conduct could be excused only by the motive of *triuwe* (Parz. 409, 15), which fortunately saves both

---

[1] The *runzît*, which was used by sergeants and for carrying baggage, might be a mare, but the heavy *kastellân* or *destrier* which the knight used on the battlefield had to be a stallion, cf. G. Köhler, *Die Entwicklung des Kriegswesens und der Kriegsführung in der Ritterzeit*, Breslau 1887, vol. 3, part 2, pp. 77ff. Frappier, in *La Technique Littéraire des Chansons de Geste*, Colloques, Liège 1959, p. 89, points out that the *chansons* represent Saracens, but not Christians, as riding mares, and Faral in the discussion following Frappier's contribution suggests that the intention was to ridicule the Saracens.

[2] Terramer's horse is called *Brahâne*, from *l'aufage brahaigne* (cf. p. 55). The meaning of *brahaigne* is 'sterile mare' (it is the feminine form of *brehain*, 'sterile', see E. Gamillscheg, *Etymologisches Wörterbuch der französischen Sprache*, Heidelberg 1969², under *brehaigne*).

Gyburg and Antikonie. Wolfram also preserves Irmschart's offer to don armour and ride to battle with her son (Al. 2717ff; Wh. 161, 5ff; cf. Singer, pp. 62, 83f), though his Willehalm (unlike Guillaume) quickly refuses her offer and is glad to accept money instead (nothing comes of it in *Aliscans*, so there is no clash with the source). Despite Wolfram's own attitude to armed ladies, which is that of his time (cf. the condemnation of Kriemhild in the *Nibelungenlied*, the restraint of Isolde in *Tristan*), Wolfram does not omit the motif or criticise Gyburg and Irmschart for *unwîpheit*[1] (though he does allow himself a harmless joke on the subject, Wh. 243, 23); instead he praises these ladies for their *triuwe*.

Wolfram cannot approve of the forward behaviour of the princess Aelis when she sends for her father's kitchen-boy and kisses him (cf. Singer, p. 77), but he preserves the episode and expresses his misgivings:

> 213, 13 wan daz mirz d'âventiure sagt,
> des mæres wær ich gar verzagt...

He then explains away the embarrassing scene by having Rennewart's visit prompted not by the princess's initiative but his own native courtesy (*von arde ein ʒuht im daʒ geriet*, 213, 5); first he politely takes leave of Loys and the Queen (independently of *Aliscans*), then he goes to Alyze, and he remains on his very best behaviour throughout. Wolfram also makes the episode, which was quite unimportant in the source, into a major event and an important motivator for Rennewart's later activities (cf. pp. 152ff). Wolfram also preserves the episode in which Rainouart kills Guillaume's chief cook by roasting him over his own fire (Al. 4370–403; Wh. 198, 18 – 199, 14), although it contradicts his own characterisation of Rennewart, and Wolfram's version is certainly no less distasteful than its source. Here again Wolfram has

---

[1] Gyburg is even praised for conducting herself like a man (95, 3: *manlîche sprach daʒ wîp,/als ob si manlîchen lîp/und mannes herʒe trüege*; 226, 30: *manlîch, ninder als ein wîp/diu künegîn gebarte*). Nevertheless, Gyburg and her ladies promptly resume their femininity when Willehalm returns (247, 1ff, independent of *Aliscans*). The troops of Nöupatris and Tesereiz apparently agree that ladies have no place in war, since they refuse to fight while Willehalm is away.

expanded the embarrassing scene and made it prominent, important and unusual. Hardly less embarrassing than this is Willehalm's behaviour towards his sister at Munleun, when he publicly insults her, jumps over the table at her with his sword drawn, shakes her till the crown falls from her head and is prevented from killing her only by the prompt intervention of their parents. Here, too, Wolfram makes no attempt to reduce the impression of violence or the force of the insults (Al. M. 2772ff: *Tas te putein, dist il lise provee,/ Tibauȝ de Rabie vos a soiornee/Et maintes fois com putain desfolee*; Wh. 153, 1: *die minne veile hânt, diu wîp*...; 18f *er jach, Tybalt der Arâboys/wære ir rîter manegen tac*...; 22f: *er hât si dicke schône/mit armen umbevâhen*), although his respect for his audience's sense of propriety forbids him to translate them all:

> 153, 4 die namn het ich bekennet,
> ob ich die wolte vor iu sagen:
> nu muoz ich si durh zuht verdagen.

The German poet is free to choose his own mode of expression, and he does not repeat words like *tas te putein!* and *lise provee!*; instead he finds a circumlocution (*die minne veile hânt, diu wîp*) and with it expresses the full sense and the full force of the original. Wolfram himself does not dare to utter the insults, but he assures us that Willehalm did. It must have been a dreadful rage indeed that made Willehalm address to his own sister and the queen at the court of France words which Wolfram himself has to suppress in polite society. Willehalm's public assertion that his sister, the queen of France, has been sharing the bed of Tybalt, who has lately arrived in Provence from Arabie and whose advent is still unknown to the French court, is really quite preposterous; it is the result of a confusion in *Aliscans* of the Saracen king Tiebaut with a French courtier of the same name, who is known to us as Tedbalt de Beürges from the opening episode of the *Chançun de Willame* (see p. 8), where Tedbalt's cowardly behaviour serves as a foil to Vivien's fortitude, an episode not related in *Aliscans*.[1]

[1] First noted by Singer, *Die Wiedergeburt des Epos und die Entstehung des neueren Romans* (*Sprache und Dichtung*, Heft 2), Tübingen 1910, in a footnote to p. 47.

Guillaume's accusation was a foolish and distasteful error on the part of the author of *Aliscans*, but rather than contradict his source Wolfram translates it fully and is satisfied with making excuses to explain Willehalm's unwontedly bad behaviour (Wh. 163, 4–10). Here one might have expected Wolfram to use his reference to propriety (*nu muoʒ ich si durh ʒuht verdagen*), a propriety demanded by his audience, to justify a variation from the source, but in fact the force of the episode is faithfully conveyed and Wolfram's reference to terms which *ʒuht* forbids him to translate only adds to the impression of Willehalm's violent and improper behaviour.

Wolfram is again highly embarrassed when Rainouart kills his brother and very nearly kills his own father, while Desramé, severely injured by his son, flees in terror from him (Al. 121c, 48–54). But his fidelity to the source is such that he includes even this, though his account of the battle is unusually evasive and bears witness to his embarrassment:

> 443, 3 Wie diu fluht dô geriet![1]
> wie daz kint von sîme vater schiet!
> wie schiet der vater vonme kint!
> seht wie den stoup der starke wint
> her und dar zetrîbe.
> wer dâ schiet von dem lîbe,
> wer dâ ze ors ze scheffe entran,
> über al ich des niht kan
> iuch zeim ende bringen
> und die nennen sunderlingen.
> wan der admirât wart sêre wunt
> geleit ûf sînen tragamunt,
> der nie mêr schumphentiur enphienc.

Even when he has misunderstood his source completely, Wolfram may do his best to render it faithfully; thus he introduces to his language the word *preymerûn*, which according to Lexer occurs only in Wolfram's *Willehalm* and denotes a kind of tent. In the

---

[1] Leitzmann edits with question marks instead of exclamation marks, which gives a more satisfactory reading (cf. Singer, p. 125).

source Guillaume had invited his father and brother to a fine banquet:

> 4261   Et dist Guillames: 'Un don vos voiel rover:
>   Ko moi prengiés cest prumerain souper'.

Here the word means 'first-class'.[1] Wolfram has:

> 245, 13   Heimrîch und iegeslîch sîn sun
>   under einem preymerûn
>   dâ vor im sâzen al zehant.

They dine beneath a *preymerûn*, because that is the term that occurred in the source.

Wolfram thus prefers to follow the source when change is unnecessary or can easily be avoided, and we must not assume he approved of everything he has allowed to stand. In view of this we should attach all the more significance to the changes which he has made when adapting the poem, for he will not have made important changes lightly and unnecessarily. The changes concerning Rennewart are collected below under four headings, to deal with Wolfram's differences with his source in the structure, the style, the characterisation and the religious attitude the poems express.[2]

The structure

The episodes of *Aliscans* are held together mainly as members of a chronological sequence of events; for the *jongleur* the great battle is a sufficient purpose to justify the long succession of episodes that leads up to it and particular events are often weakly motivated if they are motivated at all. Wolfram imposes much stricter order upon the narrative by linking the great events both to each other and to the less important scenes; he achieves this by

---

[1] Wolfram's form *preymerûn* suggests that his source had the more common French form of the word, *premerain*, though at that point none of the extant *Aliscans* mss has it. *Aliscans* does have the form *premerain* twice (1033f and 1692), but it prefers forms with *u*.

[2] Many of the points made in the following about Wolfram's treatment of his source could be demonstrated equally well by reference to other parts of *Willehalm* and *Aliscans*, but a close comparison of the whole of the two texts would make this chapter unduly long and add little to my study of Rennewart. Consequently, I take my examples mainly from the comparison of those parts of *Willehalm* and *Aliscans* that have to do with Rennewart.

adapting the episodes so that they can be used to motivate each other and by introducing or drawing attention to symbolic parallels between them. In this way each episode becomes indispensable through its reference to the others, making the particular event more significant than it was in the source, and the narrative thus becomes a closely-knit unity through the interdependence of its parts.

Al. 3148–85: Rainouart, crossing the courtyard from the kitchen, becomes involved with some young squires and kills one of them. He is carrying something which is very heavy (*si grant fais porte*), but we are not told what it is.[1] Wolfram's Rennewart (188, 1–190, 20) has to cross the courtyard to fetch water for the cooks, this being one of his duties, and the squires tip up the water. When this has happened twice, Rennewart kills one of them. Since *Aliscans* otherwise represents Rainouart as using his *tinel* to carry water and other burdens for the cooks (Al. 3207–8; 3248–9), the poet may have meant the same to be assumed here, but his text is far from explicit. Wolfram's version, however, does clearly show Rennewart performing his ordinary duty as a kitchen-hand; it also illustrates both the indignity of this mode of existence and Rennewart's long-suffering *ʒuht*, since he at first ignores the affront.

Al. 3281–91: Guillaume asks Louis for Rainouart, and Louis gladly gives him the boy. Al. 3326–41: Rainouart, angry over his mean rôle in Louis' kitchen, comes to Guillaume and begs to be taken to the battle. He does not know he has already been given to Guillaume, and Guillaume at first refuses the request (3342–54), although this had been his express purpose in asking for Rainouart. Wh. 191, 19–194, 30: As soon as the boy is given to him, Willehalm sends for Rennewart and asks him to come to the battle, which Rennewart gladly promises to do. Wolfram has overcome

---

[1] *Fais* means 'weight, burden'. Al. 3154 has in M the reading: *si grant fust porte* (i.e. it is his club), but this is unlikely to be original, since the reading *fais* has the support of all other mss and is the *lectio difficilior*. M presumably introduces the club here because *fais* is not explicit and the club is what Rainouart is usually carrying. Like the other mss, M has *fais* two lines earlier (Al. 3152). M is unusually rich in errors and nonsense readings. Since Wolfram does not appear to understand the original nature and function of the *tinel* (he sees it simply as a club strengthened with iron bands), it seems likely that he was prompted to supply water-carrying as Rennewart's duty by a line occurring later in *Aliscans*: *iiii. muis d'aige li ai veü porter* (Al. 3207; cf. Mergell, p. 48).

the implicit contradiction in the source and has linked the two short scenes by making the earlier one, where Willehalm asks for Rennewart, motivate the later conversation between them about Rennewart's going to the battle.

Al. 4370–403: At Orange Guillaume's chief cook sets fire to Rainouart's beard, which annoys him so much that he roasts the cook over the fire. Wolfram motivates Rennewart's extreme anger by introducing the motif that the beard had been 'sown' by Alyze's kiss, so that its singeing is an insult to Alyze which requires revenge (287, 11–17). Thus the importance of both the kiss and the beard is increased by their reference to each other.

Al. 4442–584: A scene follows in which Guibourc takes Rainouart to her room and gives him a sword and armour. Wolfram (289, 16–30) makes far more explicit the vague hint in the source (Al. 4434–5) that her purpose is to soothe his passion over the singeing of his beard, thus supplying a good reason for the scene and for the private talk between Rennewart and Gyburg. Wolfram thus gives meaning to this exhibition of Gyburg's kindness to Rennewart.

Al. 4765–80: On the way to the battle Rainouart forgets his club and when he returns for it finds it burnt. Wolfram links this to Rennewart's previous lapses of memory by making Rennewart very angry at the thought that this is the third such occasion and saying that it has brought *herzenleit* upon him (317, 3–9). Rennewart now thinks God may be testing him (317, 22–30). Thus Wolfram prepares the way for Rennewart's employment as the instrument of God at Pitît Punt (325, 3f), gives him the motif of *herzenleit* for his deadly purposefulness in the second battle and suggests a symbolic parallel between the burnt but strengthened club (319, 1f) and the warrior, shamed by *herzenleit* but strengthened in his purpose (cf. p. 162).

Al. 5337–53: During the battle Rainouart remembers the Christians who had been taken prisoner in the first battle and leaves the battlefield to go to the ships and free them. He goes alone and is prompted only by his memory, which at other times was not his strongest faculty, and we are not told how he manages to jump straight into the correct ship, the whole Saracen fleet being assembled in the harbour. Wolfram fits this episode into the account of the Saracen retreat. Rennewart's army is engaged against that of Halzebier. Under the pressure of Terramer's attack the six Christian armies are driven together so closely that many men have to follow a flag different from that to which they had originally been assigned (405, 13–19); in consequence, there are many of Willehalm's men among those who follow Rennewart. With this force, Rennewart pursues Halzebier's army, which retreats to the ships. The prisoners, who are being kept on one of the ships, hear the cry '*Munschoye!*' and shout it themselves so that Rennewart knows where they are (414, 17 – 416, 12). Wolfram has motivated the episode by fitting it in structurally to the encounter with Halzebier, and he has prepared well in advance for the prisoners to recognise the cry '*Munschoye!*' – for they could not have recognised the cry of Rennewart's men, which is '*Rennewart!*' – by telling at some length how the Christian armies merge under the pressure of Terramer's attack.

It is typical of Wolfram's technique that the important events are prepared for in advance as the last of these examples illustrates. Shortly before Rennewart's club breaks and he is forced to use the sword (429, 22) Wolfram tells us that the club is suffering from the violent blows it has had to deliver (423, 18–23). We are prepared for the episode in which Rennewart tries to capture horses for Berhtram and the other prisoners he has freed but crushes the horses together with their riders (416, 27 – 417, 26) by a passing reference to Rennewart's method of employing the club and a brief mention of Berhtram (388, 20–25: *swer im dâ ʒorse vor gesaʒ,/ʒeime hûfen er den sluoc...Berhtram was im sippe niht*). The very important scene after the battle, where Matribleiz is sent to supervise the embalming of the fallen relatives of Gyburg (462, 13–465, 30), is prepared for by a reference to the 'Saracen' custom of embalming at 451, 17–30; indeed, Wolfram seems to prepare us for this scene as early as 257, 1–10, where Terramer offers the Christians peace terms with Matribleiz to implement them (cf. his later function as mediator between Willehalm and

Terramer) and Gyburg praises the *stæte* and *triuwe* of Matribleiz in the warmest terms. Pitît Punt, important in Book VII, is mentioned briefly in Book V (232, 26). The quarrel between Willehalm and the Queen (147, 6–28) is prepared for at 129, 28–130, 2, when she, not Loys, has the gates closed against her brother (cf. Singer, p. 53). Willehalm's knowledge of heathen languages, which enables him to win Rennewart's sympathy at their first meeting (192, 6–24), is mentioned independently by Wolfram at 83, 18f, where it helps him escape after the first battle. Wolfram's preparation for coming events is sometimes achieved by symbolic prefiguration: we are made aware of a parallel between two events, so that an important episode seems to be prefigured by an earlier, less important one. This link, like that of motivation, makes the various episodes more significant through their interdependence.

In the course of Rainouart's encounter with the squires at Laon we are twice told, very briefly, that the cooks have blackened his face with soot and clipped his hair (3158–9; 3214–15). *Aliscans* tells us nothing of his reaction to this treatment, but in *e* he later smashes the cooks' pots (*e*, 3379, 23ff). Wolfram, possibly knowing the version of *e*, dissociates the brief allusions to his clipped hair from the encounter with the squires, links them with the smashing of the pots, and thereby produces a complete new episode (198, 18–199, 14), in which the cooks at Munleun singe Rennewart's hair and clothes and Rennewart in anger smashes their pots and nearly kills the chief cook; Willehalm finds him lamenting the indignity of having his hair and clothes singed by the cooks and consoles him, offering him better clothes and a proper haircut. This new episode which Wolfram has supplied serves to prefigure the scene at Orange (286, 3–296, 24) where the chief cook singes Rennewart's beard and Rennewart kills him; Gyburg comes to him at Willehalm's request, finds him lamenting his singed beard and consoles him, giving him better clothes and armour. This scene is most important for the Rennewart action (as is indicated by the author's invention of a scene to prefigure it) and includes the episode involving Gyburg's cloak (see pp. 173ff).

The scene in which Gyburg wraps Rennewart in her cloak seems to be prefigured by another motif of Wolfram's invention, 274, 11–14, where she sits beside him at high table and spreads part of the tablecloth over him. This motif, which occurs shortly before the event it seems to prefigure, has otherwise no purpose, apart from illustrating Gyburg's graciousness and Rennewart's *zuht*, which are both so adequately demonstrated elsewhere that a special invention independent of the source would appear superfluous.

A further hint of prefiguration is found where Willehalm agrees to wait for Rennewart while he returns to Munleun for his club. Willehalm says:

> 201, 15   ich beit dîn, wilt du schiere komn.
> hâstu iemen hinder dir vernomn,
> der mich an winde,
> dem sage daz er mich vinde:
> rîtr und ander soldiere
> brinc mit dir wider schiere
> und vergiz niht dîner stangen.

There is no reference in the source to the possibility of Rennewart's bringing troops back with him to Willehalm when he returns to his club, and he does not bring any either in the source or in *Willehalm*. The words only serve a purpose if we see them as a prefiguration of the later occasion when he turns back for his club and returns to Willehalm bringing the imperial army (329, 21–330, 26).

The desertion of the imperial army before the second battle, which is of central importance for the Rennewart action, has also been supplied with a prefigurative scene independent of the source. During the council of the army leaders at Orange prior to the departure for battle the leaders of the imperial army sent by Loys advise that the battle should be abandoned because the Saracens have already withdrawn from Orange (302, 1–30). These are the officers who desert with their men just before the battle, and Wolfram suggests very strongly that the one event was constructed to prefigure the other by a reference at 302, 1–17 to the subsequent desertion of the French soldiers as the reason why their names are not given.

The advance reference that prepares us for an important event may be a brief and apparently casual remark. Shortly before the squires tip up Rennewart's water Wolfram remarks that their boisterous game would hinder anyone who tried to cross the courtyard (187, 20–2). As Rennewart goes to battle we are reminded in a single line of the sword at his side (315, 11). Such comments from the narrator appear trivial, but derive their significance from the later events to which they refer.

Thus Wolfram relates the episodes of *Willehalm* to each other by introducing new motivation and new symbolic prefiguration; he reorganises the poem to make the narrative a unity and its parts significant through their relation to each other. This may be observed particularly in his treatment of the great battle, which must be studied as a whole and apart from the rest of the Rennewart action, since Wolfram has made a structural unit of it. In the battle narrative, too, Wolfram's great contribution is order, though the great wealth of names and varied characters to go with them, and the many different activities occurring closely together, make that order difficult to recognise. Its structure is compared by M. O'C. Walshe with 'the ordered chaos of a kaleidoscope'.[1]

The structure of the battle narrative has been completely re-organised. Rennewart's release of the prisoners, which occurred near the beginning in *Aliscans*, is placed at the end during the Saracen retreat (Al. 5337–5578; Wh. 414, 18–418, 15). At the very beginning of the battle in *Willehalm* we find the translation of a line that occurs much later in the battle in *Aliscans* (Al. 5891: *tantes ensaignes de paile, de bofus*; Wh. 367, 26: *der tiure pfellel pôfûʒ*, also 364, 27). In *Aliscans* the Christians are at their weakest very soon after the beginning of the battle (Al. 5197f; 5251–9; 5280–7), while in *Willehalm* they are at their weakest after the attack of Terramer, about half way through (405, 3–30).

The battle is seen in *Aliscans* as the development of a single encounter. Baudus kills Gui, and so Aïmer kills Baudus. Aïmer is

---

[1] M. O'C. Walshe, *Mediaeval German Literature. A Survey*, London 1962, p. 172.

quickly surrounded by Saracens, who hope to avenge Baudus, but Aymeri and Guillaume's brothers come to his rescue. Sinagon then brings large numbers of Saracens into the fray, while Rainouart goes away and frees the imprisoned Christians. As soon as they are equipped, these ride to the rescue of Aymeri and Guillaume. When Desramé attacks Guillaume, Rainouart intervenes and puts his father to flight, upon which the Saracens retreat in disorder to their ships, most of which Rainouart has already destroyed. After this, Rainouart is engaged in private battles with the Saracens who are left behind, notably with Baudins (*Baudus* in most mss), whom he ultimately converts to Christianity. On to this framework a number of personal encounters are fitted, as may be seen from the synopsis.

In *Willehalm* the battle develops through the opposition of groups, not individuals. As the Saracen armies come into battle, each of them engages one of the Christian armies until all six of Willehalm's armies are involved. Then the remaining four armies of Terramer come in, one at a time, to bolster up the Saracens' weak points. The seventh army goes to the aid of the second (led by Tybalt and Ehmereiz) because this group is unable to resist Rennewart's army alone. The intervention of Terramer's other armies accounts for the weak position of the Christians about half way through; the attack led by Terramer is a disaster for the Christians, not because of his strength or his fearful appearance (thus Al. 5906–26) but because he commands an immense number of troops (Wh. 399, 7 – 401, 19). The Christians manage to maintain their resistance, and Rennewart's army forces Terramer's first army (under Halzebier) to withdraw to the ships, where the Christian prisoners are freed and Halzebier is killed. The flight of the first Saracen army spreads to the others, but the Saracens cover their retreat until they are back on the ships. A few escape to the moors and the rest leave Provence in the Saracen fleet.

The order in Wolfram's narrative has been produced largely by the introduction of tactics in place of the ferocity of a few individuals; instead of a series of single encounters followed by a sudden Christian victory we have moves of opposing armies which advance and retreat as groups. Wolfram observes the movements from the point of view of a general, who can see the battle as a whole and is interested in tactics, while the French poet sees them from the point of view of a soldier in the Christian army, whose involvement makes him one-sided and who sees only the great individuals. Thus Mergell (p. 74f) comments on the battle narrative in *Aliscans*:

Die Anteilnahme von Dichter und Hörern ist einseitig den christlichen Helden zugewandt. Die Heiden werden lediglich als Gegenspieler gesehen, die besiegt werden und dann durch erneute Überzahl das Eingreifen des nächsten christlichen Helden motivieren.

Wolfram has overcome this one-sidedness by showing from a superior point of view the steady build-up of the Saracen forces reaching a climax with the intervention of Terramer and the consequent Saracen advance across the Larkant (which in his version is a river),[1] executed with such force and speed that the Saracen gods are left behind; this is followed by the recovery of the Christians, also expressed tactically in their advance to the ships. These movements are antithetical to those of the first battle: in the first battle a period in which the Christians hold the Larkant is followed by their retreat and annihilation when the Saracens surround Orange; in the second battle a period when the Christians retreat and cross the Larkant is followed by their steady advance as far as the Saracen ships.[2]

Wolfram's method of replacing personal encounters by tactical

---

[1] In fact l'Archant probably is derived from a river-name, though it occurs only as a battlefield in the *chansons de geste*. It has been convincingly identified with *Argentona*, a place near the coast 32 kilometres north-east of Barcelona on a river which was called *l'Argent* and from which the town derived its name with the common local suffix *-ona*, see A. Terracher, 'Notes sur "l'Archant" dans les Chansons de Geste sur Guillaume au Court-Nez', *Annales du Midi* 22 (1910), pp. 5–16; cf. Riquer, p. 169, who supports this identification. It seems unlikely, however, that Wolfram could have known this.

[2] Cf. Bumke, p. 41f. The parallel with the first battle is noticeable from the reference to the troops of Nöupatris and Tesereiz who hope to avenge their fallen leaders, as well as the often-expressed need for revenge for the dead of both sides (particularly Vivianz, Mile, Pinel, Arofel, Poufameiz) and the appearance of the familiar names of those who survived (Halzebier, Tybalt, Margot, Gorhant). The first battle, however, follows the source more closely and in it more attention is paid to personal duels and less to general tactics than in the second.

moves is sometimes to deal quickly with the personal encounters, since to dwell on them as *Aliscans* does might make us lose sight of the general picture. Most of the single encounters are dealt with briefly at the beginning of Book IX, while *Aliscans* spends the whole battle narrative on them and sometimes gives a whole *laisse* or more to single battles of Rainouart (e.g. *laisses* 116, 118, 121, 121c, 168–75), his duel with Baudins occupying eight *laisses*. Wolfram's reduction of the rôle of Rainouart, on which Bumke commented (pp. 41–3), may be to a large extent explained by this desire to replace individuals by battalions, for the army that Rennewart leads quite clearly plays the decisive rôle in Wolfram's version.

The introduction of tactics is often effected by consistently showing the great warriors of *Aliscans* as the leaders of the groups to which they are assigned by Willehalm and Terramer. The scenes in which the two supreme commanders divide their armies and assign leaders to the groups, scarcely more than a muster parade in *Aliscans*, are expanded considerably by Wolfram, particularly that of Terramer, which grows from a *laisse* of 27 lines in *Aliscans* (5069–95) to 567 lines (Wh. 341, 4–359, 30). The promotion of Tybalt and Ehmereiz to the leadership of the second army (342, 7–343, 27) in place of Ector de Salorie (i.e. Ektor von Salenîe, who becomes Terramer's standard-bearer), bears witness to Wolfram's realistic grasp of the situation: Tybalt is far more important than Ektor, being the real cause of the war, and so he must have his own men, and his importance in Wolfram's version is demonstrated when he promptly leads his army against that of Willehalm and is able to engage both Willehalm's army and that of Rennewart, which is still fresh, for the greater part of the battle.

The characters who played minor parts in *Aliscans* or were little more than names gain most in stature by being integrated into the structure of the armies; many of them, particularly the Saracens, are at the same time integrated into the noble families by being related to the chief characters and are provided with fiefs or kingdoms (cf. Singer, pp. 105ff). All this gives them a quite specific function and makes them important for their contribution to the whole action rather than as individuals. *Alipantin* (Al. 5153) is Wolfram's *Aropatîn von Gampfassâsche* (the name of the country is taken from *Parʒival* 770, 28) who rules from Gêôn to Poynzaclîns (382, 1–12), commander of Terramer's sixth army. Among his men are *Gloriôn von Ascalôn* (Al. 351, M: *Grorion*; the country from Parz. 772, 17) and *Matribleiʒ von Scandinâvîâ* (Al. 1778, 6364; both mentioned 348, 21–30; 382, 27–383, 14), who is a relative to Gyburg and king of Scandinâvîâ, Gruonlant and Gaheviez (461, 26f; 348, 24f). *Josués de Mautiste* (Al. 488) is now *Josweiʒ von Amatiste*, commander of Terramer's seventh army, cousin to Gyburg and son of Matusales (350, 3; 389, 14f; 349, 1–30); his men include *Corsant, Rubbûâl, Pohereiʒ* and *Talimôn* (Al. 490 mentions only *Corsus* and *Buhereʒ*; *Talimôn* cf. Al. 598: *Telamons*), whom Wolfram provides with fiefs: Corsant's fief is *Janfûse* (from Parz. 770, 23), Rubbûâl's is *Nouriente* (Parz. 770, 25), Pohereiz's is *Ethnîse* (Parz. 374, 26) and Talimôn's is *Valpinôse* (*Rolandslied* 8104: *Valle Penûse*; this fief distinguishes him from *Talimôn von Boctân*, who fell in the first battle, 56, 18–57, 4); all of them hold their fiefs from Josweiz. *Synagûn*, commander of the third Saracen army, becomes king of *Bailîe* (Al. 5076f: *Sinagon*; 344, 1–3; place name invented after Al. 5077: *bailie*). *Baudus d'Aumarie* (Al. 5087), commander of Desramé's seventh army and son of Aiquin, becomes *Poydwîʒ von Raabs*, commander of the eighth Saracen army and son of Oukîn, also leading the armies of Tenabrûn, Libilûn and Rubîun (350, 12–30; 412, 10–12). *Mallars* (Al. 5079a), leader of Desramé's fourth army, becomes *Marlanʒ von Jerikop*, who commands Terramer's ninth army and has *Margôt von Poʒʒidant* (Al. 5700: *Margot de Bocident*) and *Gorhant von Ganjas* (Al. 72ff; *Gorhant*; *Ganjas*. Parz. 517, 28, probably from *Lucidarius*, see Singer, p. 17) as his vassals (351, 4–15).

Several of the minor characters become prominent as standardbearers. *Gybôêʒ* (probably Al. 184c, 25: *Giboé*) becomes *der schahteliure von Cler* (a land ruled by Tybalt, cf. Al. 1199: *Tiebaus l'Escler*) and standard-bearer to Tybalt in the second Saracen army (365, 1f). *Trohaʒʒabê von Karkassuon* (not in Al.) is a duke

and standard-bearer to Ehmereiz in the second Saracen army
(365, 8f; 367, 21). *Tedalûn von Kaukasas* (not in Al.) is *burcgrâve*
of *Tasmê*, one of the three kingdoms of *Poydjus von Frîende*; he is
responsible for the forest Lignalôê and standard-bearer to the
fifth Saracen army under Poydjus (375, 22–30; *Tasmê* and
Lignalôê from Parz. 629, 21 and 230, 11). *Ektor von Salenîe* (Al.
5071: *Ektor de Salorie*, who leads Desramé's second army)
becomes a vassal of Terramer and standard-bearer to the tenth
Saracen army (353, 9–11; 401, 19f). *Esserê* (possibly Al. 5537:
l'amirant Estiflé, M: *estele*) becomes an *emerâl* under Halzibier in
the first Saracen army. *Landrîs* (Al. 4931: *Landris*), standard-bearer
to the third Christian army under Bernart (329, 11; 373, 1f) becomes a count. Iwân von Rœms (not in Al.) from Normandy is
standard-bearer to the imperial army under Rennewart (424, 24f).

Others, whose particular office in the army is not mentioned,
are given a fief or kingdom (often supplied from *Parzival*) and
sometimes relatives; they are placed under a specific commander
in one of the armies and are mentioned only in connection with
the other men under its flag. Keeping track of all these characters
is no mean achievement on Wolfram's part. Under the imperial
flag and in Rennewart's command we find *Gandalûz* (not in Al.;
Parz. 429, 20), count of *Schampân* (366, 16), count *Milôn von
Nivers* (possibly Al. 5162: *Milon*; 413, 18) and *Kîûn von Bêâvais*
(possibly Al. 4714: *Guion*, or 5155: *Guion d'Auvergne*), who is
burcgrâve of *Bêâvais* and related to Heimrîch der Schêtîs (412, 1).
Gyffleiz (369, 28; not in Al.) is a count and vassal to Arnalt,
fighting with the first Christian army. In the immediate service of
Terramer we find *Grôhier von Nomadjentesîn* (Al. 5192: *Gohier*,
M: *Gorhier*; *Nomadjentesîn* from Parz. 770, 8). *Oquidant von
Imanzîe* (Al. 5446: *Malquidant*, M: *macudant*), *Samirant von
Boytendroyt* (Al. 5447: *Salmuant*; Al. 5783: *Boutentrot*), *Bohedân
von Skipelpunte* (not in Al.; *Skipelpunte*, Parz. 770, 6), *Akkarîn von
Marroch* (Al. 1428: *Acarin*, M: *a chemin*; *Marroch*, Parz. 15,
17), who is related to the *bâruc von Baldac* (73, 19–21), *Clabûr*
(not in Al.) a relative of Tybalt, *Kanlîûn von Lanzesardîn* (not in
Al.; *Kanlîûn* see p. 93, note 1; *Lanzesardîn*, Parz. 770, 22), who is

Rennewart's half-brother, and the unnamed kings of *Barberîe* and *Hipipotiticûn* (Parz. 687, 9); all of these support his left flank (356, 1–358, 20). On his right flank (358, 21–360, 12) Terramer is served by *Purrel von Nubîant* (Al. 1778: *Borrel*), *Cliboris von Tananarke* (not in Al., possibly *Rolandslied* 2543: *Cliboris*, variant *Oliboris* and 2619: *Tarmarke*, see Bacon, p. 122), *Samirant von Bêaterr* (not in Al., probably after *Samirant von Boytendroyt*; *Bêaterr* could be invented), *Oukidant von Norûn* (not in Al., probably after *Oquidant von Imanẑîe*; *Norûn* from *Noiron pré*, *pratum Neronis*), *Crôhier von Oupatrîe* (not in Al., probably after *Grôhier von Nomadjentesîn*; *Oupatrîe* cf. *aupatris*, a Saracen leader), *Samûêl* (Al. 5447: *Samuel*), *Môrende* (Al. 5489: *Morindes*), *Fabûr* (Al. 1777: *Faburs*), *Haropîn von Tananarke* (not in Al.), father of Cliboris, and *Cernubilê von Ammirafel* (not in Al.; cf. *Rolandslied* 2682: *Zernubele*), who is Terramer's trumpeter (360, 1–12; 407, 20–23). Wolfram also supplies some of the army leaders with heraldic devices: Willehalm has a golden star, Heimrich a tau cross, Josweiz a swan, Aropatin a rook,[1] Poydjus an *ecidemôn* and Cliboris a bark.

Terramer himself is given the rank of *admirât* over all the Saracens (438, 23) and *vogt ẑe Baldac* (434, 2–5) and a father *Kanabêûs* (from *Rolandslied* 8129) and he becomes cousin to Baligan (*Rolandslied* 7150) and heir of Pompeius (338, 26f, Parz. 14, 4; 101, 29), which places him in historical perspective among the Saracen emperors.

By giving each soldier a definite place and function within the structural framework of the armies, Wolfram has changed the narrator's viewpoint from that of the individual French soldier to that of the tactician, interested in the organisation and deployment

---

[1] Wh. 382, 2 ff: *in sînem vanen stuont ein roch:/daẑ bedûte sînen wîten grif,/daẑ im diu erde unt diu schif/volleclîche gâben rîchen ẑins.* Although *roch* commonly means the chess castle or rook, Singer (p. 111) believes that Wolfram may mean the bird *rokh* of the Persian fairy tale; this is an enormous bird which flies great distances over land and seas, and so would accord with Wolfram's explanation of the significance of Aropatin's device. On the other hand, Wolfram uses the word *roch* in *Parẑival* to refer to the chess piece (Parz. 408, 29) and we have no evidence that he knew any Persian fairy tales. Since the rook in chess is and was able to move freely any number of spaces forwards, backwards or sideways (though not diagonally), it can represent Aropatin's *wîter grif* just as well.

of forces and in the effect of large-scale actions. Thus Wolfram supplies a new perspective, and the single event is seen not merely for its own sake but in relation to others as a part of the whole battle. The events are interrelated and well motivated, and by imposing order upon the subject-matter Wolfram has also been able to give significance to every part of it. In the battle narrative of the last two books of *Willehalm* Wolfram is at the height of his powers as a poet, and his achievement deserves, as great literature, to be placed beside the finest passages of his *Parzival*.

Another major structural change which makes Wolfram's poem more orderly than its source is the subordination of the Rennewart action to that of Willehalm, which is achieved mainly by making Rennewart as a person less prominent. Some of his activities are omitted, others are reported in less detail, and all are made to contribute to the main action. Wolfram's reduction of the Rennewart action has been commented on by both Mergell (p. 47) and Bumke,[1] but both of them have greatly exaggerated this reduction through not considering the variants of *Aliscans*; if Wolfram's source was similar in content to manuscript M of *Aliscans* and agreed roughly with the synopsis I have given, then Wolfram's Rennewart action does not differ very greatly in *matter* from its source, though it differs considerably in treatment. Mergell and Bumke both give Wolfram credit for having cut out Rennewart's battles against Walegrape, Flohart, Agrapart and other monsters and giants that occur in *laisses* 122–65 (cf. Mergell, *loc. cit.*, and Bumke, pp. 40–2), though it is highly improbable that these *laisses* occurred in the archetype or in Wolfram's source. The same applies to Bumke's contention that Wolfram has eliminated all the battles of Rainouart which are related after *laisse* 121b.[2] The only ones which do not occur in the *laisses*

---

[1] Bumke, pp. 41–3. Bumke explains that Wolfram needed to reduce Rennewart and Vivianz in importance in order to isolate the epic from its cyclical source. His reviewer H. Fischer, GRM 13 (1963), pp. 97–9, describes the actions of Vivianz and Rennewart as 'die Pufferstücke zwischen Branche und Zyklus' (p. 97).

[2] Bumke, p. 42: 'In *Aliscans* wird die Schlacht in 70 Laissen erzählt (L. 106–76). Die einzige taktische Bewegung, die – wie bei Wolfram – die Schlacht entscheidet, ist Desramés Flucht; sie steht in Laisse 121b. In fünfzehn Laissen ist die Schlacht bis zur Entscheidung gelangt; dann folgen noch 55 Laissen, die im wesentlichen mit Rainoarts

122–65 not in M are the last two, fought against Baudins and the Saracens who failed to escape to the ships, and there is reason to suppose that Wolfram originally intended to narrate a battle against Poydjus and explain what happened to the Saracens who had fled to the moor, but broke off before these last battles were reached (see pp. 232ff). Mergell remarks (p. 50) that Rennewart is hardly mentioned during Book V of *Willehalm*, but the same can be said for the corresponding *laisses* of *Aliscans*; such references as do occur in them are mainly predictions and repetitions which Wolfram in any case generally omits (cf. p. 94). Book V is concerned with Willehalm's arrival at Orange and the welcome extended by Willehalm and Gyburg to Willehalm's relations, who arrive at Orange one by one with their contingents of soldiers; Rennewart is not required here. The mention of Rennewart in Book V on several occasions when there is no need to mention him suggests that Wolfram did not intend to cut down Rennewart's rôle here; few of the following would have been missed had they been omitted:

225, 9   er (Willehalm) huop sich an die vart,
          mit im sîn vriwent Rennewart
          und swer an sîme ringe lac.
226, 12–15   When Willehalm sees Orange in flames and rides to the rescue, Rennewart is running behind.
227, 5–11   Rennewart, following Willehalm, sees the Saracen siege-engines and longs for battle.
230, 12–21   Gyburg asks who Rennewart is and Willehalm tells her.
232, 3–12   Rennewart goes to the stables to attend to Volatin (not in the source).

Here, as elsewhere, Wolfram is by no means as concerned with cutting down the Rennewart action as has generally been assumed hitherto.

But although Wolfram has not reduced Rennewart's action as drastically as Mergell and Bumke believe, there is no doubt that

Kämpfen gefüllt sind. Wolfram dagegen hat die Entscheidung an das Ende der Schlachtschilderung gesetzt und hat alles, was vorhergeht, auf dies Ende bezogen. Die ganze Serie von Kämpfen, die Rainoart nach Desramés Flucht besteht, hat er einfach gestrichen.'

he has reduced it. The following events recorded in *Aliscans* have been completely omitted by Wolfram:

Al. 3210–80   The squires torment Rainouart until he throws four of them violently to the ground.

Al. 3377–429   Rainouart chops down the fir tree from which his club is to be made.

Al. 3458–69   Rainouart tells Guillaume it is time he left Laon and set off for Orange, whereupon Guillaume immediately arranges for the army's departure.

Al. 3838–45   Rainouart sees Guillaume riding towards him and prepares for a trial joust, but Guillaume quickly assures him that that was not his intention.

Al. 3846–68   Rainouart washes his club in a stream and wipes it dry with his coat. Aelis, looking on, instantly falls in love with him, but her mother expresses disapproval.

Al. 4664–75   Rainouart tells Guillaume it is time to leave Orange and advance to battle, and Guillaume prepares for departure.

Al. 4715–34   Gui and Guibourc try to lift Rainouart's club but have to call for help and have it loaded on to a wagon. When the wagon reaches Rainouart he grabs the club with such excitement that the wagon collapses. (Wh. 315, 25–30 only states that the club was brought to Rennewart by wagon.)

Al. 5280–7   Rainouart calls his men together and threatens to crush any one of them who flees from the battle.

Al. 5310–32   A messenger tells Desramé about Rainouart and advises him to flee at once. Baudins silences the messenger and boasts that he will kill Rainouart.

Al. 5840–51   Rainouart boasts that he has killed his cousin and intends to kill any other relative who refuses to believe in Jesus Christ.

Al. 121b, 10–58   Baudins is specially equipped with a club by Desramé to go and look for Rainouart.

Al. 121b, 66–138   Rainouart argues with Haucebier, induces him to fight by saying that Guillaume is already dead, and kills him. (Wolfram transfers the motif that Rainouart's club breaks in this encounter to the later battle against Purrel.)

Wolfram may have intended to include some of these events which concern Baudins; his poem breaks off before that battle takes place, and some of these early references to him might be better accommodated in the narrative of his encounter with Rennewart.

Together with the above omissions, the names of two Saracens killed by Rainouart do not appear in *Willehalm*, viz. *Jambus* (Al. 4392; 121c, 50) and *Elinant* (Al. 5437; M: *elmant*). Jambus appears to have been replaced by Kanliun, who does not appear in *Aliscans*.[1] Wolfram may have misunderstood *Elinant*, possibly reading it as a present participle, or his version of *Aliscans* may have lacked both these names, for the comparison with M does not suggest that Wolfram made any attempt to eliminate men who are named as having been killed by Rainouart in the source. The only exception is Haucebier: while he is killed by Rainouart in all *Aliscans* manuscripts, he is killed in *Willehalm* by the Christian counts who have been freed by Rennewart.[2]

Most of this Rainouart matter which Wolfram has omitted is of a very trivial and incidental nature, and the serious cuts are few. Wolfram avoids dwelling on Rennewart at the expense of the main hero not so much by eliminating Rainouart matter and giving him less to do as by organising the Rennewart matter differently. The Saracen heroes whom Rennewart kills are sometimes mentioned very briefly in short lists, dealing with three or four names in a few lines, while the source narrates separately and with monotonous repetitiveness the defeat of each of them.[3] Thus in lines 413, 26 – 414, 1 we are told that Rennewart kills Fabur, Samirant, Samuel, Oukidant and Morende. At 442, 21–30 he kills Kanliun, Gibue, Malakin, Cador and Tampaste. Rennewart is still left with other battles which are narrated individually, but since many of the battles are dismissed quickly in list form Wolfram is able to shift the emphasis in the battle narrative from the individual feats of Rennewart to the heroism of the whole army.

---

[1] Kanliun's name seems to be derived from *Chançun de Willame* 3170: *Tabur de Canaloine* (see p. 31); the person probably arose from a misunderstanding of Al. 6584d: *Son fil encontre, Rainouart, devant soi*. Wolfram has read *Rainouart* as a nominative and understood 'Rainouart meets his (=Desramé's) son', while the French really means 'he (=Desramé) meets his son Rainouart'; cf. Mergell, p. 91, note 36. Wolfram may possibly have known of the tradition that Rainouart kills his half-brother, which might be the cause or the consequence of his alleged illegitimacy (cf. p. 21, note 2); that would explain why Wolfram's Kanliun is the eldest of the brothers, son of Terramer's first wife (358, 16f).

[2] The reason for this change could be their blood relationship, for both are grandsons of Kanabeus (he is nephew to Terramer, 341, 4, and maternal uncle to Synagun, 27, 14 etc., who is also Rennewart's nephew).

[3] There is one short list in the source, Al. 5446 f: *Malquidant, Samuel, Samul, Salmuant.*

Further reduction of the Rennewart action is achieved by the elimination of all the references to him that occur in *Aliscans* before he takes an active part in the narrative (i.e. when he is first seen by Guillaume at Laon); most of these references are brief and of a predictive nature. Such references can be found at Al. 289–91, 368, 404,34, 1392, 1488, 1547, 1786, and 3005–25. Wolfram also omits the lines of *Aliscans* in which the Saracens are so terrified of Rainouart that they wish to capitulate before the battle has started (Al. 5024–41; 5312–22); instead Wolfram only hints at Terramer's fear that Loys may be leading the imperial army against him (337, 14–21; cf. 340, 16ff; 367, 13f). *Aliscans* also adds to Rainouart's prominence by mentioning, when introducing some of the Saracens, that they are later to be killed by Rainouart (e.g. Al. 5066–8; 5074f; 5104f; 5110c). Wolfram omits the reference to Rennewart in every case. Wolfram gives the account of Rennewart's early history and his coming to France once (282, 28ff), not twice (Al. 3197ff and 3258ff). He shows less interest than his source in Rennewart's club, which had been almost a character in its own right, chosen out of a forest and loved by Rainouart, and very often embraced and kissed by him. Where *Aliscans* devotes 43 lines to telling how it was made (Al. 3377–429, with extensive additions in the variants), Wolfram only tells us how Rennewart asked for it (195, 28ff; 196, 20ff) and adds, much later:

> 429, 27 Kîun von Munlêûn der smit
> mit vlîze worht die stangen.[1]

He omits all reference to the washing of the club (Al. 3846–59) and to the efforts of Gui and Guibourc to lift it (Al. 4715–34). While it is Rainouart who tells Guillaume when to begin the march for Orange (Al. 3458–69), Wolfram, always correct in military matters, eliminates Rennewart and describes instead the correct procedure (Wh. 198, 9–11: *des küneges rüefær al den scharn/gebôt, si solden smorgens varn/gein Orlens ûf die strâ*z*e*). It is indicative of Wolfram's reduction of the rôle of Rennewart compared with

---

[1] Cf. also Wh. 195, 30f; 196, 20–30.

Willehalm that while in *Aliscans* the first Christian army is led by Rainouart and the second by Guillaume, in *Willehalm* the first is led by Willehalm himself, the next four by his brothers, and Rennewart leads the sixth and last. In the battle narrative Wolfram does not tell how Guillaume turns and flees from Margot de Bocident until he is rescued by Rainouart, who kills him with one blow of the club (Al. 5740–69). Wolfram especially takes pains to avoid describing the battle in which Rainouart attacks his father Desramé and puts him to flight (cf. p. 225);[1] Wolfram's Rennewart kills Kanliun instead, while it is Willehalm who fights with Terramer and wounds him. Wolfram cannot deny that Rennewart also fought with his father, since the source is here quite explicit, but he prefers not to discuss the matter and his brief reference to it (443, 3–15) is evasive and ambiguous. The comparison with *Storie Nerbonesi* (I, 526) suggests that Wolfram's source included the burial of Rainouart's brothers 'according to Saracen custom',[2] performed in honour of Rainouart. If this was in fact in the source, and if it was there too performed by Christians to honour Rainouart (this is doubtful, see p. 59), then Wolfram has eliminated Rennewart by transferring the motif to Gyburg's relatives (462, 13–30). Such changes show that Wolfram did intend to subordinate the Rennewart action to that of Willehalm, though he has not taken the liberties with his source attributed to him by Bumke and Mergell.

There is an important difference between Wolfram and his source which underlies this subordination of the Rennewart action: the poet of *Aliscans* is interested in Rainouart for his own sake; he delights in the escapades with the cooks and the squires and he narrates them at length, he is fascinated by Rainouart's extraordinary size, strength and appetite and above all by the unusual weapon, and his goal is Rainouart's vindication, his marriage and his baptism. Wolfram, however, is interested in

---

[1] Bumke, p. 45f, notes that the motif has been blinded rather clumsily.

[2] In fact, embalming was always quite foreign to Islam as it is to Judaism. Wolfram, however, mentions embalming elsewhere (Parz. 427, 17; 476, 2; 789, 21 ff; 808, 29; Tit. 21, 2) and he may have met it in the *Eneide* (9486ff) as well as in his version of *Aliscans*.

Rennewart for the sake of his contribution to the main action; his theme is war between religions and Rennewart derives his importance from the part he plays as the chosen instrument of God in gaining the Christian victory. This has been fully recognised and demonstrated by Bumke, pp. 41–5. Rennewart's battles are no longer intended primarily to bring him personal glory, but they are distinctly represented as service to the Christian cause (cf. Wh. 285, 13: *sîn hant vaht sige der kristenheit*; Wh. 325, 1–4). His defeat of five kings (413, 27–414, 16) is now used to motivate the retreat of Halzibier's army. His pursuit of Halzibier now leads to the release of the Christian prisoners, who bring about the death of Halzibier. His defeat of Golliam and Gyboez is seen as the final blow which causes the whole Saracen army to retreat. The early part of the action prepares him for his future service to Christianity; the scene where Willehalm and his brothers try to lift his club, used in *Aliscans* purely to show off Rainouart's strength, ends in *Willehalm* with a line not prompted by the source which illustrates Wolfram's own attitude to Rennewart:

> 311, 30   sîn kraft den kristen kom ze staten.

In this way the treatment of Rennewart corresponds to that of the other characters who take part in the battle. He exists, not for his own sake, but to serve a quite specific purpose, which at once subordinates him to a cause greater than himself and raises him by giving him a place and a purpose in world history and a direct relationship to God (as the tool that executes the divine will) to which the Rainouart of *Aliscans* could not aspire.

In Bumke's opinion Wolfram introduces a parallel between Rennewart and Vivianz, both being subordinated to the main action. This supports his contention that the Rennewart action has been drastically reduced, because to make such a parallel clear Rennewart must become comparable in stature to Vivianz, whose active part in the narrative is very limited. Bumke's opinion follows not only from his belief that Wolfram had a whole cycle of *chansons* for his source and needed to isolate from it a limited action, with a clear beginning and end and with one definite hero, but also from his theory that Wolfram has made out of *Aliscans* a religious epic, e.g. p. 44f:

Die Vergeistlichung Rennewarts steht durchaus parallel zu Vivianz' Märtyrerrolle. In diesen Nebenfiguren bereits kündigt sich an, dass Wolfram aus der wilden *chanson* eine *süeʒe rede* (5, 10), ein religiöses Epos gemacht hat.

Wentzlaff-Eggebert, whose interpretation of *Willehalm* appears to be based on that of Bumke, regards Vivianz and Rennewart as parallel representatives of the type of the young crusader, serving as a foil to Willehalm, and concludes.[1]

Der Vivianzepisode im ersten Teil entspricht die Rennewartepisode im zweiten Teil.

It is clear that there is similarity between the two characters; this is necessarily so, for they fight on the same battlefield against the same enemy under the same commander, both are very young[2] and both innocent of the causes of the war.[3] It would not be difficult to draw an explicit parallel between the two actions. But the presence of these important similarities given in the source argues against Wolfram's intention to draw a parallel, for he has done very little to make the similarities more explicit or to add to them. Instead, some of the parallelism which was given in the source has been dropped. Whereas in the source Rainouart is the avenger of Vivien (who had been killed by Haucebier), Wolfram contradicts the source by having Halzebier killed not by Rennewart but by Berhtram and the other Christian prisoners. Bumke claims that Willehalm's lament for Rennewart is parallel to his lament for Vivianz:[4]

Rennewart ist deutlich als eine Gegenfigur zu Vivianz gestaltet, und die Klage um ihn nach der zweiten Schlacht steht in direkter Parallele zu der Klage um Vivianz nach der ersten.

---

[1] F-W. Wentzlaff-Eggebert, *Kreuzzugsdichtung des Mittelalters, Studien zu ihrer geschichtlichen und dichterischen Wirklichkeit*, Berlin 1960, p. 262.

[2] Vivianz' beard had not started to grow (67, 15): Rennewart's had only just begun to grow (270, 29f).

[3] 67, 9–30. Cf. 388, 25: *Berhtram was im sippe niht.*

[4] Bumke, p. 94. Also W. J. Schröder, p. 414.

But Wolfram has not attempted to make the two laments similar, as he might have done very easily had a parallel been intended. Willehalm's lament for Vivianz, expressed largely in religious terms, is concerned with Vivianz' death as a Christian martyr and with his own guilt in having raised him to knighthood and led him to battle at such an early age. The lament for Rennewart is an expression of Willehalm's pain at being bereft and unable to reward the man to whom he owes victory; it is far less religious, and where religious thought does occur it is less orthodox than in the earlier lament; indeed it includes a blasphemous attack on Jesus (456, 1–3), blaming him for the disaster in a tone reminiscent of Walther von der Vogelweide calling the archangels to account for failing to help in the battle against the heathens (Walther 79, 1–16). Willehalm's grief in the lament over Rennewart seems even more intense than at the death of Vivianz: it makes his victory into everlasting defeat, the equal of hell-fire (454, 18), it rouses within him for a moment a resentment against God scarcely less intense than that of Parzival following the curse of Cundrie (Parz. 332, 1–8)[1] and it cannot possibly be compensated by the love of Gyburg, as the loss of Vivianz and the other men who fell in the first battle could be (279, 6–12; 280, 2–9; contrast 454, 12–14; 456, 14–17). The bitterness of the lament for Rennewart appears still more significant when one considers that it is aroused not by his death but only by the possibility that he may be dead. In the course of the epic Rennewart seems to replace Vivianz in the affection of Gyburg, but Wolfram does not ever refer to this and does not draw any parallels between them in relation to Gyburg. The growing love between Gyburg and Rennewart is depicted at much greater length than her concern for Vivianz, and it is an important motivating factor for the Rennewart action; we can expect it to become still more prominent and significant when the two at last recognise each other as brother and sister;[2] they are united by the closest natural bond (children of the same parents

---

[1] Willehalm, however, conquers his feeling immediately and the proper religious answer follows upon his blasphemy (456, 19–24).

[2] A recognition scene is promised, 291, 2–3.

share a single heart, 119, 24–9; 301, 17–20), while Vivianz was not even a remote relation to Gyburg. The enthusiasm and detail which Wolfram devotes to depicting the extraordinary virtues and beauty of Alyze contribute to the Rennewart action in a way which has no parallel in the Vivianz action. Vivianz fights alone under Willehalm's command, while Rennewart is the commander of an army. These differences, which suggest that Rennewart is far more important for the whole epic than Vivianz,[1] reflect the relative prominence of the two in its structure: Vivianz only appears in two books, and even there he is far from prominent, while Rennewart is for the greater part of the whole narrative so much in the foreground that there is danger of his becoming the main character, as he does in the second part of *Aliscans*.[2] Wolfram's reduction of the Rennewart action is prompted far more by the need to prevent a subsidiary character from obscuring the true hero and the principal plot than by any desire on the author's part to draw a parallel between Rennewart and Vivianz.

A parallel between Rennewart and Roland is observed by Palgen:[3]

Rennewart sollte ein Ebenbild Rolands werden, er sollte nicht nur episodische Bedeutung haben, sondern eine centrale Stellung gewinnen. So erklärt sich die ausgedehnte Klage Wilhelms, die die Verdienste Rennewarts rühmt und ihm den errungenen Sieg zuschreibt. Dies ist überschwenglich und nur durch den Einfluss des Rolandsliedes zu erklären, wo tatsächlich Roland Siege erringt.

It has long been known that *Willehalm* owes much to Wolfram's knowledge of the *Rolandslied* (and possibly the *Chanson de Roland*) and no one has quarrelled with Bacon and Palgen over the many parallels which they found.[4] Wolfram has undoubtedly

---

[1] Dante seems to have recognised this when he found a place in Paradise among the great heroes who died fighting for the faith for Rainouart (or Rennewart?) and Guillaume, but not Vivien, *Paradiso* 18, line 46: *Poscia trasse Guglielmo e Renoardo* (cf. Frappier, p. 232). They follow immediately upon Charlemagne and Roland (line 43).

[2] Mergell, p. 75, commenting on this writes: 'Rainouart au tinel ist der eigentliche Held der zweiten Schlacht, dies erweist die Analyse durchgehend. Die Formel der Chanson, *se diex ne fust et Rainouars li ber* ist mit innerem Recht geprägt.'

[3] R. Palgen, 'Willehalm, Rolandslied und Eneide', PBB 44 (1920), pp. 191–241.

[4] Bacon pp. 121–5; Palgen, pp. 191–222. Cf. also Singer, p. 6 *et passim*; Bumke, *passim*, especially pp. 134–42.

introduced many names and many motifs from the *Rolandslied* and he has linked the two poems by relating Terramer to Paligan and by introducing frequent references in *Willehalm* to Karl's battle against Paligan. Palgen argues in his comparison of the two works that Rennewart is modelled on Roland and an explicit parallel is intended.

Aliscans does not note any similarity between Rainouart and Roland. Although the *Chanson de Roland* leaves its mark on several of the *chansons* of the Guillaume cycle, especially the *Chançun de Willame* (cf. Becker, p. 21f; Frappier, pp. 148ff), only Vivien is seen parallel to Roland. This comparison is very marked both in the *Chançun de Willame* and the *Chevalerie Vivien*. Frappier, describing the essentials of the Guillaume *geste* and its relationship with the *Geste du Roi*, writes (p. 11): 'Guillaume est comme un petit Charlemagne, dont le Roland est Vivien et le Roncevaux la bataille de l'Archamp ou des Aliscans.' Just as Roland is betrayed by Ganelon but too proud to call Charlemagne to his aid, so in the *Chançun de Willame* and the *Chevalerie Vivien* Vivien is betrayed by Tedbalt de Beürges but too proud to call Guillaume to his aid. As Charlemagne arrives too late and weeps for Roland, so Guillaume arrives too late and weeps for Vivien. Roland's tragic fault is pride, expressed in his refusal to blow his horn, Vivien's is pride expressed in his refusal to retreat from the Saracens under any circumstances; in both cases the poet condemns the hero's pride, which causes his death:

Ch de Rol. 1725	Mielz valt mesure que ne fait estultie.
	Franceis sunt mort par vostre legerie.
Chev Vivien 38	Qui s'i oublie ne doit autrui amer:
	Bone est la fuie dont li cors est sauvez.

Tedbalt, like Oliver, climbs a hill to see the size of the Saracen army. Vivien's death, like Roland's, is styled as martyrdom (Ch de Rol 1522f; Ch W 547). In either case the hero's behaviour is represented as heroism in the favourable light of military standards, but the possibility of its condemnation as pride by religious standards is entertained.

The clear parallel between Roland and Vivien precluded for

Wolfram's source the possibility of drawing a parallel between Roland and Rainouart; the parallels found in *Willehalm* have been introduced by Wolfram and must therefore indicate his intention. Rennewart, like Roland, leads the emperor's men under the emperor's banner and defends the Christian Empire: *Aliscans* has no conception of a Christian empire and does not mention Rainouart's flag.[1] Wolfram had Karl's lament for Roland in mind when he wrote Willehalm's lament for Rennewart, as the following verbal echoes show:

Wh. 452, 19f	er sprach, 'in hân noch niht vernumn,
	war mîn zeswiu hant sî kumn'
Rol. 2973	mîn neve Ruolant
	was mîn zesewe hant.
Rol. 7517	thu wâre mîn zesewiu hant.
Ch de Rol. 597	Dunc perdreit Carles le destre braz del cors.
Wh. 453, 10	wan du'rvæhte mir diz lant.
Rol. 7538	Thiu lant thiu mir elliu thwunge
	thu ervâhte.

Since Rennewart is not necessarily dead the lament is less apt in *Willehalm* than in the *Rolandslied*, which speaks for Wolfram's indebtedness to the *Rolandslied* where Rennewart is concerned. The lament draws attention to the fact that Rennewart's service to Christianity is the same as Roland's, though his deeds are quite different in detail; the Roland parallel is not applicable to every part of the Rennewart action, only to its climax and its function in Wolfram's poem.

A good test of a deliberate parallel is that it should be recognisable to the audience. Since Wolfram knew the *Rolandslied* when he was working on his *Willehalm*, it is likely that it was part of the repertoire at the Wartburg, and so Wolfram's audience might be expected to know it as well as Wolfram and recognise the parallel. Nevertheless, Wolfram supplies references to Roland just before the lament (434, 16–21; 441, 4–7; 447, 1–5) and actually within it (455, 6–14), so that at this point there can be no

---

[1] Palgen, p. 206, compares the lines in which Karl presents his imperial banner to Roland and those in which Willehalm presents the imperial banner to Rennewart, Rol. 3135, 3181 and Wh. 212, 17.

doubt of a deliberate comparison. Wolfram's introduction of a parallel between Rennewart and Roland raises Rennewart's importance compared with the source and with Vivianz and makes quite clear what new religious and historical significance Wolfram has given to Rennewart.

Narrative technique ·

Wolfram handles his subject-matter very differently from the author of *Aliscans*. While he has tampered very little with the factual account of the events as given in his source, he has taken full advantage of his freedom to tell the story in his own way. Although at the level of syntax Wolfram has an unusually complicated style, he takes considerable trouble to achieve greater clarity and simplicity than his source in his treatment of the events. To this end countless minor alterations and omissions have been made, and many confusing and unimportant details have been excluded.

Wolfram omits most of the repetitions of *Aliscans*; if a line occurs several times in *Aliscans*, Wolfram translates it only once,[1] and the same applies to a number of phrases, which occur several times in *Aliscans* as clichés but are not used more than once by

---

[1] The following lines occur at least twice in *Aliscans* and are translated by Wolfram once or not at all: *Sire Guillaumes, gentix, nobles et ber* (2513, 3332); *Grant ot le cors et regart de sangler* (3150, 184d,54); *Molt le vit grant et corsu et quarré* (1169, 3211, 184c,2); *Sainte Marie, ou fu cis fus trovés?* (3448, 4108); *Par cel apostle, c'on quiert en Noiron pres* (3464, 7594, cf. 1642, 3074); *Grans fu la joie el palais seignorés* (3497, 4327, 2619, cf. 1881); *Des armes est la terre estincelee* (4020, 4766); *Tos en seroit .i. cevaus encombrés* (4105, 4422, 5317); *En Gloriëte fist on l'aige corner, Cil cevalier vont ensamble laver* (4265, 4602–3, 7503–4, cf. 7840a–41); *Se diex ne fust et Rainouars li ber* (4579g, 5689); *Le tinel lieve, devant lor vient ester* (4819, 4841); *Mais Rainouars, ki les malvais chastie/Li peçoia le chief dusqe en l'oïe* (5074, 5085f); *Paiens nel voit ne soit espoontés* (5298, 121b, 194, cf. 207); *Li plus hardis est en fuie tornés* (5309b, 7600, 3435, 4336); *Par mautalent a le tinel levé* (5486, 5517, cf. 4334, 5753; 121b,127); *Toutes ses armes li ont petit duré./ Dusque en la sele l'a tout esquartelé* (5493, 5521–2); *N'ot si felon de ci k'a Duresté* (5538, 5822); *A Loëis ferai le chief coper/Por la cuisine que il me fist garder* (7520l, 7778a–b). The same applies to the following lines, which recur with only very slight differences: 3158–9 cf. 3214–15; 3188–9 cf. 4297–9; 3217–18 cf. 4102–3; 3361 cf. 4881; 3440 cf. 121b,43; 121b,70a; 3528 cf. 3883; 3815 cf. 5835; 3994–7 cf. 8330–7; 4010 cf. 4781; 4148 cf. 4176; 4205; 4857–8 cf. 4878; 4883; 7358–9; 5295–6 cf. 5427–8; 7520h–m cf. 7777–8b.

Wolfram's Wimar dines with the knights once (175,30), while in *Aliscans* Guimars and his wife dine with the knights on two different occasions (3032ff; 3490).

Wolfram.[1] Most of the numbers which occur in *Aliscans* have also been eliminated by Wolfram. As a rule these refer to the size of the armed forces; many of them are greatly exaggerated or contradictory, and Wolfram omits nearly all of them. When describing the Christian army in the second battle he says nothing about the number of men in each group, while *Aliscans* constantly gives numerical details:

> 328, 27 wie manec tûsent ieslîch schar
> het, des wil ich geswîgen gar.
> waz touc diu hant vol genant
> gein dem her ûz al der heiden lant?

Wolfram also differs from his source here in his insistence that the Christian army is still small, while *Aliscans* has several references to the steady growth of Guillaume's army before the second battle (e.g. lines 2593, 4148, 4176, 4205). Wolfram's elimination of specific numbers is by no means confined to this account of the armies, however, and may be found at any point in the narrative.[2] By eliminating such useless and repetitive detail Wolfram has made the action easier to follow.

In the many slight differences between *Willehalm* and *Aliscans* we may also detect Wolfram's concern with realism (a concern which he expresses in the Prologue, 5, 12–15, cf. 10, 21–6). Rennewart's deeds, though still extraordinary, are not totally incredible, his enemies are not giants or whole armies, but strong

---

[1] Such phrases may be found in the following lines of *Aliscans:* 3177 cf. 3236; 3182 cf. 3189; 3797; 3813; 3830–1; 4299; 3207–8 cf. 3275a–b; 3326 cf. 4698; 7635; 3329 cf. 3366; 4744; 4124 cf. 4336.

[2] Within the narrative of the Rainouart action, the following lines in *Aliscans* contain numbers which have been omitted by Wolfram: 3207; 3217; 3239; 3259; 3275a; 3300; 3305; 3317; 3376; 3379c, d, e; 3426; 3481; 3482; 3491; 3492; 3502; 3540q; 3743; 3744; 3776; 3891; 3929; 3930; 3938; 3944; 4084; 4102; 4130; 4153; 4157; 4186; 4216; 4234; 4241; 4242; 4323; 4350; 4355; 4388; 4389; 4408; 4460; 4483a; 4529; 4565; 4630; 4669; 4728; 4729; 4731; 4799; 4808l; 4838; 4844; 4845; 4847; 4910; 4912; 4915; 4930; 4935; 4941; 4958; 5003; 5039; 5044; 5050; 5054; 5060; 5061; 5062; 5070; 5079; 5081; 5081b; 5088; 5090; 5092; 5095; 5099; 5100; 5113; 5150; 5196; 5201; 5226; 5246; 5258; 5279; 5295; 5300; 5318; 5320; 5328; 5330; 5346; 5354; 5370; 5404; 5498; 5499; 5562; 5594; 5579; 5579a; 5580; 5602; 5621; 5624; 5647; 5713; 5763; 5779; 5788; 5794; 5799; 5800; 5805; 5813; 5815; 5820; 5827; 5859; 5860; 5870; 5874; 5882; 5886; 5912; 5970; 121a,17; 121b,8,23; 30, 42, 69, 70, 81, 122, 133, 144, 145, 153, 181, 189; 121c,53; 6788b; 6821; 6855.

men, and most of the gross exaggerations and contradictions of
the source have been resolved. Wolfram keeps assuring us that he
does not exaggerate:

188, 4   ob ich sô von im sprechen sol
       daz mirz niemen merke,
379, 21   war umbe solt ich des verzagn?
       ich getarz als wol gesagn
       sô si den strît getorsten tuon.
426, 24   diz mære uns niht betriuget,
       daz sult ir hân für ungelogn.

The concern for realism indicated by such remarks is made
explicit in his reference to contemporary heroic literature:

384, 23   ich hœr von Witegen dicke sagn
       daz er eins tages habe durchslagn
       ahtzehen tûsent, als einen swamp,
       helme. der als manec lamp
       gebunden für in trüege,
       ob ers eins tages erslüege,
       sô wær sîn strît harte snel,
       ob halt beschoren wærn ir vel.
       man sol dem strîte tuon sîn reht,
       dâ von diu mære werdent sleht,
       wan urliuge unde minne.
       bedurfen beidiu sinne.

Wolfram avoids exaggeration in practice as well as in theory.
He completely omits a number of the grossly exaggerated statements of *Aliscans*.[1] Like his source he often refers to the great
wealth of the Saracens, but he shows a sense of proportion in
restricting their precious stones and metals to dress, helmets and
the face of shields and omitting every reference to golden armour
and golden shields (these may be found at Al. 4143, 4503, 4961,
4966, 4999, 5157 and 5720 in the second battle narrative alone).
Rainouart in anger hits a pillar in the great hall so hard that it
breaks in two:

4317   Si fiert .i. marbre, par mi le fait croissir,
      K'aval la sale fist les pieches saillir.

---

[1] Thus lines 4560; 3743–5; 3776–82; 4317; 4503–13; 4844–8; 5050; 5295; 5320; 5435;
5594; 5602; 5579–80; 121b,42; 5346; 6855 and 6954.

4338   Si fiert .i. marbre que par mi est froués,
          En .ii. moitiés rous et escartelés.

The pillars that supported the upper stories of a mediaeval castle were not built to collapse at a single blow of a wooden club, even with Rainouart's weight behind it, and so Wolfram's Rennewart only makes sparks fly to the ceiling (276, 27–9). The extraordinary feat at Pitît Punt, where Rainouart alone attacks and overcomes a whole army (which is later to bear the brunt of the battle), is made a little more credible by Wolfram's explanation that they were cornered in a narrow place and not wearing their armour, since they did not expect to fight (324, 23). In the battle Rainouart kills eight or ten Saracens with every blow (Al. 5294–7), while Wolfram's Rennewart kills them only one at a time (compare Al. 5602 with Wh. 388, 20f). Rainouart single-handed kills the fifty heathens guarding Guillaume's relatives (Al. 5354ff) and destroys all the Saracen ships except one (Al. 6793–6800); Wolfram gives no numbers (415, 7: *er schufft dâ manegen über bort*) and a fleet three *raste* long[1] escapes after the counts have been freed. At Al. 5970 Rainouart puts Desramé to flight despite the intervention of 20,000 Persians on Desramé's side, while in *Willehalm* only Kanliun intervenes to help his father, who is engaged with Willehalm as well as Rennewart.

As well as in the omission of incredible details which the source contained, we can see Wolfram's realism in the many casual details which his own imagination prompts him to add: how the children at Munleun follow him through the streets and ask who he is going to fight with (132, 4–7), the smoke and smell left on Alischanz by the heathens (240, 9ff), Heimrich and Gyburg at the banquet so engrossed in conversation that they forget their food (265, 22ff), how much Terramer must have paid the mariners for transporting so great an army (339, 22ff), the wild rush for the ships, when nobody waits for his brother but kings leap on board and seize the oars in order to save their own skin (438, 14f),

---

[1] For the value of the *raste* see my article 'German *Rast* as a Measure of Distance', MLN 80 (1965), pp. 449–53.

the Christians' drinking orgy after the victory (448, 3–30), and many others.[1]

Wolfram's concern with the credibility of his tale becomes still more apparent when we look at the many contradictions, inconsistencies and improbabilities which are found in *Aliscans* but have been resolved in *Willehalm*.

In *Aliscans* Louis tells Guillaume that he bought Rainouart in Sicily (3260: *Desous Palerne*), while elsewhere it says he was bought in Spain (4120, 6372); Wolfram mentions neither Sicily nor Spain but says he was sold at Tenabri in Persia (191, 11–13; 284, 18). The squires and the cooks in *Aliscans* are always terrified of Rainouart's anger (3255; 3434; 4335–6; 4612–13), and yet they persist in provoking him (3158–63; 3228–32; 3502–5; 3786–804; 4294–302; 4310–11; 4370–2). Only once in *Willehalm*, early in the Rennewart action, does anyone who has experienced Rennewart's quick anger and violence provoke him again (201, 27f), and here the episode is dealt with very quickly indeed and a motive is supplied independently of the source (the cooks are angry because he has spent the night in the kitchen without their permission). On the next occasion the danger is avoided by the complete omission of the lines 3210–55, where Louis' cooks and squires attack him again, and at Orange we are told that the squires here do not realise how dangerous his anger is:

> 282, 2   in müeten hie genuoge
> die niht bekanten sînen zorn.

Guibourc is generally represented as an extremely brave woman, the bold defender of her husband's castle (thus 1902–62; cf. *Guibours au vis fier*: 4488, 4715, 4719). Nevertheless, when she sees Guillaume's army approaching Orange, she is terrified because she thinks they are Saracens:

> 4022   Dame Guibours s'en est espaontee,
> Quida ke fuisent de la gente meserree
> Ki ja se fust de l'Archant retornee.
> La gentix dame s'est forment desmentee...
> A icest mot chiet a terre pasmee.

---

[1] Cf. G. Weber, *Wolfram von Eschenbach, seine dichterische und geistesgeschichtliche Bedeutung*, Frankfurt 1928, pp. 9–14.

Guillaume is consequently locked out of his own castle until she recovers. A general who faints with terror at the sight of his own troops in the distance is not likely to have been effective (as Guibourc has been) when surrounded by an overwhelmingly superior enemy. When she has recovered and admitted Guillaume, she trembles with fear at the sight of Rainouart:

> 4047 La gentix dame se va espaontant
> Por Rainouart, ke ele vit si grant.

In *Willehalm* Gyburg is consistently brave (cf. 95, 3–5; 226, 25–227, 2; 243, 23–30); she rushes to the battlements sword in hand when she hears of the approaching army (227, 12: *nû stuont vrou Gyburc ʒe wer/mit ûf geworfenem swerte,/als op si strîtes gerte*), but when they draw nearer she faints for joy to see that it is not the Saracens but Willehalm that stands at her gates, and so Willehalm has to wait until she recovers. Thus Wolfram leaves events unchanged, but reinterprets motives and characters.

It is also inconsistent that Guibourc, who helps to bring out the noble strain in Rainouart's character and gives him his sword, should also be personally responsible for the return of his club (Al. 4715–34); Wolfram makes no mention of Gyburg in the latter context and the club is retrieved by *ein wol geriten sarjant* (315, 25). It is strange, too, that Rainouart should throw away the sword when Guibourc gives it to him, despise it and forget it in the battle, and yet wear it only for love of Guibourc, whom he loves more than any other woman (Al. 4872–3 presumably excludes Aelis too), and think affectionately of Guibourc as the lady who gave him his sword. Again Wolfram overcomes the inconsistency. There is another odd scene where Aelis asks Rainouart to forgive her for all the wrong she has done him, and he graciously does so (3915–20). It is perfectly clear that she has been consistently kind to him and has no cause to ask for forgiveness. In *Willehalm* (213, 18–20) she much more sensibly asks Rennewart for her sake to forgive her father for all the wrong that has been done to him.

Rainouart, unlike Wolfram's Rennewart, makes no attempt to

conceal the fact that he is the son of Desramé. He shouts it aloud at Orange, after the singeing of his beard, and he frequently refers to it publicly during the battle; at Al. 5849–54 Guillaume answers one of these exclamations and shows that he understands who Rainouart is. Nevertheless, there is a final recognition scene. Wolfram's Rennewart is too proud to reveal his identity, and so this inconsistency cannot arise. During the second battle Wolfram's Willehalm does not find the corpse of Vivianz still awaiting burial four months after his death, as Guillaume does (Al. 5370). In all these changes it is clear that Wolfram seeks to overcome his source's inconsistencies while altering as little as possible the factual matter that was related in the source.

Not only order and realism but a sense of urgency is gained when Wolfram modifies the sequence of events of *Aliscans* by placing events chronologically side by side which in the source had simply followed each other. Wh. 305, 1–30 tells, independently of the source, how the soldiers in the various armies clean and prepare their armour while their leaders debate. 296, 15–24 (also independent) tells how Rennewart is entertained by court ladies, who admire him in his new armour, while Gyburg goes to church. In Book V Gyburg is engaged in the religious dispute while the army is steadily coming nearer to Orange. Wolfram's masterly handling of the time dimension in *Willehalm* has been discussed in detail by Hans-Hugo Steinhoff,[1] giving particular attention to his technique for co-ordinating events which take place at the same time, and Steinhoff finds this art more subtly and more successfully employed in *Willehalm* than in any other Middle High German work he has studied; this very important part of Wolfram's artistry contrasts very strikingly with the source, where the relationship of the events to each other in time has scarcely been considered.

Much in Wolfram's technique may be the consequence of his desire to distance himself from the events he narrates. Wolfram's view of the battle and his interest in the characters is far less one-

---

[1] Hans-Hugo Steinhoff, *Die Darstellung gleichzeitiger Geschehnisse im mittelhochdeutschen Epos*, Munich 1964 (*Medium Aevum, Philologische Studien*, vol. 4), pp. 19–43.

sided than that of his source, where the poet shares with his main characters a fanatical nationalist and religious zeal. Wolfram's desire for objectivity always affects his narrative technique and it is possible here to quote only a few of the more striking examples of his practice, which may be noted in the details at any point in the comparison of *Aliscans* and *Willehalm*. A greater distance from the events is in fact generally characteristic of the German adaptations of Old French epic poems. Jean Fourquet[1] calls this a '*fatalité du genre*'; the German poet is not simply telling a story but working on a source; he is necessarily '*sentimentalisch*', in Schiller's sense, where the original may be '*naïv*'. It is his business to reflect upon the events and interpret their significance for his audience, and he inevitably makes his presence felt more keenly than the narrator of his source had done.

Wolfram devotes much attention to the thought of his characters, while *Aliscans* is mainly interested in their action. Consequently, Wolfram's speeches are longer, more deliberative and more significant than those of *Aliscans*. In the scene where Gyburg comes to Rennewart in the kitchen (Al. 4442–584; Wh. 289, 20–296, 21) Wolfram places the emphasis upon the conversation between them while *Aliscans* is mainly interested in the gifts she gives him and the respect she offers him; in *Aliscans* Guibourc opens the conversation by offering gifts:

> 4446 Dame Guibors fu molt de france orine,
> Les lui s'asist; belement le doctrine:
> 'Venés ent, frere, en ma cambre perine,
> Je vos donrai une peliche ermine,
> Et si arés mantel de sebeline,
> Puis me dirés auqés de vo covine.'

The gifts then dominate the episode and fill the discussion, while Wolfram does not mention them until 293, 21 and leaves the presentation until 295, 1–28. The corresponding episode in *Willehalm* is almost entirely conversation, concerned with Rennewart's attitude to Gyburg and Willehalm, and with his religious

---

[1] J. Fourquet, *Hartmann d'Aue: Erec, Iwein*, Paris 1944 (*Bibliothèque de Philologie Germanique*, no. 5), p. 29.

position. When Rainouart meets the deserters in *Aliscans*, the speech of their leader concerning the pleasures of life in France occupies ten lines (4822–31) and leads very promptly to Rainouart's action; in *Willehalm* the same speech is broken into two parts and occupies altogether 67 lines (323, 17–324, 7; 325, 24–327, 9). Wolfram introduces many speeches in which major characters express their motives, intentions and feelings quite independently of the source.

There is a great deal of direct speech in *Aliscans*, and many of the speeches are short and unimportant. Wolfram either omits such speeches or treats them briefly as reported speech or thought. This may be observed by comparing Wh. 289, 22–6 with Al. 4446–54, or Wh. 290, 19–22 with Al. 4467–8, 4492–8. Wh. 277, 13–278, 13 illustrates Wolfram's avoidance of direct speech, though there is no corresponding passage in *Aliscans* to compare with it. Examples of Wolfram's treating unimportant direct speech by reporting the main idea very briefly as a thought may be found by comparing Al. 3164–71 and Wh. 190, 3f. or Al. 4696–709 and Wh. 314, 18–20, 25–7.

The stylistic consequences of Wolfram's desire for objectivity are particularly noticeable in the forms of verbs he uses. While *Aliscans* conveys a sense of urgency and involvement by using the active voice and the present tense throughout, Wolfram always uses the past tense and very often the passive voice.[1] Many active verbs are avoided by using circumlocutions, which are often passive in form.[2] Where active verbs are retained, the tense is

---

[1] Examples of Wolfram's use of the passive voice to narrate action can be found at Wh. 190, 7; 196, 5; 197, 1; 198, 14; 272, 4; 277, 5–6; 285, 28–30; 311, 14; 313, 11; 315, 25–6; 316, 25; 317, 10; 324, 29; 366, 21; 367, 15,24; 370, 4; 372, 5; 373, 18; 374, 1,6,19; 375, 1,8; 376, 1–2; 380, 4,24; 383, 4,7; 388, 29; 391, 8–12; 397, 2,6; 405, 4; 409, 11; 411, 2–3; 412, 27; 414, 3; 418, 24; 421, 22; 422, 15; 429, 17,19; 431, 22; 432, 26; 442, 21. All these examples after Wh. 324, 29 occur in the battle narrative. Excluded from my list are all cases where the passive is the normal form and might be expected, e.g. 424, 4–5: *sô vil was der heidenschaft,/daʒ nie geprüevet wart ir ʒal,* or 428, 3–4: *swâ man des vil von künegen sagt,/dâ wirt armmannes tât verdagt.*

[2] Examples of this device occur at Wh. 190, 10; 191, 24; 198, 18; 279, 6; 282, 9; 284, 13–15; 316, 5; 318, 26, 29; 324, 9–11; 333, 18–22; 379, 30; 381, 1; 384, 9; 387, 18; 388, 22–3; 390, 29; 391, 1–7; 392, 18; 410, 4–5; 411, 28; 412, 2; 415, 27; 417, 14; 419, 7; 431, 18; 440, 15–17; 441, 25; 456, 25–7.

often altered, so that the action is seen in completion, for example, Al. 4903–41 shows us Guillaume dividing up his army into fighting units, while Wolfram's corresponding passage (328, 6–24) tells us that Willehalm's army has been divided up and explains how it has been done. There are many examples of this.[1] The use of the past tense, the passive and reported speech are basic features of Wolfram's style which he shares to some extent with the other German courtly poets, while vivid narration in the present tense and the active voice with plenty of lively dialogue is typical of the style of the *jongleurs*; Wolfram cannot have given thought to every change of this kind, but introduces them as an unquestioned part of the act of translation. They express his own attitude to the subject matter, a less involved and more objective attitude than that of his source, and transform the material by introducing distance between the poet and the events.

The main effect of these peculiarities of Wolfram's narrative technique is to introduce greater consistency and stricter order. Order, as well as realism, is promoted by the elimination of unnecessary detail, repetition, exaggeration and inconsistency, and by the careful treatment of the time dimension. The new perspective which Wolfram derives from his greater distance from the events is largely a consequence of his style, with its passives and indirect expressions and its regular use of the past tense. The adoption of a new and more objective perspective is a feature very comparable to that noted in the preceding section, where Wolfram views the battle as a whole from the superior point of view of the tactician rather than with the immediacy and involvement of a particular soldier.

But while Wolfram's objectivity and his greater distance from the events are typical features of the German courtly epic in contrast with the *chansons de geste*, his marked concern for realism and credibility is in contrast with the mood of German courtly literature no less than with the *chansons*. The courtly poets are

[1] Wh. 198, 20–2, 26; 201, 25–7; 202, 1–5; 232, 5; 271, 28–30; 272, 7–10; 273, 28–30; 290, 13; 311, 8; 313, 1–5; 314, 26–9; 316, 8,10,28; 319, 5–7; 324, 10–11; 334, 6; 419, 10–11; 422, 24–30; 424, 21–2; 428, 25,27.

not usually embarrassed by exaggerations and improbabilities, or by giants and monsters, but delight in such things: the image of chivalry has always been colourful and romantic, and much inclined to fantasy. But unreality does appear to embarrass the great poets who stand at the end of the courtly culture. Gottfried von Strassburg censures the tale for being incredible when it speaks of a swallow that brought a golden hair from Isolde in Ireland (*Tristan* 8601ff) and he treats with a superior, ironic humour the episode involving a dragon. Walther von der Vogelweide questions and compromises the noble fiction of courtly love (in a crisis Hartmann had already drawn attention to its unreality – *daʒ iu den schaden tuot, daʒ ist der wân*, MF 218, 22). Wolfram goes still further in his regular elimination of the fantasies and improbabilities of his source in all but a few details (e.g. the horned troops of Gorhant, Purrel's unbreakable armour, the golden Kaukasas mountains – all marvels of the distant East). The great courtly poets are not becoming less receptive to the ideals or the imaginative fantasies of chivalry, but they are disquieted by their remoteness from reality. Wolfram has himself paid memorable tribute to the romantic splendour of knighterrantry, to adventure and the thrill and glitter of the tournament, in the career of Gahmuret Anschevin, who lives out with zest the ideal of a generation that had produced the living romance of Richard Lionheart. But the world about Parzival himself is already more problematic, while fantasy and romance, intrinsic to the tale, adhere mainly to Gawan. For Parzival knight-errantry is inadequate and the Round Table a mere stage on his way; however sincerely he admires his father and his friend, Parzival himself must find a vindication of chivalry that really faces up to the religious problem. In *Willehalm* Wolfram again seeks the proper relation of God and chivalry, this time in more realistic terms than the ideal of the Holy Grail.

The new concern for reality in the most penetrating minds of the age grows with the awareness that the brief heyday of chivalry is over. The nobility could afford to take as their highest ideal the noble games of courtly love and knight-errantry only as long as their position as the ruling class was unassailable, for in these games chivalry is absorbed in itself, idealising its own existence and feeling no need of a fuller purpose in service to something outside itself. But when the real self-sufficiency of chivalry was undermined, when the knights began to lose their overwhelming military and political power, then the self-sufficiency of their ideal was doomed. The knights now had to justify their ideals convincingly in generally acceptable terms, and Wolfram, like Walther, has to subordinate chivalry in a realistic way to the still valid Christian purpose. While the serious literature of chivalry is driven thus towards realism (or else to become less serious and merely entertain), there is a flourishing religious literature, backed by a new popular piety, which has no need to justify itself in realistic terms and can revel in miracles and mysteries; in religion all things still were credible, while the authority of chivalry was no longer strong enough to silence its critics.

The characterisation

The most striking differences between *Willehalm* and its source lie in the portrayal of character. All the main characters differ very considerably from their prototypes in *Aliscans*, but in the present context Wolfram's method must be demonstrated mainly by comparing Rainouart with Rennewart.

Rainouart is characterised by his extraordinary strength, his crudity and his appetite for food, strong drink and fighting; Scherer writes:[1]

Der Heide Rennewart ist bei dem Franzosen ein gefrässiger, trunksüchtiger, plumper Riesenflegel, der seinen Gesellen zur Zielscheibe ihres rohen Spottes dient und ihnen dafür tüchtige Schläge versetzt.

He is constantly shouting threats and insults (*gloton! fil a putain! je te lairrai ans .ii. les iex crever!* are among his favourites), particularly at cooks and Saracens (Al. 3735–42; 3772; 4299; 4313; 4383; 4840). His club is far more important in *Aliscans* than *Willehalm* (cf. p. 94 and Mergell, p. 51) and it appears

---

[1] W. Scherer, *Geschichte der deutschen Literatur*, Berlin 1883, p. 184.

independently of Rainouart in a list of the main characters (Al. 4579nn: *Sor tos les autres voiel del tinel parler*). Rainouart embraces and kisses, washes and sleeps with his club (Al. 3847–54; 3885–92; 4365–7; 4406–8). Wolfram, however, has seized upon the motif of Rennewart's high birth and noble rank among the Saracens, emphasised it and endowed him with hereditary aristocratic qualities (notably a desire for *minne* and *êre* and a sensitivity to *smâcheit*, together with the will and perseverance to overcome it), and has exchanged Rainouart's boorish stupidity for *tumpheit*, the natural folly and inexperience of youth, which conceals a saint-like simplicity and single-mindedness that unites him with Parzival. Rainouart fits quite well into his environment at the beginning of *Aliscans*, when he is a kitchen labourer, but he is comic later when, thanks to his ferocity, he is promoted to join the nobility (cf. the comic scenes at Al. 7654–95f; 7763–87; ms *a*, 7805–10; 7845–58; ms *C*, *laisses* 189b–e). Wolfram's Rennewart, however, is conspicuously out of place at the beginning in Loys' kitchen and finds his proper station finally as leader of a great army.

Rennewart's new character may be illustrated by following Wolfram's differences with *Aliscans* through the text. When Guillaume accepts Rainouart as a gift from Louis, Guillaume promises to feed him well (Al. 3286: *je li donrai a mangier a plenté*); *Willehalm* on the same occasion offers to guide him to a nobler way of life (Wh. 191, 22f: *waʒ ob ich, hêrre, im sîn leben/baʒ berihte, op ich mac?*), and Rennewart remarks that he will not use up much of Willehalm's food:

> 194, 28 ir muget die kost lîhte hân,
> als ich nu ger von iwerr hant,
> swie iwer marke sî verbrant.

Shortly afterwards, Rennewart begs Guillaume to take him to the battle, basing his plea mainly on his ability to cook:

> 3332 Sire Guillaumes, gentix, nobles et ber,
> Por amor dieu, laissiés m'o vos aler;
> Si aiderai le harnois a garder,
> Molt savrai bien un mangier conreer
> Et faire .i. poivre et .i. oisel torner.

> En toute France n'en a mie mon per.
> Je ne criem homme d'une char escumer,
> Et se ce vient as ruistes cos douner,
> Par cele foi, ke je vos doi porter,
> Pior de moi i porriés bien mener!

Rennewart at this point does not mention food at all (194, 9–23). Wolfram also omits the later lines:

> 3856   Li quens Guillaumes s'en prist molt a irer,
> Saint Juliën commença a jurer:
> Se Rainouart nes va del fust fraper,
> Ne mangera de pain a son disner.

Rainouart's appetite accounts for his love for the kitchen; Wolfram drops both motifs, since they are not becoming to a man of noble birth. Whereas Rainouart immediately upon his arrival at Orange makes for the kitchen, carrying his club with him, Wolfram's Rennewart at this point goes directly to the stables in order to attend to Willehalm's horse; these lines occupy exactly the same position in the narrative:

> 4098   En la quisine est Rainouars entrés,
> El plus bel lieu fu ses tineus posés.

> 232, 3   bî dem orse Rennewart beleip:
> ungerne in iemen dâ von treip,
> unz erz gestalte schône.

Rennewart is interested in Willehalm's horse more than his kitchen and wishes to serve Willehalm rather than to feed himself. In place of Guillaume's short speech about Rainouart to Aïmers at Orange (4283–9), Wolfram introduces a long account of him, spoken by Gyburg to Heimrich (272, 2–30), which stresses his good behaviour and his nobility and completely ignores the lines of the source:

> 4286   Mais trop desire en quisine a caufer,
> Le fu a faire et la car escumer.

Wolfram omits the whole of *laisse* 96 (Al. 4616–44), which relates in detail how much Rainouart manages to eat at one sitting in the kitchen, and tells instead how ashamed Rennewart is at having been in the kitchen (Wh. 192, 3–4; 193, 23–30). When Wolfram cannot avoid telling how Rennewart enters the kitchen (for an important episode requires it), he describes it as humility on Rennewart's part (Wh. 282, 13f: *sîn edelkeit des geruochte,/daʒ er die küchen suochte*) and contrasts Rennewart using his club as his pillow, with his wealthy nephew Poydjus who lives in luxury. Typical of Wolfram's Rennewart are the lines (not in *Aliscans*):

> 314, 28 er was halt von dem ezzen
> geloufen durch bûsîne krach.

As soon as Rennewart is introduced, his new *ʒuht* is revealed. Rainouart is teased by squires when crossing the courtyard, loses his temper and kills one of them who had hit him (Al. 3145–90). In *Willehalm* (187, 30–190, 20) the squires tip up water which he is carrying for the cooks; on the first occasion he takes their practical joke good-humouredly:

> 190, 1 Daz vertruog er als ein kiuschiu maget,
> unt wart von im ouch niht geklaget.
> 'in schimpfe man sus tuon sol,'·
> dâht er, und brâht in aber vol.

Not until the same happens again does he become violent (190, 11: *dâ von im kiusche ein teil ʒesleif*). Loys then remarks that it is most unusual for him to lose his temper:

> 190, 26 ez ist im selten ê geschehen
> daz man in fünde in unsiten.
> er hât von kinde hie gebiten
> in mîme hove mit grôzer zuht:
> er begienc nie sölh ungenuht.

When the army leaves Laon Rainouart oversleeps and is left behind and when he does wake up he forgets his club; the reason is that he has drunk too much the night before:

> 3529 En la quisine est Rainouars remés;
> Il se dormoit, car tot fu enyvrés.

Wolfram does not mention his drunkenness, but only his over-sleeping (Wh. 200, 30: *in het der slâf verirret*). On catching up the army, Rainouart tells Guillaume he must return for his club, and boasts:

> 3540i En la quisine est mes tineus remés;
> Si je la lais, petit vaut tes barnés;
> En la bataille seras desbaretés.[1]

Wolfram's Rennewart at this point thanks Willehalm for reminding him of his club:

> 201, 8 Ez was ein helflîchez wort,
> daz mich der stangen hât gemant.

The ensuing battle between Rainouart and the cooks at Laon for possession of the club is reduced from over a hundred lines (Al. 3723–837) to ten (Wh. 201, 24–202, 3); when the cooks complain of his violence, Guillaume says: '*de fol et d'ivre se doit on bien garder*' (Al. 3834). His stupidity is then demonstrated when, seeing Guillaume ride to greet him and help him carry his club, he imagines that Guillaume intends to attack him and prepares for defence (3840–5). Wolfram has blinded this motif rather clumsily:

> 202, 8 nu het ouch sîns geverten
> gebiten dort der markîs.
> den dûhte daz daz selbe rîs
> sölhen würfen wær ze swære.
> sus kom der starke soldier:
> vor hunden ein wildez tier
> wær niht baz ersprenget.

At Orange Rainouart again drinks too much (Al. 4306f; 4330) and, when teased by squires, he smashes a marble pillar (4303–42). This time Wolfram explains his drunkenness by telling us that Rennewart is not accustomed to strong drink:

> 276, 8 die starken wîne gevieln im baz
> danne in der küchen daz wazer.
> die spîse ungesmæhet azer:
> ouch lêrt in ungewonheit,

[1]Cf. also *laisse* 121b, 169f:

> 'Sire Guillaume, et car me secorés!
> Se je i muir, molt grant perte i avrés.'

117

> daz starke trinken überstreit
> sîn kiusche zuht und lêrt in zorn,
> den edeln hôhen wol geborn.

Aliscans, however, lists drinking among his habits (3349: *Et le vin boire, engloutir et laper*). The violent episodes are then balanced by a scene in which the squires tease Rennewart but he does them no harm (Wh. 281, 25–30; not in *Aliscans*).

When Rainouart's beard is singed in Guillaume's kitchen, he boasts that since he is the son of Desramé he is not afraid to kill the cook of Guillaume, and addresses the cook thus:

> 4383 Fiex a putain, mauvais musars provés,
> Qidiés vos dont ne fuise si osés,
> Ne vos touchasse por Guillaume au cort nes?[1]

Wolfram motivates Rennewart's violence at this point by introducing Rennewart's feeling that Alyze, whose kiss planted his beard, is insulted when it is singed; consequently the episode illustrates his pride and his concern for honour and not his contempt for Guillaume. When Guibourc comes to the kitchen to calm Rainouart down he greets her with abusive remarks about the cooks:

> 4453 Cil pautonier sont de molt pute orine
> Je ne gart l'eure k'en face desepline.

Soon he is comforted by Guibourc's generosity and is overcome with delight by the gifts she gives him and the respect these gifts express (Al. 4580–7). Wolfram's Rennewart says nothing about the cooks and expresses concern lest too much respect be shown to him; he thanks Gyburg not for her gifts but her *güete* (cf. p. 171) and refuses the fine clothes she offers him (Wh. 289, 20–296, 21). Whereas Rainouart, after accepting the gifts, promptly asks Guibourc to let him go away (Al. 4583), in *Willehalm* it is Gyburg who asks Rennewart for leave to go (296, 19–21).

After leaving Orange Guillaume notices that Rainouart has again forgotten his club and Rainouart angrily blames Guillaume

---

[1] Cf. 7691:   Quidiés vos ore avoir trové bergier?
Ne vos osasse por Guillaume toucier;
Je ne sui mie lievres a esmaier.

for not reminding him of it, so that Guillaume feels obliged to send for it himself (Al. 4698–714). Wolfram's Rennewart is here so apologetic and ashamed of himself that Willehalm sends for his club to spare the sensitive youth the shame of turning back from the advancing army (314, 18–315, 30). The reason for Rennewart's forgetfulness is not that he has slept too long in the kitchen, but the more noble motive of his interest in Willehalm's army (314, 1ff; 315, 6: *vil manec geflôriertiu schar/Rennewarten dar ʒuo brâhte/daʒ er gar überdâhte/ob er ie stangen hêrre wart*).

Rainouart's lack of respect for Guillaume is seen again when he tells Guillaume that it is time for the army to leave Laon, and later Orange, and Guillaume meekly obeys each time (Al. 3459–68 and 4664–70, both omitted by Wolfram). When he meets the deserters he claims that he has a right to lead them since he is a king's son and keeps boasting about his high rank (Al. 4857, 4878, 4883) until they remark: '*Os dou deable, com il set sermouner!*' (4888). Wolfram's Rennewart tells no one but Alyze of his high rank among the Saracens and politely asks Willehalm for permission to lead the deserters. Rainouart attacks the deserters until in fear they promise to follow him (Al. 4851–5), whereas Wolfram's Rennewart stops because:

> 325, 17 die rîchen und die armen
> begunden in erbarmen.

This new *ʒuht* is also shown in the battle when Rennewart does not attack the unarmed Nubians who guard the Christian prisoners.[1]

> 416, 2 von arde ein zuht in daz hiez,
> sît si âne wer dâ lâgen
> und swert noch pogen pflâgen.

In *Aliscans* he had shown no sign of such inhibitions (cf. 5354–7; 5404–12). Similarly Wolfram does not translate a brief encounter with another Saracen, whom he attacks from behind:

> 5832 Sachiés de voir, ne l'a pas salué,
> Par de deriere li a grant cop doné,

---

[1] Wolff, p. 535, mistakenly attributes this episode to Willehalm.

El haterel l'a molt bien assené,
A son tinel l'a tot escervelé,
Devant ses piés l'a mort acravanté.

Aliscans demonstrates Rainouart's stupidity by showing at
length how difficult it is for him to learn how to unhorse an
enemy without destroying both man and horse at one blow
(5427–537),[1] whereas Wolfram's Rennewart is successful at his
first attempt once the method has been explained to him (417,
4–418, 9). *Aliscans* spends well over 100 lines describing the
crushing of horses (5427–527; 5751–62; *laisse* 121b, 135–6), while
Wolfram only mentions this briefly in passing (364, 14; 365, 21;
416, 27). His Rennewart is interested in horses (cf. 232, 3–5) and
kills them only accidentally, while Rainouart boasts before the
battle of his intention to kill horses:

4535   Se je n'oci et lui [any Saracen] et le destrier,
        Ja mais Guillaume ne me doinst a mangier.

He even kills a horse after he has learnt how to avoid doing so
by thrusting with his club (Al. 5759). As a nobleman by birth
Wolfram's Rennewart cannot intend to kill horses.

Although Wolfram's Rennewart still fights against his kinsmen
and kills his brother, Wolfram supplies for him the motive that
he believes he has been abandoned by his kinsmen (285, 1ff) and
justifies him finally as an instrument of the true God (see p. 197).
Wolfram has further complicated the characterisation of Rennewart by introducing a steady development from promise to fulfilment (see pp. 142ff), while Rainouart remains the same throughout, never losing his love for the kitchen, his crudity and his
aggressiveness.

Thus Wolfram has made Rennewart's character more noble.
He has eliminated gluttony, drunkenness and stupidity, reduced
his crudity to a mere superficial consequence of his environment

---

[1] It is in keeping with Rainouart's limited intelligence that when Bertrand advises him to
thrust, '*Sire, si ferés en boutant*' (5476), he answers: '*Ore vois jou aprenant;/Des ore
irai mes cox plus adoućant*' (5478f). The only line which contains a glimmer of hope for
Rainouart's intelligence is missing from M. In the other manuscripts he prays to God at
his baptism: '*Que il me puist sens et valor doner*' (184d, 25).

at Laon, and supplied instinctive *zuht* and modesty in his dealings
with Gyburg and Willehalm as well as a knight's feeling for *êre*
and care for horses.

Many of the changes which Wolfram has introduced to
ennoble Rennewart's character affect other characters as well and
almost all of them are also ennobled for their own sake. The Old
French poets, even up to Chrétien, do not feel responsible for the
moral conduct of their heroes and make little effort to idealise
their characters (though they freely pass moral judgement and as
storytellers they will naturally prefer a hero who is brave and
true); the German translator, however, constantly measures his
heroes against the courtly standard and feels bound to defend their
honour no less jealously than he would his own. Wolfram shows
this concern for his heroes' morals and dignity to a marked
degree. Rennewart's deference to Willehalm allows a more
flattering characterisation of Willehalm than was possible in the
source.[1] Willehalm commands his army without awaiting direc-
tives from Rennewart. By blinding the motif that Guillaume
hastily declines the offer of a trial joust against Rainouart
(Al. 3840–5) Wolfram has not only avoided a demonstration of
Rennewart's stupidity but also rescues Willehalm from an un-
dignified exhibition of fear. He omits the episode where Guillaume flees in terror from Margot de Bocident and has to be
rescued by Rainouart (Al. 5740–66). Wolfram avoids the implicit
crudity in Guillaume's character, as in Rainouart's. When Guillaume receives a deputation of cooks complaining that Rainouart
has killed the chief cook, he finds Rainouart's behaviour amusing:

> 4428   Ot le Guillaumes si s'en est ris assés.

Killing cooks is good fun by the standards of *Aliscans* (cf. also
Al. 3281; 7725). Wolfram ignores line 4428 and hints that the

---

[1] Typical of Rainouart's attitude to Guillaume are the lines (not reached in Willehalm):

> 7758   Li quens Guillaumes le prist a apeler
> Molt doucement sans point de ramprosner:
> 'Rainouars, Sire, laissiés m'a vos parler!'...

> 7763   Dist Rainouars, 'Sire, laissiés m'ester!
> Je ne dorroie un chien de vo parler.'....

cooks, having overheard something of Rennewart's origin, make Willehalm wonder whether Rennewart is of noble birth, whereupon he sends Gyburg to placate him (Wh. 289, 11–19). Wolfram's Willehalm does not ever accuse Rennewart of cowardice (cf. Al. 3540f–g). He humbly expresses gratitude to Rennewart for bringing back the imperial army (Wh. 330, 27–331, 12), while Guillaume does not thank him at all. Willehalm arranges for Rennewart to be equipped, while Guillaume leaves Rainouart to find and make his own weapon. With these changes Wolfram has made Willehalm's character consistent, avoiding the discrepancy in his source between the hero of the first battle, who boldly challenges the Emperor Louis at Laon, and the pathetic puppet general of the second battle whose main concern is to keep on good terms with the lowest of his foot-soldiers, who terrifies him.[1]

Fear of Rainouart is also shown by Guibourc and Aymeri (Al. 4047–51; 4281–2); in these cases too, Wolfram replaces fear by kindness and respect (Wh. 271, 27–272, 30; 274, 2–14; 289, 20–296, 21; 312, 6–8). The Emperor Louis is made considerably more noble by Wolfram. In *Aliscans* Louis is a villain ready to betray the Christian cause, a type regularly met with in the earliest *chansons de geste* (compare Tedbalt de Beürges in *Chançun de Willame*, Isembard in *Gormont et Isembard*, Ganelon in the *Chanson de Roland*), and as such has no redeeming features. He hates and fears Rainouart for his strength (3263–5; 3276–80) and he refuses to let him be baptised although he knows of his noble rank (3274); he is visibly pleased to be rid of Rainouart when Guillaume asks for him (3287–8). Wolfram's Loys regrets that Rennewart will not accept Christianity and would release him from the kitchen if only he would be baptised; Loys is still a bad King, but he does not commit the terrible sin of condemning a soul to hell by refusing baptism. He praises Rennewart highly and refuses to part with him until implored to do so by Alyze (191, 1–28). The nobility Wolfram has introduced into Alyze's character is most noticeable in his handling of her love for Rennewart. Aelis falls in love suddenly when she sees Rainouart strip

[1] For Guillaume's fear of Rainouart cf. Al. 3842–4; 7626; 7630–1; 7758–63; 7787.

off his tunic to wipe the dung from his club, although even the French soldiers and Guillaume are disgusted by his behaviour (Al. 3855–9), and she is sorry her father will not keep him in France where she could look at him again:

> 3861   La fille au roi l'en prist a regarder,
> Ens en son cuer le prist a enamer;
> Dist a sa mere: 'Ves, com biau baceler!
> Je ne cuit mie, k'en c'est ost ait son per.
> Bien li avient cel tinel a porter.
> A deu de gloire le puisse commander;
> Nel verrai mes, tant me doit plus peser.
> Mal fait mes pere, quant il l'en lait aler'.

Wolfram's Alyze has been fond of Rennewart from childhood (284, 13: *dô mann ir ʒeime gespilen gap,/ir ʒweier liebe urhap/vol-wuohs*) and is herself responsible for his leaving France to prove his worth. The warriors of both sides gain from Wolfram's suppression of the boasts and exchanges of insults that precede a battle and the heaping of derision upon the defeated enemy afterwards, features that *Aliscans* shares with most heroic literature (where they are a spur to valour and a proper reward for victory) but are unworthy of a nobleman by Wolfram's courtly standard. The Christian army in *Willehalm* also gains somewhat from not requiring the constant threat of Rennewart's club to prevent it from deserting (cf. Al. 5280–7).

The Saracens gain most of all from being ennobled by Wolfram. While the *Aliscans* poet introduces each of the major Saracens with curses and abuse and tells us how fierce, ugly and evil he is, Wolfram generally mentions his courage, wealth and chivalrous qualities, thus:

Aerofles	Li Sarrazins fu molt de mal pensé (1171, 41)
	Molt le vit grant et hideus et corsu (1298)
Arofel	Gyburge güete was geslaht
	von im: er hetez dar zuo brâht,
	daz ninder kein sô miltiu hant
	bî sînen zîten was bekant (78, 19–22)
Ector	N'ot si felon dusqe a la Mer Rogie (5072)

123

Ektôr	Ektôr, der ie bewart was vor aller zageheit (433, 4f)
Haucebier	En tot le mont n'ot paien si felon (355) Molt estoit fel et de grans crueltés (121b, 71a)
Halʒibier	sîn hôher prîs vor schanden was ie mit werdekeit behuot: in wîbe dienste het er muot (46, 10–12)
Baufumés	Un roi paien de molt grant cruauté (5508)
Poufameiʒ	der junge clâre süeze gast (55, 15)
Baudus	N'ot plus felon jusque as vaus d'Alemaigne (1401) . . . li cuivers de put lin (5164)
Poydwîʒ	der manlîch und der hôch gemuot (389, 21)
Putećaingne	C'est un paiens ke damediex soufraingne (5001)
Putegan	der wol geborne (353, 25)
Danabrus (M)	Onques el siecle n'ot rois, ou tant mal ait (1087a)
Tenabrun	. . . ûz prîse nie getrat (350, 17)

Wolfram's attitude to the Saracens is regularly the opposite of that of his source; he respects and admires them, while *Aliscans* despises them. If a man is a Saracen, he must be despicable (cf. 1443: *Li Sarrasin sont de pute maniere*).[1] *Aliscans* delights in the capacity of the Saracens for sudden anger; Rainouart seems to have inherited this quality from his father, thus:

> 4981 Desramés l'ot, molt en est aïrés,
> De maltalent est tains et enbrasés.
> Les iex roueille s'a les sorciex levés,
> Estraint les dens s'a les guernons crollés.
> Nus ne puet dire, com est grans sa firtés,
> Nus ne l'esgarde n'en soit espaentés.
>
> 5042 Desramés l'ot, pres n'a le sens dervé.

Rainouart sometimes behaves very similarly (Al. 3178–89; 3735–45; 4333–9), and foul tempers are, of course, not restricted to

---

[1] There are some very rare examples of praise in *Aliscans*:

> 6783 *Un fier paien de grant nobilité* (Triboé)
> 7182 *Molt ot prodome en Baudus l'Arabi* (M=Baud. *li A*)

This praise is doubtless explained by the imminence of Baudins' conversion to Christianity.

Saracens (cf. Guillaume outside the palace at Laon, 2493ff). At
Al. 3805–17 Rainouart loses his temper and kills the chief cook
expressly because he is called *fil a putain* (son of a whore) by him,
although this is a term he frequently uses himself (e.g. 3765,
4383, 4840, 7690); even his father Desramé calls Rainouart *fil a
putain* (121c, 33) and *he* is best placed to know. Wolfram replaces
the scene in which Desramé works himself up into a fury against
the Christians (4981–8) by a conversation in which Terramer
finds out about the size and disposition of the enemy contingents
before dividing up his own army (334, 19–339, 2). The *Aliscans*
poet always sides with the French,[1] while Wolfram is objective
and can allow the Saracens to show as much *zuht* and nobility as
the Christians.

The greater simplicity of Aliscans is particularly striking in the
characterisation, which is so different from Wolfram's. Its characters either enjoy the poet's unbounded sympathy, as do Guibourc,
Guillaume, Vivien and Rainouart, or he despises them as he does
Louis, the chief cook and the Saracens. We should not on this
account charge the *Aliscans* poet with undue naïvety, for the
simple portrayal of characters in black and white is the general
rule in the epics of the twelfth and thirteenth centuries. Even with
so great and thoughtful a poet as Hartmann von Aue it is generally
true to say that some characters are good, like Iwein and Erec and
most courtly knights, while others are bad, like the Count of
Limors or Harpin (though a good man may temporarily err or be
enchanted), and it is quite understandable that Kalogreant should
wish to enquire of the Wild Man which of the two categories he
belongs to. Thinking in terms of opposites was common, and it
was doubtless promoted by the Church, which constantly presented men with the same simple choice: God or Satan, good or
evil, salvation or damnation, heaven or hell. But Wolfram does
not conceive reality in such simple terms as these. People are not
black or white, but generally they are *parrieret*, mottled like the
magpie of the *Parzival* Prologue. Wolfram's characters in *Parzival*

[1] He refers to the French as *nostre gent, les nos, nos Frans*, and to the Saracens as
li cuvert mescreant, cuivert de put lin, la gens haïe, cf. Mergell, p. 14.

and in *Willehalm* are not decidedly good or bad but all basically good, though liable to fall into sin. This must be so, for God created everyone – including the heathens – and all are exposed to the Devil's tempting.

Wolfram's considerable changes in characterisation may in part be due to the change of *genre* which his material must undergo when he treats it. *Aliscans* is representative of the national heroic epic of France. *Willehalm* is not heroic literature; it may owe much to its heroic source, but it is quite unlike the heroic epics of either France or Germany. Wolfram has transformed a heroic *chanson* into a courtly epic. The characters in heroic literature are individuals; their highest concern is for the integrity of their own personality and their only bond is to their *sippe* or *lignage*, which reflects their personal glory and will preserve their reputation. Such characters are typical of heroic literature, where heroes strive to preserve their own personality and independence against all odds. Roland dies for his personal honour, not for Christianity or for *la douce France*: he has only to sound his horn to be sure that the Christians will win and the rearguard be saved, but this conflicts with his personal sense of honour. The age that remembered him as the defender of Christendom was not truly heroic; he was conceived as a really heroic character, whose personal reputation is his deepest concern and whose personality is unique. Types may be found in heroic literature, but the main characters are unique and transcend the types. Vivien certainly resembles Roland as regards *demesure*, but both are more than a personification of this fault – Vivien is young and inexperienced and saintly; he has no lady-love but is cared for by Guibourc; Roland is betrothed to Alde and has a companion Oliver, he is a councillor with fiefs, and a proven warrior, and he incurs guilt through his insulting speech to Ganelon. There is only one Hagen, one Siegfried and one Dietrich von Bern, while there is any number of Gaweins or approximations to Gawein. The great heroic character often has a unique feature to express his unique personality; Roland has his horn, Guillaume his short nose, Rainouart his club and Vivien his fatal vow. In German literature one may think of Siegfried's vulnerable spot or Hildebrand's age or Hagen's political wisdom and grim loyalty to his king. In his concern to stress his hero's individuality the poet may sometimes seem more interested in a particular feature which expresses that individuality than in the person himself; we have already seen (p. 94) that *Aliscans* seems more interested in the club than Rainouart. The courtly character, on the other hand, tends to represent a courtly ideal, and the ideal may be shared by many others, who by approximating to the same ideal resemble each other: any gentleman whose ideal is that of chivalry will approximate to Gawein, and so the famous Arthurian knights tend to be similar types of the same ideal – hence the need for a Keii, who does not conform, to serve as a foil to them by negating some of their positive qualities. The great personalities of heroic literature are derived from an unsettled age of conquest, when every community was in constant military danger and survival depended on the few outstanding men who could inspire confidence in their followers; but when a firm social order has been established, heroes are required who will defend that order and fight for a common cause, like Christendom or chivalry, not for the glory of their unique personalities.[1]

This reduction of individuality and a subordination of character to ideals is detectable in Wolfram's courtly adaptation of *Aliscans*. Vivianz, no longer characterised particularly by his unique vow,

---

[1] Cf. Sir Maurice Bowra, *From Virgil to Milton*, London 1945, p. 9f, who reaches these conclusions from a comparison of Homer and Virgil: 'The heroic world holds nothing so important as the prowess and fame of the individual hero...In his more than human strength he seems to be cut off from the intercourse of common men and consorts with a few companions only less noble than himself. He lacks allegiance, except in a modified sense, to suzerain or cause. What matters is his prowess. Even morality hardly concerns him; for he lives in a world where what counts is not morality but honour...This ideal, outmoded though it has long been in most parts of the world and intolerable as it is in civilised society, had its uses when peoples were on the move, as the Greeks were in the dawn of their history or the Angles and Saxons when they came to England from their continental homes. In such times the hero, the superman, is the leader who inspires and commands others in the work of war which precedes the establishment of a new order.' The heroic personalities of French and Germanic literature date from the interval of chaos between the collapse of the Roman civilisation and the establishment of the Frankish Christian order, as the Homeric heroes date from the 'time of troubles' (to use Toynbee's language) between the fall of the Minoan civilisation and the establishment of a settled Greek civilisation.

represents the Christian martyr and can differ only in his degree of conformity to this ideal from the other Christian soldiers, who in their dedication, courage and death resemble him. Willehalm is the Christian lord defending the frontier against the infidel, a tower of strength to his liege men and loyal to his king and his religion; his brothers and his father are not essentially different. Even Rennewart, a strikingly unique character in the source, becomes God's chosen instrument for the defence of Christendom, and is thus subordinated to God's purpose rather than moved by his own private passions (cf. pp. 197ff). The poet is scarcely interested in Willehalm's nose and Vivianz' vow, and Rennewart's club is for him far less important than his willingness to learn that he must modify his unique crudity and become a gentleman like other people. Not one of the characters lives for himself and asserts his private personality as he did in the *chanson*, but each makes his contribution towards achieving the ideals of the society into which he is integrated. The court epic expresses the age of gradualism, when a man derives his importance from social integration and when individuality and non-conformity could only be understood negatively as extra-social and therefore anti-social energies which must be suppressed. In thus making the main characters constructive as contributors to an ideal, Wolfram has deprived them of much of their uniqueness: Willehalm, the Christian leader, is now comparable to Charlemagne, and Rennewart to Roland and to Parzival, while such comparisons would not hold in the French sources. The loss of their strong individuality should not be regarded as a fault in Wolfram, living as he did in an age which believed in the ideals he has made his characters conform to, when a specific function within society was more to be admired than a bad temper outside it. Through his courtly adaptation of heroic subject-matter Wolfram has found it possible to express the ideas and ideals of his age through specific characters in a specific action which is no longer self-sufficient but is a meaningful contribution to the slow realisation of God's purpose on earth.

Religious content

Both *Aliscans* and *Willehalm* are very much concerned with the clash of religions; consequently considerable differences arise out of the different religious attitudes of their authors. Wolfram has given much thought to the religious implications of the conflict in *Aliscans* and has altered the story to agree consistently with a more complicated theory of religion.

For *Aliscans* the conflict poses no religious problem. God is a Christian and sides with the French, and the Saracens are God's enemies:

> 1058   Puis que li hom n'aimme crestiënté,
> Et qu'il het deu et despit carité,
> N'a droit en vie, je le di par verté
> Et ki l'ocist, s'a destruit un malfé.
> Deu ai vengié, si m'en set molt bon gre.
> Tuit estes chien par droiture apelés,
> Car vos n'avés ne foi ne leäuté.

Ne foi ne leäuté. Religion and morals go together; they are two sides of the same coin. Whoever hates God hates love (*qu'il het deu et despit carité*), and though a Saracen may be strong, and even brave, he cannot share the high moral qualities, like love and loyalty, that the Christians derive from the only good God. The Saracen gods, of whom there are many, are not illusions, but very real demons hostile to God, though they are less powerful and so predestined to defeat. Similarly, the Saracens do not disbelieve in God, but hate him (1058–9; 6021; cf. 31: *C'est une gent ki vers deu n'a amor* and 1257 (introducing Aerofles): *Grans fu et fors, mais onqes dieu n'ama*). The final defeat of the Saracens proves that their gods are weaker. The Christian God often intervenes in favour of the French.[1] The Christians are God's people and call

---

[1] Thus Al. 7147:   Dist Rainouars, 'Sainte virge honoree
                       Secorés moi, reïne corounee.'
                       A icest mot est sa vertus doublee.

Cf. also the immediate effect of Rainouart's prayer 7076–119 and the ineffectiveness of Saracen prayers (e.g. 5775). God intervenes for the Saracen Baudins (7223–4) so that he may become a Christian. Jesus Christ saves Guillaume from death at the hands of Desramé (5952). Wolfram generally avoids such intervention, though Terramer

him *nostre sires*, while the Saracens are *la gent Tervagant, la gent a l'Antecris*. The poet of *Aliscans* uses *diex* only to refer to the Christian God, while Wolfram uses *got* (both singular and plural) to refer to Saracen gods as well. All Saracens go to hell when they die (5767: *Mort sunt paien et livré a torment*; cf. 1141–2), and, when rare praise is spent on a Saracen (Baudins) we are told he is the fairest devil in hell: *Dedens enfer n'a de plus biaus malfés* (7266). It is the Christian's duty to exterminate as many of God's enemies as possible; for this reason Rainouart vows to kill any relative, including his father, if he will not accept Christianity (5768; 5842–51; 121c, 11–15; 6978–83). In its attitude to religion, *Aliscans* does not differ in any important way from the *Chanson de Roland*: *Paien unt tort e chrestïens unt dreit* (1015).

With this simple, dualistic view of religion, *Aliscans* could not allow Rainouart to be a Saracen. Several times he rejects Muhammad and swears he is a Christian:

121b, 98   Mahon ferai desbrisier les costés,
            Si ferai faire eglises et autés
            Dou grant avoir qui i est amasés.
            La iert Jhesus esauciés et levés
            Et li suens cors benoïs et sacrés,
            Molt n'ert haucie sainte chrestïëntés.

121c, 27   Ne croi Mahon ne que un chien pandu.

6898   (Baudins) 'Or croi Mahon, si seras acordés.'
            Dist Rainouars: 'Ja n'i sera pensé.'

6921a   Et se ne sui baptisiés ne levés,
            Je croi en dieu et ses saintes bontés,
            Et la pucele kil porta en ses les
            Tant com jo vive n'en ert mes cuers tornés,
            Car Mahomet ne vaut .ii. oes pelés.

6933   Dist Rainouars: 'Diex soit mes avoués,
            Et li miens cors en ses mains commandés!'

Guillaume does appear to slip up when he tells Guibourc that

considers it a miracle that so few Christians could do him so much harm in the first battle (107, 18ff) and the miraculous presence of stone coffins on the battlefield is the work of the Christian God (357, 22ff; 259, 8ff).

Rainouart is not a Christian, but this is an answer to her question as to whether he has been baptised:

> 4118 'Ne sai s'il est baptisés ne levés.'
> 'Nenil voir, dame, n'est pas chrestiënés.'

This illustrates the dilemma in which the *Aliscans* poet found himself. There was no disputing the tradition that Rainouart had never been baptised, particularly as the baptism of Rainouart at the end of the tale had always been an important scene, to judge by the *Chançun de Willame*. And yet it was commonly accepted that a man became a Christian by virtue of the mystery of baptism, so that baptism itself was regarded as the essential mark of a Christian. In the *Chançun de Willame*, Rainouart says on one occasion that he has been baptised (line 3252) and on others that he has not (3360, 3389, 3487). *Aliscans* adopts consistently the paradoxical position (though without considering its interesting theological implications): he believes in Christ and despises the Saracen religion, but through no fault of his own has been denied baptism. Guillaume's expression, *n'est pas chrestiënés*, strictly means that he has not been made Christian,[1] and it may intentionally express the contrast between his unbaptised condition and his inner conviction. Rainouart employs the word *Sarasin!* as a term of abuse (121b, 73; 7433c); he expresses his Christian creed in a prayer (7076–119), and prays to the Virgin Mary (121a, 29–30; 7147–8). As well as frequently invoking God, he calls upon and swears by Christian saints, especially Paul, Thomas and Denis,[2] and a man's oaths are a sure guide to his true faith. Nevertheless, the shallowness of Rainouart's Christianity is revealed when he quarrels with Guillaume: he promptly reverts to Islam and begins to swear by Muhammad (7592; 7655).

Despite the simplicity of the religious faith of *Aliscans*, the poet manages to make mistakes. Apart from the historical errors

---

[1] The verb *chrestiëner* means 'to baptise' or 'to convert', cf. M. Gildea, *Expressions of Religious Thought and Feeling in the Chansons de Geste*, Washington 1943, p. 14f, and A. Tuschen, *Die Taufe in der altfranzösischen Literatur*, diss. Bonn, 1936 (unpublished).

[2] Al. 3733; 3736; 3739; 3769; 4402; 4530; 4641; 4642a–43; 4704; 4837; 5305; 5483; 5879; 121b, 116; 7073; 7312; 7387; 179, 19, 26; 8056.

or representing Islam as a polytheistic religion and having the Saracens worship idols,[1] a conception shared with the *Rolandslied*, he confuses the religions even in the terms of his own simple dualism. Although the Saracens are the devil's people, they use the term *deables* for abuse as the Christians do;[2] they even describe the Christian Trinity as holy.[3]

Wolfram is not able to accept the naïve form of Christianity found in his source. His faith, though Christian, is not exclusive, for the Saracens are also children of God (307, 25–30; cf. 450, 19). Gyburg's plea that heathens should not be slaughtered unnecessarily, and Wolfram's own statement that the slaughter of heathens was sin, are based not so much on a feeling of common humanity as upon the religious belief that the heathens are also the handiwork of the only true God; out of reverence for their own God the Christians must spare the heathens.[4] Gyburg brings non-Chris-

---

[1] Runeberg, p. 149, points out that the Saracens in fact made no images but the French, who did, imagined that the Saracens must do the same. Possibly the Old Testament has contributed to this assumption by its condemnation of the unfaithful who worship idols and through the divine commandment that God's people shall make no graven image. The picture of the Saracens is also influenced by the pagans of antiquity, who worship many gods and have images of them; thus in *Willehalm* Saracens like Nöupatris bear the banner of Amor (24, 5) and the Saracen pantheon often includes Jupiter and Juno, cf. H. Naumann, 'Der wilde und der edle Heide', *Festgabe für G. Ehrismann*, 1925, pp. 80–101. The ascription of embalming to the Saracens is perhaps also due to confusion with the pagans of antiquity (cf. p. 95, note 2). It is also noticeable that the heathens in *Willehalm* are far less interested in astrology than in *Parzival*, where Wolfram seemed to give some credence to their claims to be able to read the stars. Perhaps Wolfram has been persuaded that astrology cannot predict truthfully on the grounds he must have met in the *Kaiserchronik* (in the dispute between Clemens and Faustinianus), that gods would be totally powerless in the pre-determined world that astrology presupposes, and so one cannot believe in gods *and* astrology.

[2] Al. 235, 475, 1650, 6785–7. The prize-winning example of this error is the remark of the heathens in *Chevalerie Vivien* when they see the Christian knight Vivien approaching them: *Dist l'un a l'autre: 'Qui est cist Antecriz?'* (527); cf. Ch. Viv. 1576: *Diables est, si est fiz a jaiant.*

[3] Al. 1190a: 'Par Mahomet! ne me vient pas a gre
             Ke nus homs croie la sainte trinité.'

Cf. 6883–5:   'Et se tu crois Jhesum de maïstés
             Ki fu destruis od les larons provés
             En Jhrusalem et en la crois penés,
             Tout l'or dou mont, je te di verités
             Ne te garroit ke ne fuisses tués.'

[4] Cf. Schwietering, p. 178: 'Lebendiges Bewusstsein von Gottes Schöpfergrösse verbindet sich mit dem Erlebnis der Gotteskindschaft zu franziskanischer Frömmigkeit, aus der heraus Wolfram seiner Vorlage...widerspricht.'

tians within the scope of God's plan of salvation, both by naming certain heathens who have been saved by grace (307, 1–15) and even by hinting that circumcision might be a racially conditioned variant of baptism (307, 23f). Admittedly, Wolfram dare not commit himself to such opinions, and he does say the heathens are damned and the Christians saved (38, 29f; cf. Gyburg to Terramer, 110, 24f), but his sympathy with the views expressed through Gyburg is unmistakable and he shows his own personal concern for the salvation of the heathens (20, 10–12).[1] This salvation can be spoken of only as a hopeful possibility, but Gyburg's hope is firmly based on the continued mercy and grace of God, which has saved before and may save again, and upon the love which he must have as a father for all his children:

> 307, 26   dem sældehaften tuot vil wê,
> ob von dem vater sîniu kint
> hin zer flust benennet sint:
> er mac sich erbarmen über sie,
> der rehte erbarmekeit truoc ie.

> 309, 12   sîn erbarmede rîchiu minne
> elliu wunder gar besliuzet.

Gyburg's attitude here reminds us of *Parzival*, where Wolfram shows concern for the salvation of Belakane and Razalic (Parz. 28, 14–19; 43, 4–8). The view that baptism, the sacrament by which the individual man obtains his share in the benefit of Christ's redemptive death, is one certain way, but perhaps not the only way to salvation, and that it may be unsuitable for some races, makes it possible for Wolfram to show his Rennewart as a Saracen who refuses to be baptised instead of a Christian by conviction to whom baptism is unjustly denied (Al. 3271–3; contrast Wh. 193, 19: *nu ist mir der touf niht geslaht*). And whereas the Saracens of *Aliscans* believe in God and hate him

---

1 Mergell, p. 109, notes that the religious dispute between Guibourc and Desramé in *Prose Aliscans* contains several references to the damnation of all heathens, while Wolfram's corresponding passage (215, 10 – 221, 26) does not contain any of them.

(Al. 31; 1190a–93; 6021), Wolfram's are at worst foolish and misguided (Wh. 20, 10–12; 217, 8; 218, 2ff; 352, 14ff; cf. Parz. 454, 4ff).

By avoiding the dualism of his source Wolfram is able, even in religion, to find common ground between Christians and heathens rather than see only the irreconcilable differences. While in *Aliscans*, as in the *Chanson de Roland*, and the *Rolandslied*, Christian standards are the only criteria by which a man's worth can be judged, *Willehalm* also has a chivalric set of values according to which Saracens and Christians may be compared on equal terms.[1] Since chivalry is part of the divine order, instituted by the only true God, who created both heathens and Christians, a heathen may please God more through his excellence in chivalry than in his religious observances, which are based on error; thus Tesereiz can share with Vivianz the miracle, elsewhere attributed only to saints and martyrs, of giving off a sweet odour as he dies (88, 1–11), and Kanliun shows his real worth when he abandons the gods, which are in his care, in order to follow his father into danger and save his father's life at the cost of his own (404, 12ff). A Christian could never earn praise from Wolfram for putting another duty above his religion, but Kanliun does, and in this he resembles Rennewart (fighting against his gods and his kinsmen for the sake of honour and a Christian princess) and Gyburg (who would stay with Willehalm even if her father's gods were stronger), or in *Parzival* Feirefiz, forsworn for Repanse de Schoye, and his mother Belakane, who would gladly have abandoned her religion for *minne*. It is this relative unimportance of his duty to his religion that most strikingly distinguishes the good Saracen from the good Christian.

The view of religion underlying *Willehalm* is thus more complicated than that of *Aliscans* in several respects:

[1] Cf. Schwietering, p. 174. It is an exaggeration, however, when Schwietering claims (p. 177f) that the Saracens are more chivalrous than the Christians because the soldiers of Nöupatris and Tesereiz, apparently placing chivalrous values above their religion, will not attack the lady Gyburg. Since Christians never find themselves in this situation we do not know they would have responded less nobly; noble Christians also receive generous praise in *Willehalm*.

1. The simple dualism with heathendom seen simply as the negation of Christianity has been abandoned.

2. The Saracens are foolish and misguided, but not deliberate enemies of the only true God.

3. God cares for all his creatures, not only for the Christians, and there is hope of salvation for all.

4. Religious values are complemented by chivalric ones, valid for all knights, according to which a Saracen may be equal in worth to a Christian despite his religious error.

III · RENNEWART'S DEVELOPMENT

THE POSSIBILITY OF DEVELOPMENT IN 'WILLEHALM'

It is characteristic of Wolfram that he likes to show the development of important characters. This is a central theme in *Parzival* and may be seen not only in the hero, but in Sigune and Gawan, who gradually realise ideals quite different from that of Parzival. Since it is far more prominent in *Parzival* than in its source, we may expect Wolfram when adapting another French poem to seize upon such opportunities as it offers for tracing the development of character, both in the main hero and others. Accordingly, scholars have given much attention to character development in *Willehalm*. Mergell describes 'Willehalms Reifwerden zu höchster, religiös gegründeter Menschlichkeit' (pp. 96, 128ff, 176), which for him is the main theme of the poem.[1] On this point Wolff is entirely in agreement, but he shows more interest than Mergell in the development of other characters. Schwietering traces Willehalm's gradual realisation of a religious consciousness of brotherhood with all men, which links him with the heathens as children of the same God.[2] Ranke comments on the progress of Willehalm and Gyburg through their sufferings to a new humanity.[3] Maurer illustrates this progress, comparing Willehalm's behaviour after the first battle, when embittered by the loss of Vivianz and Mile he takes cruel and unnecessary revenge on the innocent Arofel, and after the second, when despite the loss of Rennewart, which has hurt him much more deeply, he entertains no thought of revenge but honours the Saracens in the final scene with Matribleiz.[4] The pattern of development that leads from Willehalm's uncouth

---

[1] '(Die) Entwicklung Willehalms, die den eigentlichen Sinn und die geistige Einheit der deutschen Dichtung ausmacht', Mergell, p. 128.

[2] Schwietering, p. 173: 'Wolfram gelangt über solche Ansätze [the education of the hero in *König Rother*] weit hinaus, indem er die seine Dichtung beherrschende Gestalt des Helden sich von der Stufe einer stark höfisch gefärbten Gesittung über das Bewusstsein seiner Verbundenheit mit der Sippe zu vertiefter, im Gefühl der Gotteskindschaft gründender Frömmigkeit entwickeln lässt.'

[3] Ranke, p. 61.   [4] Maurer, pp. 181–98.

behaviour at the imperial court and his boasting over Arofel's death to his respectful treatment of Gyburg's relatives after the second battle has more recently been studied by Werner Schröder.[1]

According to Bumke, however, there cannot be any development of character in *Willehalm*, and several scholars have adopted his position.[2] His argument is based upon a distinction between heroic and courtly literature. Wolfram's *Willehalm* is not derived from a *roman cortois* like the other German court epics, but from a *chanson de geste*. The *roman cortois* is interested in the adventures of a particular character, who gives the poem its structural unity and whose progress to ever more difficult adventures tends to suggest and reflect his inner development as a person, while the *chanson de geste* records national history and is interested in events rather than characters. Even the main hero may fall out and be replaced, as in the *Chanson de Roland* and the *Chançun de Willame*, because the structural coherence of the poem lies in the chain of events. Where there is development it lies in the events and not the characters. And so in *Willehalm* the action develops, as the conflict grows and becomes more significant, but the characters do not change. Willehalm's generous behaviour after the second battle is conditioned by his victory: in defeat he had sought revenge, victorious he shows magnanimity. His behaviour is in either case proper from the Christian point of view: the idea of revenge was perfectly acceptable when fighting heathens, indeed it contributes greatly to the motivation of the second battle. Scholars have been misled by the comparison with *Parʒival*, which is truly courtly and does show development of characters, and have overlooked the fact that *Willehalm* conforms to very different structural principles which it has inherited from the *chanson de geste*.

This theory, at least as far as the *chanson de geste* is concerned, seems to be borne out if we look for evidence of character

---

[1] Werner Schröder, 'Zur Entwicklung des Helden in Wolframs Willehalm', *Festschrift für Ludwig Wolff*, Neumünster 1962, pp. 265–76.

[2] Bumke, pp. 56–64; cf. W. J. Schröder, PBB 82 (1960), pp. 411–21; Wentzlaff-Eggebert, p. 265; Walshe, p. 173; M. Wehrli, *Wirkendes Wort* 10 (1960), p. 344; H. Fischer, GRM 13 (1963), pp. 97–9.

development in *Aliscans*. Guillaume's character certainly does change – he is a formidable hero until Rainouart appears, and then he very quickly loses his courage and self-reliance and endures Rainouart's uncouth behaviour with such humility and polite submissiveness that he appears ridiculous and cowardly. But this change is decidedly for the worse, and it is sudden and unexplained; it is not development but inconsistency. In Rainouart's case there are a few indications of a possible development. Soon after his first appearance he expresses a strong desire to escape from Louis' kitchen and find fulfilment in battle, as he tells Guillaume:

> 3355   Dist Rainoars: 'Or me laissiés parler.
> Sire Guillames, je me vuel esprover.
> Trop longement m'ai laissié asoter.
> Si m'aist diex! nel puis mais endurer.
> Ja en cuisine ne quir mais converser,
> Se diex plaisoit, ains vaudroie amender.
> Mal soit dou fruit, ki ne veut meürer!'

There is a strong hint of development in that image of the fruit that must one day ripen, *Mal soit dou fruit, ki ne veut meürer!* When he does leave the kitchen and the chief cook tries to make him return to his duties, he proves able, despite his prodigious appetite, to resist even the temptation of a meal ('*Quant vos voliés, bien poüés disner*'). And later, as the troops are being drawn up ready for battle, Rainouart again takes up the image of the ripening fruit and looks forward to the coming fulfilment:

> 4878   'Fiex de roi sui, si doi firté mener.
> Or mais vaurai ma force demostrer.
> Trop longement m'ai laissié asoter:
> De hait ait fruit qui ne veut meürer,
> Et hons si ait, ki n'a soing d'amender.
> Nes sui de roi, bien m'en doit ramembrer.
> Li bons se prueve, dire l'oi et conter.'

But these few hints are quite inadequate to show that the *Aliscans* poet intended to portray any development of Rainouart's character. Rainouart often refers to his noble parentage and his desire to prove his true worth in battle (*ma force demostrer*); in the kitchen this desire is frustrated and he is therefore always dissatisfied with his lot. His proper place, as seems evident from his strength and his aggressive instincts, is in the battle, but as a strong man, not a knight. He may be given a place in the army and can prove his worth in a crisis without undergoing any development; in battle he finds scope for his strength without changing as a character. Although when his club breaks he learns to use the sword, the knightly weapon, he is quick to abandon it when another club becomes available, as it is too small for him and only kills one Saracen at a time. Although he learns to use his club like the knightly lance to unhorse his enemy, he reverts to his former tactic of crushing man and horse together with blows from above as soon as the urgent need of horses is satisfied. Rainouart's attempts to behave like a knight, particularly when he mounts a horse back to front, are comic interludes, after which he reverts to his true character. At the end of the epic he is no more a gentleman than at the beginning, as may be judged from his behaviour at his investiture and his baptism. At the victory feast we are told in manuscript *a* how he objects to being seated at high table with the knights and longs to return to the kitchen, and manuscript *C* relates how he runs away and hides when he is threatened with the prospect of marriage to Aelis. And when in the *Moniage Rainouart*, which continues his story, he retires to a monastery, it is precisely the contrast between his changed environment and his unalterable character that provides the comic interest; Guessard and Montaiglon write (p. lxviii): 'dans le moûtier Saint-Vincent...il est accueilli à peu près comme un oiseau de proie qui s'introduirait dans une faisanderie.' Rainouart proves unadaptable; he is as much a misfit in the monastery as he had been in the kitchen. He rises socially as his fortunes change, but he cannot develop to suit new situations and new demands that are made on him.[1] The unity and the interest of *Aliscans* do not lie in any dominant character but in the action of the two battles, the chain of events leading from Desramé's landing in France to his defeat and flight.

---

[1] One scholar has claimed that Rainouart's character develops: W. Comfort, 'The Character Types in the Old French Chansons de Geste', PMLA 21 (1906), pp. 402–4.

When we come to Wolfram's *Willehalm*, however, Bumke's theory no longer applies. Wolfram gives such prominence to the development of character (as we shall see in Rennewart's case) and he portrays it so sympathetically that it cannot be dismissed on grounds of theory as the imagining of modern scholars. In the case of Willehalm himself a fairly detailed study of the development of his character has been written since the appearance of Bumke's book.[1] The reason why Bumke's theory has proved unsatisfactory on this point does not lie in any weakness of the theory but in its application to *Willehalm*. It is broadly true that characters do not develop in the *chansons de geste*, or indeed in heroic literature generally, but it is absurd to treat *Willehalm* as though it were a *chanson de geste* and expect it to conform to structural principles of heroic literature. A *chanson de geste* is a French poem, treating French heroic sources, which may be historical or legendary, in assonating *laisses* of varying lengths, produced by a *jongleur*, who is usually anonymous. *Willehalm* is a German epic in rhyming courtly couplets, composed by a well known poet whose other works are courtly lyric and Arthurian romance and whose declared intention is to adapt a French source to please a German courtly audience. It is, for all its heroic sources and its possible affinities to legend or heroic literature, a German courtly epic. It is not a *typical* courtly epic – not an Arthurian romance with Celtic ancestors, rich in fantasy and adventure – but its authorship and the circumstances of its origin, above all its form and the nature of the audience and the patron it was produced for, compel us to regard *Willehalm* as a legitimate, if distinct, member of the German courtly epic tradition. Bumke's own statements when he treats *Willehalm* as a heroic epic suggest that he is embarrassed by facts that will not conform to his pattern. He mentions the external similarity of *Willehalm* to the court epics and refers to it as the only attempt in Middle High German to raise a *chanson* to the higher artistic level of court epic (p. 59), and he has to concede that the technique of court epic has been used (pp. 59, 64). When, as Bumke argues, Wolfram made one

[1] Werner Schröder, 'Zur Entwicklung des Helden...'

single epic out of a heroic cycle he could not avoid introducing
development, which would give unity to his work, but he avoided
the usual course of making the events refer to the hero's development and devised instead the strange technique of making the
conflict itself develop, from a quarrel over Gyburg's *minne* into a
clash between the Christian Empire and all heathendom (p. 82):

> Um dies zu erreichen, hat sich Wolfram einer merkwürdigen und, soweit
> ich sehe, innerhalb der mittelhochdeutschen Epik einzigartigen Technik
> bedient.

There is no need to quarrel with Bumke's own terms 'merk-
würdig' and 'einzigartig', which illustrate the improbability of
the theory (cf. Meissburger's review, ZfdP 81, pp. 112ff). Bumke
finds good reason why development should be introduced but
then avoids the consequence by introducing the unlikely hypothesis that this development has been transferred to the conflict.[1]
He argues that Willehalm is a saint throughout the epic and does
not become one in the course of the action (pp. 101–6), thus
avoiding a development of Willehalm, and yet he claims that
Willehalm's sanctity is derived from his activities in this world,
particularly his warfare against the heathens; Bumke has to
employ considerable ingenuity to reconcile these two views, for
the second implies a development of Willehalm towards sanctity
as a result of the battles.[2] Bumke's important argument (pp. 39–

---

[1] The conflict *does* grow, both in *Willehalm* and the source, in consequence of the common narrative principle of *Steigerung*. For the growth of the Rainouart action see
Rasch, pp. xxxvii–xxxviii.

[2] Discussion of this problem has been unnecessarily complicated by misunderstanding of
the lines 2, 28f: *swenn er gediende dînen haz/mit sündehaften dingen*, which has caused
scholars to speculate over which particular sins Wolfram is referring to (cf. Maurer,
p. 195; Bumke, p. 103; Wentzlaff-Eggebert, p. 266; Werner Schröder, 'Zur Entwicklung des Helden...', p. 269). Bumke deals with the problem by translating *verdiende*
as 'verdient hätte', which makes the lines almost meaningless and can scarcely be
defended since *verdiende* stands parallel to the obviously indicative forms *vergaz*,
kunde, *was*, *brâhte*, *liez* and *gewan*. Wentzlaff-Eggebert, though following Bumke, sees
here evidence for Willehalm's development, particularly since his *wandel* is mentioned
soon after (3, 2): 'Die Vorbildlichkeit dieses Heiligen liegt...in der Überwindung der
sündhaften Dinge durch Werke der "manheit" und Wandel vor Gott.' But the line
'*mit sündehaften dingen*' can be treated more simply as an adverbial phrase (cf. *Iwein* 408:
mit eislîchen dingen, 1763: *mit etlîchen dingen*; *Engelhart* 1000: *mit herzelîchen dingen*;
Parz. 762, 8; 777, 10, and many other examples in BMZ I, 332f, under *dinc*, cf. modern

55) that Wolfram had to leave his epic unfinished because Renne-wart threatened to usurp Willehalm as its hero implies that there is, after all, a great difference between *Willehalm* and the *chansons de geste*, where heroes can come and go without interfering with the work's unity. For all this, Bumke's observations on the differences between *chansons de geste* and *romans cortois* are valuable and enlightening. If, when applying them, he had recognised *Willehalm* as a court epic, though derived from a *chanson de geste*, then he would have expected to find develop-ment of character and he might have shown how the change in *genre* has led to certain differences between *Willehalm* and its source, among them Wolfram's introduction of development of character.[1]

This development is most marked not in Willehalm but in Renne-wart. Willehalm is already a mature man when the action begins: he already has his fief and his vassals and his reputation, he is universally respected as a great leader of men and a dangerous enemy, a loyal subject of his king and strong defender of Christ-endom, and his unusual energy and strength of will are in evidence from the beginning. Rennewart, however, is introduced as an uncouth kitchen labourer and has become a great military com-mander, well on the way to fulfilling his high ambitions, by the time the work breaks off. Rennewart offered Wolfram far greater opportunity for portraying a developing character than Willehalm did, and Wolfram's practice may be studied much more easily with reference to Rennewart. In his pioneering article on *Wille-halm* Ludwig Wolff devoted several pages to Rennewart and gave most of his attention to the development of Rennewart's charac-ter, which, he says, is Wolfram's main interest in Rennewart:[2]

Das, was ihm der Gestaltung wert erscheint, ist gerade, wie der edle Keim aus unscheinbarer und hässlicher Hülle hervorbricht.

allerdings, schlechterdings). The passage does not refer to any particular sins, but to a development from early sinfulness to later sanctity brought about through the grace of God.

[1] For a stimulating exposition of the contrary view that development of a character is not possible at all in mediaeval literature see the article of my teacher F. Norman, 'The Approach to Mediaeval Literature', *Festschrift für Taylor Starck*, The Hague 1964, pp. 130–9.　　　　　　　　　[2] Wolff, p. 514.

Wolfram shows this interest as soon as Rennewart is introduced. The first time he is mentioned, in Loys' kitchen, Rennewart is compared with gold that has fallen into a puddle but will never rust, with a jacinth that may fall into dirt but can never be spoiled by it, and with a young eagle that has just emerged from the shell and gone down from the nest.[1] Later, at Orange, he is compared with a rosebud just beginning to open. In three of these images a rough outer covering has only to be shed to reveal something unsuspectedly pure and noble within, and that nobility is unaffected by its surroundings. Wolff's expression 'wie der edle Keim aus unscheinbarer und hässlicher Hülle hervorbricht' describes this admirably. The young eagle and the young rose suggest a promise that must be fulfilled in maturity. The gold, the jacinth and the eagle all possess an innate natural nobility and are shown in a setting that is not proper for them, the gold in a puddle, the jacinth in dirt, and the eagle out of the nest. They all represent Rennewart, with his noble birth and heritage, as a labourer in the kitchen, and they show that his temporary environment does not affect his natural qualities. These images are not only appropriate to his condition at the outset, but they also suggest development to a future when his circumstances will have changed. They indicate a conception of development that belongs to the courtly age and differs from that of the modern *Entwicklungsroman*. In the modern novel a young man, given talent and the will to learn, may grow towards a maturity quite unsuspected in his early days and

---

[1] It has rightly been noted (Singer, p. 69) that Wolfram has blundered over this image. Like the gold and the jacinth, the young eagle is by nature incorruptibly noble but has fallen for a time into dirt, but Wolfram introduces the image saying that newly-hatched eagles *do* sometimes fall from the nest, since the father throws them down if they do not dare to look straight into the sun (189, 9–11). This makes the image imply that Terramer has expelled Rennewart for cowardice, and Wolfram is forced to correct this impression by supplying the unconvincing explanation that in Rennewart's case the young eagle flew down voluntarily at some later date (189, 18: *Rennewart, der starke man,/was wol ins aren nest erzogen,/niht drúz gevellet, drab gevlogen/unt gestanden úf den dürren ast*). We know, however, that Rennewart's descent to Loys' kitchen was not voluntary, and the image of the fallen eaglet depends upon the knowledge that newly-hatched birds cannot fly. Had Rennewart been able to fly on to the barren branch, then he could also have left it again. For a fuller exposition of this passage, which appeared after completion of my typescript, see C. Gerhardt, 'Wolframs Adlerbild "Willehalm" 189, 2–24', ZfdA 99 (1970), pp. 213–22.

in the course of his development become a different person. Such development accords with a law of natural evolution and constant progress which since the time of Herder has been part of our own cultural tradition. But for Wolfram there is no evolution and no essential change; for him qualities of character are inherited. A man of outstanding parentage, like Rennewart or Parzival, must inherit noble qualities to an unusual degree, and his natural character, his *art*, is as noble at birth as it ever will be. In this Wolfram is typical of his time, which saw a world without progress, and of his class, with its comforting stress on heredity; a courtly poet will not look for development in a person's nature, but in circumstances that can be changed or attributes, such as knowledge or skill, that may be acquired. We recognise this easily among Wolfram's contemporaries. Chrétien's Perceval is a fool only until he is properly instructed; a few days with Gornemant in the environment of chivalry, which is proper for him, and he is an accomplished knight; his development is not a steady growth but a revelation of his true nature. The same applies to Ulrich's Lanzelet: on his first encounter with chivalry he can learn to ride excellently within minutes because it is in his nature to ride; the true chivalric qualities quickly become evident when a character finds his proper environment. Hartmann at first describes his Enite as a lily among thorns and says she *would* have been beautiful had she not been poor (*Erec* 333–8); as soon as she is raised to her proper station that innate beauty is revealed. Wolfram's attitude to 'development' is essentially the same. Sigune's great capacity for *triuwe* is not acquired through her suffering but is already evident when she first meets Parzival, or in *Titurel* still earlier, when standing on the battlements she awaits Schionatulander's return from the wars. Gawan's chivalric qualities and his capacity for *minne* are from the beginning an essential part of his nature. Parzival's natural compassion, which eventually wins him the Grail, is already present when he pleads with his mother on behalf of the birds. The images with which Rennewart is introduced show his nobility as a natural part of him from the beginning: the newly-hatched eagle is already an eagle, and the gold and the jacinth are no less noble for lying in the dirt. The qualities a noble character will reveal in maturity are present at the beginning, not only potentially, but actually, and the course of his development will consist in conquering any impediments that inhibit them (such as an unsuitable environment or a mistaken conception of proper behaviour or of God) and in putting the natural qualities into their proper order, so that each can function as it should and have its full effect. Development is not a change, but the unfolding and harmonising of the qualities that make up a character. This attitude to character is reflected in Wolfram's stylistic tendency to treat qualities of character as independent forces, often at war with each other, and to personify them, so that a man's *triuwe* or *tumpheit* may become active in his heart and determine his actions.[1] A character reaches his ideal condition not by modifying his nature but by finding the proper harmony of his natural qualities and thus being what God meant him to be. From birth a man has his own particular *telos*, the purpose for which God made him and which he must try to realise in the course of his career; Parzival is destined to become Grail King and Rennewart to lead men. Development is the progress towards that self-fulfilment. Every natural quality has its proper function to fulfil. A quality may be misdirected, as when honest simplicity manifests itself as *tumpheit* and leads a man to do foolish things, but it can ultimately find its proper, useful place in the personality when it becomes the simple sincerity of his trust in God. Rennewart's natural sense of honour and his will to fight are thus misdirected when he bullies the cooks in revenge for their taunts; they will find their proper place one day when he is a commander in battle. His aggressiveness is not to be repressed or altered, but directed properly. No man can shed his true nature, for that is within and inherited, but he can shed external factors that inhibit the true self – the dirt that clings to the gold. When Rennewart appears at Orange a development of this kind has already begun: the rosebud, with which he is compared, is begin-

[1] H. Brinkmann, 'Geschehen, Person und Gesellschaft in der Sprache des deutschen Rittertums', *Wirkendes Wort*, Sonderheft 2, 1954, pp. 24–33, especially p. 27f.

ning to open and reveal the rose within, and though Rennewart is covered with dust from the journey, some of it has been washed away by sweat and the true whiteness of his skin shines through:

> 270, 12 dâ sîn vel was besweizet
> und der stoup was drûf gevallen,
> dô er vor den andern allen
> kom als im sîn manheit riet,
> etswâ ein sweizic zaher schiet
> den stoup von sînem clâren vel,
> Rennewarts des knappen snel.
> sîn blic gelîchen schîn begêt,
> als touwec spitzic rôse stêt
> und sich ir rûher balc her dan
> klûbt: ein teil ist des noch dran.
> wirt er von roste immer vrî,
> der heide glanz wont im ouch bî.

In his whiteness of skin, which in this image has become partially visible, we may see Rennewart's true nobility, which at Orange is beginning to emerge. Wolfram distinguishes the true light (*lieht*) that comes from within and can be seen (as *schîn*) in the appearance of noble and beautiful people, from *varwe*, the deceptive artificial colouring that hides a person's true nature. Gyburg stole her complexion from the rising sun (292, 12ff) and where Herzeloyde sits there is no need to light candles (Parz. 84, 13ff), while from Condwiramurs there shines *ein liehter glast* (Parz. 186, 20); the divine light which expresses itself in a person's character as goodness shines out from him as beauty (cf. Parz. 64, 4ff; 102, 26; 187, 18; 235, 17f).[1] This is quite different from deceptive *varwe*, which is put upon him from outside and temporarily conceals his true nature – Rennewart may be *küchenvar* and Gyburg *harnasvar*, but the *varwe* can be washed off. We see again that Wolfram

---

[1] Hartmann suggests the same conception of beauty as a light from within when he says that Enite's complexion outshines the ruby on her breast (*Erec* 1560–5). It was also known to the philosophers (e.g. Witelo, *Perspectiva* IV, 148: *Lux, quae est primum visibile, facit pulchritudinem, ut videntur pulchra sol et luna et stellae propter solam lucem*; cf. Aquinas, S.Th. I, 39, 8: *Ad pulchritudinem tria requiruntur . . . Primo quidem, integritas sive perfectio: quae enim diminuta sunt, hoc ipso turpia sunt. Et debita proportio sive consonantia. Et iterum claritas: unde quae habent colorem nitidum, pulchra esse dicuntur*).

regards *varwe* as a deceptive exterior when he complains of ladies who wear a coat of paint upon their skin: *gestrichen varwe ûfe̜ vel/ist selten worden lobes hel./swelch wîplîch her̜e ist stæte gan̜,/ich wæn diu treit den besten glan̜* (Parz. 551, 25ff, cf. 776, 8ff: *manc ungevelschet frouwen vel/man dâ bî rôten münden sach/ob Kyôt die wârheit sprach*). We must consequently see Rennewart's development not in modern terms, as a process of essential change and growth, but rather as the gradual removal of a *varwe*, of all that is foreign to him, so that the noble qualities which are his royal heritage may be revealed and properly employed.

Comparisons between *Willehalm* and *Par̜ival* are at present out of favour – we have been warned that *Willehalm* is quite a different kind of work and has to be interpreted independently[1] – but Wolfram himself compares Rennewart and Parzival at the beginning of their careers, referring particularly to their hidden worth, which in either case has been unnaturally repressed:

271, 15   eins dinges mir geloubet:
            er was des unberoubet,
            sîn blic durh rost gap sölhiu mâl
            als dô den jungen Parzivâl
            vant mit sîner varwe glanz
            der grâve Karnahkarnanz
            an venje in dem walde.
            jeht Rennewart al balde
            als guoter schœne, als guoter kraft,
            und der tumpheit geselleschaft.
            ir neweder was nâch arde erzogn:
            des was ir edelkeit betrogn.

With Parzival, too, the true nature is seen as a light that shines from within and can be seen despite uncourtly dress and uncouth behaviour, and which naturally contrasts with the *varwe glan̜* of Karnahkarnanz, who looks upon him in envy and wonder.

In both cases *tumpheit* is caused by an uncourtly childhood environment and symbolised in an uncourtly weapon (Parzival's *gabylôt* and Rennewart's *stange*). Neither of them has yet learnt to subject his healthy natural appetite to the discipline of courtly

---

[1] Bumke, p. 64; Fischer, GRM 13 (1963), pp. 97–9.

etiquette, and Rennewart displays his enthusiasm for food at the banquet at Orange as unashamedly as Parzival in Jeschute's tent (cf. Singer, p. 89). The strength that each of them employs in the service of a royal kitchen is compared to that of a mule:

> Parz. 120, 7   nû hœret fremdiu mære.
> swennerrschôz daz swære,
> des wære ein mûl geladn genuoc,
> als unzerworht hin heim erz truoc.

> Wh. 188, 12   dâ drî mûle mit ir kraft
> under wærn gestanden,
> zwischen sînen handen
> truog erz als ein küsselîn.

The mule suggests not only strength but also stubbornness (seen in Parzival's refusal to stay with Herzeloyde and Rennewart's persistent refusal to accept Christianity), a quality closely related to that perseverance which, according to the Prologue of *Parʒival*, has redemptive power; *tumpheit*, too, has its positive side with religious associations[1] and helps both Parzival and Rennewart to overcome their religious *ʒwîvel* (in Rennewart's case cf. p. 205).[2] Stubbornness and *tumpheit* are negative aspects of important qualities which Parzival and Rennewart need in order to reach their proper goals. Both are *parrieret*, for they refuse to trust the Christian God yet are by nature religiously inclined and have the courage and determination (*unverʒaget mannes muot*) to strive to a noble end undaunted by setbacks. This is the quality that sustains Parzival in his long quest for the Grail, and it is this characteristic that first catches Willehalm's attention and accounts for his continued interest in Rennewart:

> 194, 1   Dem marcgrâven wol behagete
> daz der junge unverzagete
> in alsô smæhlîchem leben
> mit zuht nâch wirde kunde streben.

As well as *tumpheit*, Parzival and Rennewart share *schœne* and *kraft*, but these qualities do not develop. Other characters have

---

[1] Bumke, p. 150; Wolff, p. 514f.
[2] Cf. H. B. Willson, 'Einheit in der Vielheit in Wolframs Willehalm', ZfdP 80 (1961), p. 48.

schœne and *kraft*, and when Wolfram needs an analogy to Renne-wart's *schœne* he chooses not Parzival but Anfortas (283, 26ff, cf. Parz. 796, 5ff); development is indicated only when such qualities go together with *tumpheit*, which must change, for the images of the gold and the jacinth show that noble qualities cannot coexist indefinitely with *tumpheit*.

Wolfram's point of comparison between Parzival and Renne-wart lies in the stark contrast between a deceptive appearance and the nobility that is at first concealed; Rennewart is not comparable to Parzival in all respects.[1] By picking on this particular common feature, Wolfram indicates that Rennewart here stands, like Parzival, at the beginning of his development and that this development, like Parzival's, will consist very largely in the gradual revelation of unsuspected hereditary qualities.

In the episode with which Rennewart is introduced he loses his temper and kills a young squire. Shortly afterwards, in another fit of temper, he destroys all the cooks' pots and nearly kills the chief cook. Wolfram's Rennewart, unlike the Rainouart of *Aliscans*, does show a measure of inherited *zuht* (cf. 213, 5: *von arde ein zuht*) and keeps his temper a little longer than in the source, but this *zuht* never prevails for long against the natural passions that he has never learnt to control. He does not begin to develop until he has left Loys' kitchen. He has been with Loys since early childhood and has laboured in the kitchen for an indefinite period, always firmly resisting every attempt to make him become a Christian. A change becomes possible when Willehalm comes to take him away from this environment and treats him with unwonted kindness. In Loys' kitchen he had always suffered harsh and humiliating treatment and had naturally responded with resentment, which made him resist Loys' influence and reject the offer of baptism. Willehalm and Gyburg, however, always treat him with kindness and respect, which gradually foster trust on his part and make him willing to accept their guidance.

[1] Whereas Parzival is impatient to have a horse and armour and become a knight like the others, Rennewart resists chivalry, refuses a sword and a horse and desires only a club, rather like the *gabylôt* Parzival had to begin with.

In order to develop, Rennewart needs not only guidance, but also a goal for which to strive, and this is provided, in accordance with courtly convention, by the hope of a lady's *minne*. Rennewart is always fond of Alyze, but as long as he is at Munleun she is important to him only as a childhood playmate and friend. The relationship changes when he leaves Munleun; at their parting Alyze begs him to forget his humiliations at Munleun and think of a better future, whereupon she gives him her kiss (213, 9–30). He behaves with formal courtesy, bows deeply to Alyze and the other ladies, and takes his leave of her with respectful and moving words (cf. pp. 196ff). From then onwards the memory of this meeting sustains him in his striving for nobility; he is no longer a child, but Alyze's knight (285, 16–22; 318, 14–17; 418, 15), and Alyze is no longer a child, but a lady who can inspire noble deeds and offer *minne*.

The Rennewart action has scarcely advanced when Orange is reached, but some improvement in his behaviour is already noticeable. While his violence at Munleun was always the result of sheer bad temper at being teased or insulted, his motive for killing the cook at Orange is to avenge an insult to Alyze (see p. 152), and Wolfram supplies a new episode where, though teased by the squires, Rennewart keeps his temper:

> 281, 29 er entet ir keinem drumbe wê,
> als er ze Munlêûn het ê
> geschimpfet ungevuoge.
> in müeten hie genuoge
> die niht bekanten sînen zorn:
> der wart ouch gar von im verborn.

At Orange he shows the first sign of a soldier's interest in horses (see p. 157), and it is here that his beard, the visible sign of his manhood, begins to grow.

On the march from Orange to the battle Rennewart forgets his weapon three times. According to *Aliscans*, he forgets it the first time in his haste to catch up with the army on having overslept after excessive drinking (Al. 3530–9), the second time through the Devil's ill-will (Al. 4691), and the third time because he has fallen asleep in the kitchen (Al. 4767). Wolfram uses the motive of oversleeping only the first time (200, 30). The second and third times it is interest in the army that distracts his attention; the second time it is his fascination by its colour and pomp, which might attract the attention of any woman (314, 30−315, 10), but on the third occasion it is a close military scrutiny (cf. Singer, p. 99):

> 316, 22 er wolte prüeven dise unt die,
> schilde und ir baniere baz,
> unz er die stangen aber vergaz.

Wolfram's changed motivation introduces independently of the source a progression that illustrates Rennewart's development; each time the motive is more noble and better suited to the character and interests of a soldier and a gentleman.

In the battle Rennewart's strength and natural ability as a leader are gradually engaged as he gains steadily in importance. At first he fights against the deserters with his club as a single man, then against the Saracens as leader of one of the armies, and later he leads men of all the Christian armies in the advance to the ships to free Berhtram and the other prisoners. In performing this feat he does not, as in *Aliscans*, slaughter the fifty unarmed Nubian guards, but only destroys the ships: *sus kund er ȝühte walten* (415, 24). He goes into the battle as a strong man with a club and ends as a great commander with a sword and with the promise of a horse to come. Had *Willehalm* been finished, this progress would certainly have been taken further (see pp. 227ff). It is possible to trace its course through certain symbols which are closely associated with Rennewart's development; these are the growth of his beard, his interest in horses, and the weapons he uses.

SYMBOLS OF DEVELOPMENT

Rennewart's beard

The history of Rennewart's beard is independent of *Aliscans*. In *Aliscans* Rainouart has the beginnings of a beard throughout, but it never develops. When Wolfram's Rennewart is introduced we are told, in contradiction to the source, that he has no beard:

Al. 3218   Gernon li poignent selonc le sien aé.[1]

191, 30   der was noch âne bart.

When the cooks at Munleun set fire to Rennewart, they singe his hair and his clothes but no beard is mentioned (198, 20f); his hair is mentioned again at 199, 2, but no beard. On reaching Orange, however, the first hairs are beginning to appear:

> 270, 29   sît er von Munlêûn ûf die vart
> schiet, im wuohs sîn junger bart.

> 271, 4   man het im wol die gran gezelt:
> diene drungenn munt niht sêre.

These hairs are then mentioned several times during the sojourn at Orange (274, 23; 286, 8.28; 287, 11; 289, 13; 311, 16). At the banquet Rennewart's beard is mentioned as the most striking difference between him and Gyburg, who otherwise resemble each other in appearance very closely (274, 15–26). After this there is no further mention of the beard except a casual reference at 423, 16 (*ob sîn besenget junger bart/mit sweiȝe iht wære behangen?*), which reminds us of it during the battle.

This beard is consistently associated with Alyze and with Rennewart's desire for glory. Rennewart declares the hairs were planted by Alyze's kiss:

> 287, 11   mîne grane, die mir sint angezunt,
> gesæt ir minne ûf mînen munt,
> diu mir stiure ûf dise vart
> mit kusse gap. den selben bart
> hât ûz mînem kinne
> noch mêr gezogn ir minne
> dan mîner kurzen zîte jâr,
> ode dan der smæhlîche var
> des mich ir vater wente.

This agrees entirely with the narrator's explanation that Rennewart is not really old enough to have a beard but this one has been induced by Alyze's kiss:

---

[1] This line and Al. 4102: *Gernon li poignent, n'ot pas .xx. ans passés*, are missing in M.

271, 1   ern hete der jâr doch niht sô vil
diu reichent gein des bartes zil:
Alyzen kus het in gequelt.

It also explains why there was no sign of it at Munleun, while it is beginning to appear at Orange: Alyze kissed him when he left Munleun for Orange. A man striving for renown needs a lady's supporting and ennobling *minne*, and Alyze's kiss may be understood as the token of her *minne*, which makes Rennewart seek glory and urges him to behave more nobly. A beard is the outward indication of manhood, and in courtly literature a man's courage is generally inspired by a lady's affection, as Gyburg recognises when she advises her maids to be feminine and put their armour away:

247, 30   bi vriundîn vriunt ie ellen vant.
diu wîplîche güete
gît dem man hôchgemüete.

The notion that Alyze's kiss has sown Rennewart's beard was noted by Jakob Grimm[1] and compared with the custom of warning one's daughters not to kiss a man because his kiss may plant a moustache. A popular belief of this nature, if it existed as early as the thirteenth century, might account for Wolfram's ready association of kiss and beard, but it does not explain its significance in *Willehalm*. Rennewart, being a young man, would have no reason to fear the planting of a beard, and Alyze, having no beard, could not plant one. With the sexes reversed, the whole idea becomes absurd. The reason why Wolfram chose a growing beard as the token of Alyze's *minne* lies not in such popular beliefs, but in the manhood that a beard naturally implies,[2] and manhood *can* be sown by a lady. Alyze has awakened Rennewart's virility.

Facial hair was proof of manhood before the law. When a boy's beard began to grow, he could no longer be deprived of his

---

[1] Grimm, D Wb., vol. I, col. 1143; cf. Singer, p. 87.
[2] A beard commonly indicates manhood and strength, cf. Bächtold-Stäubli, *Handwörterbuch des deutschen Aberglaubens*, vol. I, cols. 929–31, under *Bart*.

adult right to hold a fief, according to the section on *Lehenrecht*
in the *Schwabenspiegel*:[1]

Ob ein herre nůt gelouben wil. daz daz kint zů sinen iarn komen ist. daz ez
lehenber si. dez sol swern sin nehster mag. er si von vater oder můter. ob ez die
hat. oder ob siz nьt wissen so sol sin vormunt swern sin ob er ez weiz. vnde
swerent die vůr in nůt dannoch sol er damit nьt verliesen. wen sol im griffen
oberhalp des mundes hat ez da cleinez har. daz ist ein gezivg. vindet man im
vnder den ůhsen cleines har. daz ist der ander gezivg. vindet man im vnder
den beinen cleines har an den gemehten. daz ist der dritte gezivg. da mit hat
der knabe sinь iar behebet.

Just as the *Schwabenspiegel* requires hair first of all on the upper
lip, so Wolfram implies that Rennewart's hair at Orange has
begun to grow on his lip:

> 286, 8   der koch besanct im sîne gran
>   unt verbrant im des mundes ouch ein teil.

That is, after all, the place where it was sown by Alyze. Rennewart's beard is proof of his manhood, and on this depends his
right to lead men and, if opportunity should arise, to hold a fief.[2]

This significance of facial hair is implied in Willehalm's
lament for Vivianz, when he recognises that he alone is responsible
for Vivianz' death:

> 67, 9   wê mich dîner clârn geburt:
>   waz wold ich swerts umb dich gegurt?
>   du soltst noch kûm ein sprinzelîn
>   tragen, dîner jugende schîn
>   was der Franzoyser spiegelglas.
>   swaz dînes liehten antlützes was,
>   dar an gewuohs noch nie kein gran:
>   war umbe hiez ich dich ein man?
>   man solde dich noch vinden
>   dâ heim bî andern kinden
>   billîcher dan dû hetes getragn
>   schilt, dar und dû bist erslagn.

---

[1] *Schwabenspiegel*, ed. Lassberg, p. 186 (*Iarʒal*). I am most grateful to Dr. Rosemary
Combridge for discussing Rennewart's beard with me and directing me to the books of
law.

[2] In the part of *Aliscans* not reached by Wolfram Rainouart is invested with the fiefs of
Porpaillart and Tortelose.

ich sol vor gote gelten dich:
dich ensluoc hie niemen mêr wan ich...
diu schulde ist von rehte mîn:
durch waz fuort ich ein kindelîn
gein starken wîganden
ûz al der heiden landen?

This interpretation is confirmed in Wolfram's narrative:

13, 25   ouwê daz sîniu jungen jâr
âne mundes granhâr
mit tôde nâmen ende!

Willehalm is responsible because Vivianz had not reached manhood when Willehalm knighted him at Termis.[1] The proof lies in the absence of *mundes granhâr*. The death of Vivianz lies far more heavily on Willehalm's conscience than the death of Arofel, and the reversal of this order by modern scholarship is not to be justified from the text. The killing of Arofel is not a sin, but the fulfilment of a duty: Willehalm must avenge his *swestersun* Vivianz, who has been killed by Arofel's *swestersun* Halzibier. Willehalm bears this responsibility not only as Vivianz' nearest kinsman, but as the man directly responsible for his untimely death. He therefore cannot bargain with Arofel and take payment for his life, but kills him for Vivianz (79, 28: *er dâhte an Viviânzes tôt,/wie der gerochen würde*). Vivianz' fatal vow never to flee before Saracens is a consequence of the wild impetuosity of a boy who has not yet learnt the caution and *mâze* of manhood. In the world of *Parzival* youth is no serious disability in battle (Clamide, Segramors and young Parzival are *âne bart*), but the realism of *Willehalm* will not let boys fight harmlessly with men. Vivianz has no lady, for he is not yet ready for *minne*; Rennewart, however, is guided by Alyze to proper manhood and inspired by her in the great battle. In this way we can understand why Rennewart construes the singeing of his beard by Willehalm's cooks as an

---

[1] D. Dalby, *Lexicon of the Mediaeval German Hunt*, Berlin 1965, p. 218, suggests that the reference to the *sprinzelîn* in this passage may be a pun. Vivianz is hardly old enough to have even a merlin, a small and inexpensive falcon; but *sprinzelîn* could also mean 'tiny lance', 'fragment of a lance' (from *sprinze*, splinter from a lance) – he is hardly old enough to be carrying a lance splinter into battle, let alone a proper lance.

insult to Alyze, and his consequent bitterness and violence express his sensitivity for her honour.[1] This burning of his beard may be compared with the burning of his club, for in either case the humiliating affront makes Rennewart bitter but firmer in his purpose than before (cf. p. 162).

With this interpretation we can see why the growth of the beard seems to reach its completion at Orange and is not developed further. The last mention of its growth immediately precedes the march into battle. By this time Rennewart is completely a man, ready and fit to go to war, and his beard is grown. Manhood having thus been reached, the expression of his development must be transferred to other symbols.

Rennewart's interest in horses

In the French tradition Rainouart hates horses (cf. p. 39). Horses necessarily belong to knights and are essential to their way of fighting; Rainouart fights on foot and needs no horse, and it is not until he becomes a knight after the battle that he is given one (Al. 8027–96). Similarly, the men of Gorhant, who fight on foot with iron bars, have no use for horses (Al. 82; Wh. 35, 21f). Rainouart seems too big for a horse, and he certainly can run as fast as Guillaume rides (Ch W 2768; Al. 3884, 4010, 4677, 4741–3, 4781; Wh. 202, 13–18; 226, 12–15; 272, 6f; 317, 11–17). Wolfram, however, is always interested in horses; he praises Willehalm's care for Puzzat and censures Margot for riding a mare in battle. Care for one's horse is a sign of a well bred nobleman and as such is to be expected in the court epic rather than the *chanson de geste*. We are not likely to find a hero who hates horses in a work by Wolfram.

At Munleun Rennewart has no interest in horses. When the Jew offers him one, he is quick to refuse:

> 196, 10 er bôt im dannoch mêre,
> harnasch, ors und lanzen starc...

---

[1] Cf. Singer, p. 87: 'Während er im französischen Gedicht vom Anfang an seine Milchbart trägt und seine Entrüstung über das Ansengen seines Bartes durch den Koch nur aus dem Stolz des Jünglings auf seine ersten Barthaare sich erklärt, sind diese hier das Symbol seiner keimenden Liebe geworden, und wenn er hier den Koch zur Strafe tötet, so rächt er gewissermassen seine junge Liebe an ihrem Verächter.'

196, 16   dô sprach der knappe schiere
'ich wil ze vuoze in den strît.
harnasch unde runzît
daz geb mîn hêrre den dies gern.'

Wolfram is here independent, for Rainouart was not offered these gifts. As the knights ride to Orange, Rennewart shows his independence of horses by running in front of them.

On arrival at Orange Rennewart shows his first sign of interest in horses. Here Wolfram contradicts his source: whereas Rainouart had immediately made for the kitchen (Al. 4098–9), Rennewart first attends to the needs of Willehalm's horse:

232, 3   bî dem orse Rennewart beleip:
ungerne in iemen dâvon treip,
unz erz gestalte schône.
dâ von Samargône
ein insigel was gebrant
anz orses buoc, daz er dâ vant,
dar nâch was Arofelles schilt.
den knappen hete gar bevilt
und het er sich versunnen
wie daz ors wart gewunnen.

Apart from this there is no mention of horses in connection with Rennewart at Orange.

During the battle Rennewart kills horses as well as Saracens with his club, but this is not, as in *Aliscans* (cf. p. 120), his express intention; when he has learnt how to kill his enemy without harming the horse he never reverts to his old battle technique of crushing man and horse together with a heavy blow from above. Having freed Willehalm's relatives from captivity he is quick to learn how to provide them with horses. Towards the end of the battle there is a clear indication that he is going to have a horse of his own.

420, 22   ez wart ouch Rennewarte sider
ein ors, hiez Lignmaredî.

Li Margaris is the name of the horse which in *Aliscans* is given to Rainouart at his investiture. We have already noted Wolfram's habit of preparing for an important scene by supplying a brief advance reference (pp. 80ff); this mention of Lignmaredi suggests that Rennewart's changing attitude to horses will be crowned, when he is a true knight, by possession of his own horse. Rennewart has just learnt to use the sword when this horse is mentioned, and so a horse would now be more appropriate than before. Wolfram does not reach this climax, but he does appear to be preparing for the presentation of this horse, which in *Aliscans* is among the honours Rainouart enjoys after the battle, by indicating a shift from his initial hostility towards a more chivalric concern for horses.

Rennewart's weapons

Rennewart's weapons and his use of them are also indicative of his development. Here, too, Wolfram is at variance with *Aliscans*, where Rainouart has a club throughout and his brief adventure with a sword serves only as a comic episode.[1] As soon as Baudins' club breaks in two, Rainouart is quick to seize half of it and throw away his sword (Al. 6967–72). The sword is too small for Rainouart, while his club is well suited to his strength and his uncourtly way of fighting.[2] The knights commonly use the sword just as Rainouart uses his club, to deliver crushing blows from above on an enemy's helmet (Rainouart, of course, cuts his man in half and buries the sword in the ground); given such a technique, the sword has no advantage beyond its cutting power, an advantage worthless to Rainouart, since he can always crush his enemy with a single blow. In *Aliscans* the club is always mightier than the sword, as Desramé recognises when he is arming Baudins (Al. 121b, 137). All the many improvised weapons that he uses in the long Rainouart *geste* resemble the club (e.g. a ship's mast, a

---

[1] Frappier, p. 225f, discussing Rainouart in the *Chançun de Willame*, sees that his discovery of his sword might have led to a development but that this possibility is neglected in both *Chançun de Willame* and *Aliscans*: 'elle aurait pu servir de prélude à un véritable apprentissage chevaleresque de Rainouart, mais l'auteur n'a pas pu ou n'a pas voulu tirer le parti possible de ce thème qui restera latent ou ne sera qu'effleuré aussi dans *Aliscans*.'

[2] Cf. Runeberg, p. 133f: 'Le tinel est la seule arme digne de Rainouart, et Rainouart est le seul personnage qui puisse remuer le tinel.' In a rare moment of enthusiasm for the sword Rainouart says every man ought to have four of them at his side, Al. 6788a–c (cf. Ch W 3332: *Chascun franc home deveit quatre porter*).

tree trunk, an iron bar) and all of them are referred to with the same word *tinel* (cf. Runeberg, p. 134f); no French poem can think of Rainouart parted from his club.[1]

At Munleun Wolfram's Rennewart has no weapon at all, though his aggressive instinct is very much in evidence (190, 12–20). His first desire, satisfied by the smith at Munleun, is to possess a wooden club strengthened by iron bands.[2] Although this weapon proves efficient in battle,[3] it is unusual among knights, being the traditional weapon of the extremely uncourtly giant;[4] Erec, Tristan and other good knights have occasion to fight with sword and lance against giants armed with clubs.[5] The club (*stange*) is sometimes used by Saracens (e.g. Wh. 35, 20–2; 395, 24; *Der jüngere Titurel* 3501f), but it is not their characteristic weapon; in the *chansons de geste* the Saracens use all kinds of unconventional arms[6] of which the club is only one and is most often used by Saracen giants.[7] The hero of a court epic never

---

[1] The exception, which delightfully proves the rule, is quoted by Runeberg, p. 4:

> 'Canteres sui, qu'el mont n'a tel,
> Ge sai de Guillaume au tinel
> Si com il arriva as nes
> Et de Renoart au cort nes
> Sai ge bien chanter com ge vueil.'

From '*Deux Bourdeurs ribauds*', see *Histoire Littéraire de la France*, Paris 1733–1949, vol. 23 (1856), p. 95.

[2] Walshe, p. 173, calls the *stange* an iron bar, but this does not tally with 195, 27 – 198, 1, especially 196, 20–30.

[3] A similar weapon, the Flemish *godendac*, was apparently used with success at Courtrai in 1302, see Sumberg, p. 229.

[4] The giant's club is often bound with iron hoops, cf. the giants whom Erec defeats, *Erec* 5385: *wâfens wâren si blôʒ.|waʒ ir wer wære?|ʒwêne kolben swære|grôʒe unde lange:| den wâren die stange|mit îsen beslagen.* Sometimes an iron club is used, cf. Rajna, p. 443; Grimm, D Wb vol. 10, cols. 792–802, under *Stange* (2).

[5] *Erec* 5385ff; *Iwein* 5021–6, 6677–86; *Tristan* 15976–81; *Eneide* 7136–40; *Parʒival* 570, 5f; *Herʒog Ernst* 5168–71; *König Rother* 650f; Lamprecht's *Alexander* 5077f; Albrecht von Kemenaten's *Goldemar* 4, 10–12; *Wigalois* 2114ff.

[6] In *Aliscans* Aenré fights with his teeth and a whip (*flael*), the dwarf Agrapart with teeth and claws like a cat, Baudins uses a ship's mast and a club like Rainouart's, Borrel an immense hammer, Crucados a club, Flohart has a scythe and breathes fire, Gorhant's men each have a flail with a lead ball at the end (*mache*, cf. A. Schulz, *Das höfische Leben*, Leipzig 1889, vol. 2, p. 213), Grishart has an axe, Haucebier three poisoned swords, Loquifer his *loque* (a special iron club), Margot de Bocident a *flael* and Walegrape a long hook (*croc*).

[7] In the above list (note 6) Baudins, Crucados and Loquifer are giants.

uses a club as his weapon.[1] Clubs are used by people who, like giants, are strong but uncouth, like the Wild Man in *Iwein*.[2] Widolt mit der stangen in *König Rother* (cf. Vidolf mittumstangan in the *Thidrekssaga*) is probably derived from a fairy-tale giant and may owe some features to Rainouart.[3] The club is in any case not a respectable weapon; Runeberg (pp. 105–7) quotes the Finnish tale of Kurki and Potko, where Kurki's weapon is normally the sword, but in one variant where he is the villain and is ultimately condemned to death he fights with a club. Rennewart's choice of a club for his weapon therefore characterises him as an uncouth person: it is the weapon a giant would choose. His *dörperheit* is hinted at in Wolfram's imagery: Willehalm had cut through the ranks of the heathens with his sword as the sun cuts through a dark mist with its sharp bright rays (40, 12ff), but Rennewart wielding his club is like a peasant ploughing a furrow:

> 327, 22   Rennwart die tôtlîchen furch
> mit sîner grôzen stangen ier.

For all this, Wolfram does not see the club in an entirely negative light; though uncourtly, it is a weapon, and Rennewart's attachment to it expresses his determination to help Willehalm. His willingness to return for it whenever he forgets it shows that he cannot be deflected from his purpose. This is proved when he forgets it for the third time and suffers the shame of turning back as the army advances into battle (316, 25 – 317, 20). Wolfram places considerable emphasis on this shame and on Rennewart's reaction to it, although this 'retreat', not being motivated by cowardice,

---

[1] Heinrich von Neustadt's *Apollonius* is an exception, but allowance must be made for its setting in pre-Christian antiquity, its stress on adventure and the unusual, its late date (early 14th century) and the influence of the Rennewart of Wolfram and Türheim.

[2] *Iwein* 469f. Cf. *Yvain* 293: *une grant maçue an sa main; maçue* is one of the words used in *Aliscans* to describe Rainouart's club.

[3] Cf. Rajna, p. 443; Panzer, *Italische Normannen*, pp. 76–9. J. de Vries, however, in his edition of *Rother*, Heidelberg 1922, p. xcviii, rejects the derivation of Widolt from Rainouart on the grounds that Widolt was known before Rainouart and that the evidence for linking them, being based only on the equation of the epithets *au tinel* and *mittumstangi*, is inadequate. Panzer opposes this view and quotes considerable evidence for the derivation of Widolt from Rainouart. The *Thidrekssaga* was based on Low German tales, and we know that there was a Low German version of *Aliscans* (viz. the *Kitzinger Bruchstücke*).

may not appear culpable. It needs to be seen from Rennewart's point of view: a man who is seen running away when battle is imminent may be taken for a coward (cf. 318, 1–5 and Al. 3540d–g, where Guillaume accuses Rainouart of cowardice on seeing him turn back for his club), and we know very well how hypersensitive Rennewart is where *êre* is concerned. Furthermore, Wolfram seems to regard flight more severely than his source: his Vivianz *ungerne vlôch* (41, 12), that is, he did not flee (cf. Bumke, p. 21, note 24), while in *Aliscans* Vivien really did flee and his tragic fault was his *demesure* in having vowed that he would never flee under any circumstances. Guillaume, like a wise man, had fled after the first battle:

> Al. 620 Molt par fu sages, car bien savoit fuir
> Et ou besoig trestorner et guencir.

Willehalm, however, flees only at his men's prompting (53, 15), which partially exculpates him,[1] and his flight seems to embarrass Wolfram, for as well as supplying the excuse of *sîner manne rât* he distances himself from the tale with the phrase *sus hôrt ich sagen* (53, 14). He will not mention the names of the French leaders at the conference at Orange because they are later going to turn back (302, 1–18), and when they are induced to return to the field under Rennewart's command he remarks '*ich het ouch ê der vlühte haz*' (330, 26).[2] Wolfram, a moralist as well as a soldier, seems to have abhorred the very idea of retreat. Rennewart feels that turning back for his club is so shameful that he suffers

---

[1] In mediaeval literature responsibility falls more heavily upon the prompter than the person who does the deed. Lunete is nearly burned at the stake for her advice while Laudine seems to remain guiltless – even Wolfram does not attack her. King Mark sends Tristan on a dangerous mission to Ireland and marries despite his solemn vow to the contrary because the barons advise it, whereby he is at least partially exculpated. Charlemagne, in the *Chanson de Roland*, sends Ganelon on the dangerous mission to Marsilie because the French barons have advised it (319ff). *Rûmoldes rât* makes him notorious. Sibeche can take revenge on Ermanaric by giving him bad advice. The Devil does not sin, but prompts sin; that is why man, who sins at the Devil's prompting, can yet be saved, while the fallen angels cannot, since they sinned on their own initiative, Wh. 308, 14–24 (accordingly the Basques claim to be free from sin, since the Devil, unable to learn their language, cannot tempt them). The M.H.G. language shows the same attitude in some of its idioms (e.g. *im riet sîn tumpheit*). See my article 'The Advisor's Guilt in Courtly Literature', GLL 24 (1970), pp. 3–13.

[2] Cf. the remark of Parzival: *swenne ich fliehen lerne,/sô stirb ich als gerne*, Parz. 260, 1f.

herʒeleit, an injury so grave that it can normally be effaced only by blood revenge;[1] he determines to make good this disgrace by exceptional valour in the battle against the heathen, upon whom he exacts the appropriate revenge, and so his will to fight is strengthened by the experience. When he finds his club, it is burned but has become harder and firmer:

> 319, 1   nu enruochet, was se ê wæher:
> si ist nu vestr und zæher.

The strengthening of his club in the fire is comparable to Rennewart's own experience, becoming more deadly and resolute in his purpose through the disgrace he has suffered. We soon witness Rennewart's firmness and the club's effectiveness when, returning to battle, he encounters the French deserters at Pitît Punt – willingly committing the very offence he had committed unwillingly – and conquers them and their temptations (which include the promise of *êre* and *minne* in comfortable France).

In the early part of the battle Rennewart uses his club to good effect and with it frees Willehalm's relations who had been captured during the earlier battle. Its limitations as a weapon, however, become evident when Rennewart has to provide horses for them; he is unable to kill a Saracen without crushing his horse as well. Like Parzival, and in contradiction to the source, Rennewart is willing and quick to learn, and Berhtram soon teaches him to unhorse his enemy by thrusting with the club (417, 2–21). In this way Rennewart begins to use his club in the manner of a knight's lance and fight rather more like a gentleman than before. His instant success where he had previously failed proves the value of the new method.

Rennewart faces his next crisis on meeting Purrel, whose armour is so strong that none of the knights can wound him (425, 25–426, 30). Rennewart tries to solve the problem by reverting to his old method and delivering a crushing blow from above; the blow kills the horse and shatters Rennewart's club but it only wounds Purrel, who escapes with the help of his men. The natural limit

---

[1] Cf. Maurer, *Leid*, pp. 179–83 *et passim*.

of the club's value has been passed, and Rennewart is now forced to use the sword. Quickly he recognises its superiority over the club:

> 430, 30   er sprach 'diu starke stange mîn
> was mir ein teil ze swære:
> dû bist lîht und doch strîtpære.'

The sword has been at Rennewart's side ever since he was armed by Gyburg at Orange, but he has not realised its worth until taught by the experience of battle. At Orange it had still seemed inappropriate, as Wolfram remarks:

> 312, 11   man muoz des sîme swerte jehen:
> het ez hêr Nîthart gesehen
> über sînen geubühel tragn,
> er begundez sînen vriunden klagn.

Neidhart often complains of peasants who wear the sword,[1] and Wolfram's remark here implies that Rennewart at Orange is like the peasant of Neidhart's poems; the sword is inappropriate for him as long as he does not behave like a knight. Gyburg knows that its time will come, and it is in this crisis of the battle that Rennewart reaches the maturity which makes his sword appropriate.

As Rennewart's weapons change, so does his effective rank. When we first meet him he is a kitchen-boy and unarmed. When he becomes a foot-soldier he is armed with a club. Before he leads men his club is strengthened in the fire; having distinguished himself in battle he learns to use it as a lance; and when he learns to use the sword he has become the effective leader of a large composite army of Christians who have been forced together under the impact of Terramer's attack. At the same time he is acquiring chivalry. His club suits him as long as his strength is not subordinated to the chivalric code, but it would be absurd in the hands of a knight, while his sword, like the promised horse, is indicative of his rise to chivalry.

---

[1] Neidhart von Reuental, ed. Wiessner, 41, 1f; 53, 34; 55, 30f; 59, 10; 88, 34; 90, 18. 33; 92, 7.

GUIDANCE AND 'GÜETE'

The development of Parzival and his rise to become Grail King depend more than anything else upon the guidance he receives from good men, whose advice and instruction at critical moments sets him on the proper path, and then upon his own willingness to listen to what they tell him. Parzival's readiness to follow the precepts of his mother leads him (despite the errors due to his *tumpheit*) to Gurnemanz, the gray, wise man who teaches him true chivalry; his long period of self-reliance and independence, when he is estranged from God and courtly society, is the most barren part of his career: it ends on a Good Friday when he has learnt the futility of his own efforts and asks God for help. He drops the reins of his horse and allows divine providence to guide him to Trevrizent, whose wisdom and saintliness direct his further progress. Parzival's career could only be a disaster if it were directed from the outset by his own folly; to overcome his folly he must be willing to attend to others who can guide him well, and his success depends upon the soundness of their teaching and his own readiness to heed their good advice rather than follow the promptings of his own foolish will. The Middle Ages had no great admiration for personal independence and self-assertion; they had more respect for conformity to sound, established principles, for obedience to the good authorities, for constant, loyal submission to the will of recognised superiors. No man achieved salvation by his own efforts; he had to be open and responsive to the beneficent grace of God and in Christian humility allow his life to be directed by the divine will, expressed through Holy Church, and not by an independent will of his own.[1]

That natural readiness to respect good people and be guided by them which is essential to the career of Parzival is no less important for Rennewart. Rennewart rises socially and learns the virtues of chivalry moved by the hope of Alyze's *minne* and guided by

---

[1] Cf. my article 'The Advisor's Guilt' (see p. 161, note 1). On such guidance in *Parzival* see W. Mohr, 'Hilfe und Rat in Wolframs Parzival', *Festschrift für Jost Trier*, Meisenheim 1954, pp. 173–97.

the *güete* of Willehalm and Gyburg. Rennewart needs above all else to be respected and treated kindly; when he enjoys such treatment from Willehalm and Gyburg he quickly becomes responsive to them and willing to do as they say. Willehalm and Gyburg are not motivated by fear (as so often in *Aliscans*), nor primarily by their desire to gain a valuable soldier, but by their *güete*, a natural sympathy which prompts them to be consistently kind and in their kindness to show Rennewart the respect he desires and tries so valiantly to deserve. Their *güete*, being a quality of character, never fails, even when they have good reason to be impatient or angry with Rennewart; Willehalm's apparent weakness when he seems to ignore serious misconduct (as when Rennewart kills his chief cook or delays the army by repeatedly forgetting his club) is an unfortunate consequence for the modern reader of Wolfram's emphasis on the long-suffering *güete* of Willehalm and Gyburg.

In making more noble the Rainouart of *Aliscans*, who is traditionally uncouth and aggressive, Wolfram faced an awkward problem: tradition would not allow him to exclude the rowdy episodes in which Rennewart mishandles the cooks and squires of Munleun and Orange, but these episodes were difficult to reconcile with the new character in which Rennewart's inherited *zuht*[1] was prominent, a quality which presupposes self-discipline. His known behaviour appeared to contradict his character and parentage. Wolfram meets the problem by exhibiting Rennewart's violence only on occasions when he has been treated with marked disrespect and unkindness, exceeding the limits which his *zuht* can endure; where the source had shown Rainouart to have no *zuht* at all, Wolfram explains on each occasion how his natural *zuht* is strained beyond breaking point (190, 1–11; 190, 26–30; 274, 7–14; 275, 13 – 276, 14; 281, 20 – 282, 4). When he encounters *güete*, however, Rennewart always responds with *zuht*. He says as much himself when he is asked to respect Heimrich:

> 273, 15 'hêrre,' sprach dô Rennewart,
> 'im blîbt mîn dienst ungespart,

---

[1] 213, 5: *von arde ein zuht*; also 416, 2.

und al den dies geruochent,
diez güetlîche versuochent.'
dô gienc der ellens rîche
für die wirtîn zühteclîche.

His willingness to serve the Christian cause is similarly a consequence of his gratitude for the kind and respectful treatment he
enjoys from Willehalm and Gyburg.[1] Bumke noted (pp. 150–2)
that *guot* and *güete* are important words in *Willehalm*, and the
same has been shown for Hartmann's works.[2] Wolfram applies
them so often to God and to Gyburg that Bumke reads *güete* as a
religious term referring to her sanctity. Although it has since been
demonstrated by Werner Schröder[3] that *güete* need not carry
religious overtones, it would be unwise to distinguish rigidly
between religious and secular values: the kind of behaviour
associated with *güete* includes humility and charity and so belongs
to the Christian ideal, and it cannot be dissociated from other
aspects of saintliness.[4] Koppitz equates Wolfram's concept of
güete in the *Willehalm* Prologue with the *caritas* of Abelard.[5] It
is a central moral value for Wolfram, as he indicates in the important
excursus on *vröude* and *trûren* in Book VI (280, 28 – 281, 2),[6] and
he ascribes it not only to Gyburg, but to Willehalm, Alyze,
Wimar the merchant and others (see Bumke, p. 151). Werner

---

[1] Cf. Willson, p. 48: 'Seine tapferen Kämpfe zugunsten der Christenheit ergeben sich
unmittelbar aus seinem "Liebesverhältnis" zu Willehalm und Gyburg. In seiner Dank-
barkeit für die sehr grossmütige und menschliche Behandlung, die ihm sein Herr
erweist, bekundet er eine Zuneigung, die nur als "karitativ" bezeichnet werden kann
(vgl. 195, 10–11 u. 198, 30).'

[2] M. Bindschedler, 'Guot und Güete bei Hartmann von Aue', *Festschrift für Friedrich
Maurer*, Stuttgart 1963, pp. 352–65.

[3] Werner Schröder, 'Süeziu Gyburg', pp. 62–4.

[4] Cf. G. Meissburger, 'Gyburg', where Gyburg's *güete* is discussed in some detail
(especially pp. 71f, 91ff and footnote 34). Meissburger's later article '"Güete" bei
Wolfram von Eschenbach', adds little to this. Meissburger tends to see *güete* primarily
as a mode of behaviour ('Sich der bestehenden Ordnung fügen, zugleich ihre gött-
liche Bedingt- und Bestimmtheit erkennen und sich entsprechend im Leben verhalten',
'Gyburg', p. 71, cf. '"Güete" bei Wolfram von Eschenbach', p. 163), while Wolfram
treats it as a natural quality of character (cf. such expressions as *'ir sît sô guot'*, *Gyburge
güete was geslaht/von im*, 78, 19f, et al.).

[5] H. Koppitz, *Wolframs Religiosität*, Bonn 1959, p. 267f. For a similar but not identical
definition see Bumke, p. 163, note 65.

[6] The passage is discussed in detail by Meissburger, '"Güete" bei Wolfram von Eschenbach'.

Schröder has described *güete* as 'Gnade', that is, unmerited favour;[1] this describes very well the behaviour of Willehalm and Gyburg towards Rennewart throughout the epic, provided we exclude the element of condescension which 'Gnade' generally implies, since grace comes only from a superior to an inferior. For such a relationship Willehalm is too respectful and Rennewart too proud. Rennewart invites and welcomes *güete*, but he never asks the comparable favour of *milte* (though to honour Willehalm he will accept reward, cf. 331, 13ff): *milte* wins vassals and servants, obedient while *milte* lasts, but *güete* can win the lasting respect of a friend (as Wimar's *güete* wins that of Willehalm); *milte* is for subordinates, *güete* for equals, and Willehalm is sensible enough to know which of them he must offer Rennewart.

The *güete* of Alyze is recognised by both Willehalm and Rennewart, and both of them are influenced and guided by it (for its effect on Willehalm see 156, 12–18 and p. 194). We witness its power in her ability to reconcile enemies and turn hatred into love; she alone can reconcile Willehalm with her mother and Rennewart with her father. It is her *güete* that Rennewart blesses in his last words to her as he leaves for the war (213, 27f). Willehalm's *güete* is mainly shown in his behaviour towards Rennewart, but it is confirmed in his treatment of Matribleiz after the battle. Gyburg, whose *güete* is mentioned most often, also shows this quality mainly in her dealings with Rennewart, but it is always her most characteristic feature.[2] Like Alyze she can reconcile enemies and overcome hatred: for her sake Ehmereiz is spared in the first battle and Matribleiz honoured after the second, and the healing power of her *güete* is evident in the effect upon Willehalm's brother of her famous speech to the army leaders, whose mood a moment before had been uncompromisingly aggressive (311, 1–5). While to others Rennewart appears stubborn, quarrelsome and very dangerous, his quick sensitivity and responsiveness to Gyburg's *güete* enable her to direct his energies with ease, and she remarks:

[1] W. Schröder, 'Süeziu Gyburg', p. 62.
[2] Cf. Meissburger, 'Gyburg', pp. 91ff.

272, 19   man mag in ziehn als eine maget:
          er leistet gern swaz man im saget.

The Christian victory is followed in the source by Rainouart's great quarrel with Guillaume, which can be ended only by Guibourc's intervention; Wolfram's emphasis on her *güete* and its great power over Rennewart seems also to prepare her for this task.

    The working of *güete* in Rennewart's life begins when Willehalm, having heard of his plight, asks Loys if he may take him away and treat him kindly:

191, 22   'waz ob ich, hêrre, im sîn leben
          baz berihte, op ich mac?'

This makes Rennewart's development possible, and here it begins. Willehalm's desire to improve Rennewart's lot is nearly frustrated by Loys' reluctance to let him go, but Alyze secures his release. Willehalm then sends for him, but Rennewart refuses to converse except in his own language, though he understands French perfectly well. Instead of justly punishing him for his insolence, Willehalm condescends to speak Rennewart's language and addresses him as *trûtgeselle mîn*. This is independent of *Aliscans*, where Rainouart comes to Guillaume and begs with moving humility to be taken to the war (Al. 3328–41), and it demonstrates how Willehalm's *güete* can make him appear weak to us. But by stressing Rennewart's pride and introducing this initial resistance to Willehalm's approach Wolfram draws attention to the effectiveness of Willehalm's *güete* and shows how it can win a man for the Christian cause. For Rennewart's pride dissolves in a moment; he answers politely and respectfully, confessing at once his lack of trust in his own god Mahmet. When Willehalm again addresses him with great deference and asks his help against the Saracens, Rennewart responds with gratitude and willingness to serve. His quickly increased respect for Willehalm shows clearly as he changes the form of address from *du* (193, 12, 13) to *ir* (always after 194, 10). He says he desires no great reward (for it is *güete*, not *milte*, that has attracted him) and promises to submit to correction and guidance from Willehalm:

> 194, 20 ir muget mich wol berihten
> swenne ich in swacher vuore bin
> (jugent hât dicke kranken sin)

He then expresses enthusiasm for his new lord:

> 195, 7 er sprach, 'hêr, wie sol ich nu varn?
> swaz ir heizet mich bewarn,
> des phlig ich als ich phlegen kan.
> so lieben herrn ich nie gewan:
> iwer hulde sî mîn lôn.'

Rennewart asks for Willehalm's *hulde*; *güete* is naturally experienced as *hulde* by the person who benefits from it. Rennewart's ready gratitude and goodwill here illustrate the educative power of *güete* and contrast not only with his initial coldness to Willehalm but also with the episode in the courtyard with which he has just been introduced, where he reacts with quick violence to the harsh and disrespectful treatment he suffers from the squires. The significance of Willehalm's kindness at this first meeting is recognised by Wolff (p. 515):

Ungewohnte Menschlichkeit, die sich aus tiefem Verständnis für seine seelische Lage seiner annimmt und es nicht verschmäht, ihn in seiner heidnischen Muttersprache nach seinem Schicksal zu befragen, beginnt, den Trotz, mit dem sich das Herz Rennewarts umkleidet hatte, abzuschmelzen.

Willehalm's initial respect for Rennewart may perhaps be prompted by Loys' remark '*ich weiz wol, daz er edel ist*', when explaining to him who Rennewart is, just before this meeting.

Soon after this, Rennewart's hair and clothes are singed by the cooks and Rennewart reacts with a violent fit of temper. Willehalm does not punish him, but comforts him and treats him as a friend (198, 30); he promises him new clothes and a better haircut and tells him to ignore the affront and behave with *zuht*. Here again we see Willehalm's guidance through *güete*. When Rennewart oversleeps the next morning and joins the army late, Willehalm rides to greet him personally and waits patiently while

Rennewart returns for his club, which he has forgotten. When Rennewart returns he addresses Willehalm much more respectfully than in the source (200, 26 – 201, 23, cf. Al. 3540d–u). His unsolicited care for Willehalm's horse at the end of this journey is perhaps an expression of gratitude for the *güete* which he thus enjoys by the way. At Orleans Rennewart takes leave of Alyze and rewards her *güete* with exemplary courtesy and agrees to forgive her father for her sake. With her kiss, Alyze's *minne* begins to work as the ennobling force in him, directed by Willehalm's and Gyburg's *güete*.

At Orange Gyburg shows particular interest in Rennewart. At the banquet he is specially honoured by being seated beside her at the head of the table, and responds to this honour with courtly *zuht*:

> 274, 1 Diu tavel was kurz unde breit:
> Heimrîch durch gesellekeit
> bat Rennewarten sitzen dort
> ûf dem teppich an der tavelen ort,
> bî der künegîn nâhen.
> daz enkund ir niht versmâhen.
> Rennewart saz mit zühten dar.

Der tavelen ort means not the corner (*daz ecke*), but the shorter side of the table, at the top, where the host would normally sit alone;[1] it was a special honour for a guest when the host made room for him on the *ort*,[2] and Rennewart blushes with shame. When Gyburg shows further *güete* by extending the tablecloth to reach him, he again responds with *zuht*:

> 274, 11 die künegîn des niht verdrôz,
> daz tischlachen gein sîner schôz
> si güetlîch bôt; dar zuo er sweic,
> wan daz er mit zühten neic.

[1] Cf. Parz. 176, 13: *der tisch was nider unde lanc./der wirt mit niemen sich dâ dranc./er saz al eine an den ort.* Rennewart is, in fact, off the table rather than on the *ort*; Gyburg is sharing the *ort* with Heimrich, who sits on the other side of her (265, 2–5), and there is no more room. That is why Rennewart is sitting on the carpet and needs to have the tablecloth extended to him.

[2] Cf. W. Pieth, *Essen und Trinken im mittelhochdeutschen Epos des zwölften und dreizehnten Jahrhunderts*, Leipzig 1909, p. 62.

Rennewart is thus more highly honoured than any of the guests except Heimrîch, who dines beside Gyburg on the *ort* itself, which is wide enough for two people (*diu tavel was kurʒ unde breit*), while Rennewart dines on an improvised extension of it.

Later, when Rennewart kills the chief cook at Orange and terrifies the others so that they will not work, Willehalm does not call him to account and punish him, as might be expected, but sends Gyburg to him, asking her to treat him kindly (289, 19: '*nemet mînen friunt mit vuogen dan*'). Gyburg had never been in the kitchen before (289, 20f), but goes there now out of respect for Rennewart and addresses him kindly. Rennewart's anger is quickly conquered by her *güete*, which he immediately recognises, and he promises to accept her guidance:

> 289, 27 dô sprach er, 'vrouwe, ir sît sô guot,
> swaz râtes ir gein mir getuot,
> des volg ich.'

Gyburg's offer of fine clothes calls forth gratitude and modesty in him, although he refuses them. Gyburg is most courteous when asking about his ancestry:

> 290, 19 dô sprach si 'trûtgeselle mîn,
> möht ez mit dînen hulden sîn,
> sô vrâgt ich wann dû wærst geborn,
> woltst dûz lâzen âne zorn.'

Werner Fechter,[1] surprised that a lady of Gyburg's rank should address her foot-soldier vassal in such terms, attempts to show that the phrase '*möht eʒ mit dînen hulden sîn*' is a polite cliché, comparable to modern German '*gestatten Sie bitte!*'; he quotes many examples of its use and argues that no consciousness of rank is involved. It is striking, however, that in the great majority of his examples the phrase is addressed to a person of superior rank and Wh. 290, 20 is the only case where an apparent inferior is being addressed. Fechter claims that the peasant using the phrase in *Der arme Heinrich* (line 369) is not using peasant language, but the important fact remains that he is addressing a superior. The

---

[1] W. Fechter, 'Möht ez mit iuwern hulden sîn', GRM 8 (1958), pp. 206–8.

phrase may well be a polite cliché, but it is one used when addressing superiors, and it is no more a natural way for a great lady to address a subordinate than *trûtgeselle mîn*. For Gyburg to speak thus expresses her *güete* towards Rennewart and accounts for the great politeness of his evasive answer.[1] Upon this answer follows her successful reconciliation of Willehalm and Rennewart and the symbolic expression of her *güete* towards Rennewart when, secretly guessing his identity, she wraps him in her cloak. This gesture indicates her protective care for Rennewart and is a great honour for him; its meaning and implications are discussed in the next section (pp. 173ff). In the course of this episode Gyburg is able to persuade Rennewart to wear proper armour (which he had previously refused, 196, 10–30) and even, despite his initial reluctance, to accept willingly the sword with which he will deliver the Christians in the coming battle. Gyburg's *güete* is here decisive, for it has conquered Rennewart's self-willed stubbornness, which was hitherto unshakable, and enabled him to become effective as a leader of the Christians in battle. Thus Gyburg guides Rennewart towards his proper destiny.

Rennewart forgets his club again on leaving Orange. This time he is thoroughly ashamed and apologises humbly to Willehalm; his *zuht* is now more in evidence than after his earlier forgetfulness and misdemeanours, when he did not apologise. On the previous occasion he had asked Willehalm to wait with the whole army while he collected the club (201, 10–13); this time he promises to find Willehalm's track himself and catch up with the army. Again Willehalm spares his feelings by sending a soldier back for the club.

When Rennewart forgets his club for the third time he does not tell Willehalm but returns for it himself. When he comes back, leading the imperial army, Willehalm addresses him with great courtesy and respect and receives a modest answer (330, 28 – 331, 20);

---

[1] Cf. Meissburger, 'Gyburg', p. 91: 'Die Demütige scheut sich nicht, den Gedemütigten aufzusuchen und mit ihm zu sprechen, als wäre er ihresgleichen. Gyburgs Worte besänftigen Rennewart alsbald. Er, der wie Gyburg "durh toufes twingen" (284, 29) leiden muss, spürt offenbar, dass eine besondere Kraft von ihr ausströmt, ahnt vielleicht sogar, dass sie ihr Leid, das auch seines ist, überwunden hat.'

in this willing and effective support Willehalm reaps the reward of his early, consistent *güete*. In the course of the battle we see once more Rennewart's willingness to accept guidance when he quickly learns from Berhtram how best to use the club and later takes Gibelin's advice that he should use his sword. The purpose behind his efforts is to earn Alyze's favour and it is her *güete* that sustains him in battle (here, too, 248,1f applies: *diu wîplîche güete/gît dem man hôchgemüete*). Thus inspired and led, Rennewart makes progress in realising the ideal of chivalry, and his progress is always dependent upon kindness and respect which foster in him the will to respect and obey those who treat him well.

The conclusions reached in this chapter may be summarised as follows: our knowledge of the *genre* of court epic as a whole and of Wolfram's practice in *Parzival* leads us to expect development of some major characters. Rennewart is similar to Parzival, particularly in his youthful promise at the beginning and in his obvious outward progress. By comparing the two with reference to the promise of youth, and by referring on several occasions to the coming fulfilment, Wolfram reveals his own conscious intention to portray a development of Rennewart comparable to that of Parzival. Rennewart's progress towards chivalry is shown in the development of his *zuht* and in his increasing respect for Willehalm, quite independently of the source, and it becomes explicit in his rising social position. It is implied symbolically in his changing attitude to horses and weapons. It is stimulated by Alyze's *minne*, which causes the growth of his beard, the symbol of his manhood. It is directed by Willehalm and Gyburg, whose natural *güete* overcomes his initial resistance and bitterness, earning his respect for them and his willing obedience.

EXCURSUS: *Gyburg's cloak*

The special kindness and respect that Gyburg shows to Rennewart is nowhere more movingly and effectively present than when she comes to comfort him after his unpleasant encounter with Willehalm's cooks. Rainouart's quarrel with the cooks at Orange serves in *Aliscans* as comic relief between the serious battle scenes; the cooks once again play a trick on him – this time they set fire to his moustaches while he is asleep in their kitchen – and he pays them back in his usual violent manner by roasting the chief cook on his own fire. Since Wolfram is always at pains to stress Rennewart's nobility and *zuht* this episode is very damaging for his Rennewart and, as on other occasions (see p. 74), he deals with the embarrassing matter of his source not by avoiding it but by giving it special prominence and significance. He has made Rennewart's moustaches into a symbol of his manhood and a token of Alyze's love, and so the affront is for Rennewart an insult to Alyze which honour demands he must avenge. When he has killed the cook he thinks of his noble kinsmen who are dishonoured with him and his anger turns against Willehalm, who should never have allowed his servants to treat the son of Terramer so disrespectfully (288, 1–30). His relation with Willehalm has reached a dangerous crisis, for his new lord is letting his cooks treat Rennewart as Loys' cooks had done. His anger reaches its climax when Gyburg, with characteristic humility, comes to him in the kitchen. Her kindness soon overcomes his anger; she offers him fine clothes and armour, which he refuses with great politeness, and she asks who he is. Although he tells her no more than for courtesy's sake he must (290, 24ff: *ich bin ein armer bätschelier/und doch vil werder liute fruht./des muoz ich jehen, hân ich zuht'*), she realises he must be her long-lost brother. She asks him to sit beside her and wraps part of her cloak round him:

> 291, 1 Der knappe dennoch vor ir stuont.
> der vrouwen tet ir herze kuont
> daz si niht ervuor wan lange sider.
> si bat in zuo zir sitzen nider,
> ir mantels swanc se umb in ein teil.

This gesture expresses great respect and special favour, as Rennewart immediately recognises:

> 291, 6 dô sprach er 'vrouwe, diss wære geil
> der beste rîtr der ie gebant

helm ûf houbet mit sîner hant.
swer mich alsus sitzen siht,
vil unfuoge er mir giht,
und nimt mich drumb in sînen spot:
des erlât mich, vrouwe, durh iweren got.'

The gesture also has symbolic significance, for the cloak is an ancient symbol of protection. It is generally, though not exclusively, offered by high-born ladies, and the power to offer protection beneath the cloak has been expressed in terms of a hierarchy with this ascending order: feudal superiors, ladies, pregnant ladies or virgins, saints, the Virgin Mary.[1] The symbolic gesture is best known through religious painting, since a cult of the protective cloak, particularly in connection with Mary, arose in early 13th century painting.[2]

The sense behind the symbol is indicated by the order in Schué's hierarchy: to be taken beneath the cloak is to be granted a share in the security of a person who is inviolable because of social rank, sex or divinity. It is naturally a great honour to be granted such a favour, and it occurs as such in literature. It is a sign of respect as much as of protection when Graf Rudolf is welcomed by the Queen of Constantinople with kiss and embrace and taken under her cloak.[3] This is also the case at Parz. 88, 9, where Herzeloyde allows Kaylet to sit *'under ir mantels ort'* and then attends to his wounds with her own hands and lets him lift her on to her horse without a cushion. In Konrad von Würzburg's *Engelhart*[4] a lady uses the gesture as a token of her favour and a love-scene follows. But it is as a symbol of protection rather than respect that it is understood in Grimm's Dictionary, which gives several examples, including Wh. 291, 1–5, and comments: 'Unter den Mantel ward derjenige genommen, den man schützen

---

[1] K. Schué, 'Das Gnadenbitten in Recht, Sage und Kunst', *Zeitschrift des Aachener Geschichtsvereins* 40 (1918), p. 278.

[2] Cf. the detailed study of this motif in painting by Vera Sussmann, 'Maria mit dem Schutzmantel', *Marburger Jahrbuch für Kunstwissenschaft* 5 (1929), pp. 285–351. Kienast, p. 109, recognised that it is this motif that appears at Wh. 291, 1ff.

[3] *Graf Rudolf*, ed. P. Ganz, Berlin 1964 (PSQ 19), 1b, 14.

[4] Engelhart (ed. Haupt) 3106: *er wart von ir vil zarte/empfangen an der selben stete./daz mantelîn si ûfe tete/unde empfienc in drunder.*

und in Obhut haben wollte.'[1] This is its sense in the representation of the Last Judgement in the porch of Autun cathedral, quoted by Perdrizet,[2] where little souls are hiding under the robes of the archangel because they are threatened by devils. Grimm quotes an example of the cloak as a place of refuge from the *Sängerkrieg auf der Wartburg*, where Heinrich von Ofterdingen suddenly finds himself in danger:[3]

Da nun Afterding sach, wi iz zu fur, do floch her undir den mantil der edlen lantgravin, frouwen Sophien, durch schutzes willen, den her da vant.

As a symbol of protection, the gesture sometimes gained legal validity where the right of guardianship or duty of protection was involved. Thus it was a frequent practice at weddings in mediaeval Germany for the groom to take the bride under his cloak; this practice lived on among colonies of Jews in Russia into modern times.[4] In cases of adoption the legal duty of protection is particularly important, and it is here that we most often find the cloak. A child born before the mother's wedding could be made legitimate if the mother took it under her cloak at the wedding ceremony: such a child was called a *filius mantellatus* or *Mantelkind*.[5] This practice is vouched for in 13th century England by Robert Grosseteste (1175–1253), bishop of Lincoln,[6] and it occurs in the rhymed chronicle of the Flemish poet Philippes Mouskes (circa 1220–82).[7] Similarly, the *skautsætubarn* or *knésætubarn* of Old Norse law are children legitimised by being placed

---

[1] Grimm, D Wb, vol. 6, col. 1608, under *Mantel*.

[2] P. Perdrizet, *La Vièrge de Miséricorde, étude d'un thème iconographique*, Paris 1908, p. 19.

[3] Grimm, *ibid*, col. 1608f.

[4] Perdrizet, p. 23 (after Grimm, 'Poesie im Recht', *Kleinere Schriften* 6, p. 164). Perdrizet (p. 23f) quotes some biblical parallels, such as Ruth 3, 9 (where Boaz spreads his skirt over Ruth to indicate his intention to marry her), Ezekiel 16, 8 and 1 Kings 19, 19.

[5] Grimm *ibid*, cols. 1613–14 under *Mantelkind*. Cf. *filii mantellati*, Grimm, *Deutsche Rechtsaltertümer* (4th ed.), Leipzig 1899, vol. 1, pp. 219–21.

[6] See Du Cange, *Glossarium ad Scriptores mediae et infimae Latinitatis*, vol. 5, p. 35, under *pallio cooperire*.

[7] *Ibid*. Details of Mouskes' chronicle in *Histoire Littéraire de la France*, vol. 19, pp. 861–72; the relevant lines are these: *Li duc ki les enfans ama/Gunnor adonques espousa/Et li fil ki ja furent grant/Furent entre autredeus en estant,/Par dessous le mantiel la mere/Furent fait loial cil trois frere.*

upon the knee under the cloak of the mother.[1] When Saint
Francis of Assisi formally left his father and returned to him all his
belongings, including his clothes, the bishop of Assisi publicly
took him under his cloak; the episode appears in the paintings of
Giotto, Taddeo Gaddi, Domenico Ghirlandaio and Bennozzo
Gozzoli. The great popularity of the story may be attributed to its
being understood in terms of adoption: Francesco Bernardone is
no longer the son of his father but the son of the Church. There
is possibly a biblical precedent at 1 Kings 19, 19, when Elijah
adopts Elisha by casting his mantle over him.

The theme of the protective cloak begins to appear in religious
painting during the 13th century and there are a number of
representations of Mary and of Saint Ursula protecting people
under the folds of their cloaks. The great majority of pictures
show the theme in connection with Mary, for she can offer protection more perfectly than anyone else, combining in one person
the virtues and inviolability of a lady, virgin, mother and god-
head. Perdrizet (pp. 18–26) traced the cult of Mary's cloak in
13th to 15th century painting back to a legend told by Caesarius of
Heisterbach and apparently propagated by his order, the Cistercians. A certain monk had a vision of the heavenly paradise and saw
it peopled with many saints, prophets, martyrs and monks, but
none of the Cistercian order. When he saw Mary herself and
asked her why her most devoted servants had been excluded, she
opened up her cloak and revealed the Cistercians in great numbers
and the monk was delighted to see that his own order enjoyed
her special favour.[2] Because of this story Perdrizet assumed that
the theme of protection under Mary's cloak began within the
Cistercian order, a view that was supported by 13th century
Cistercian seals, which often show Mary with her cloak spread. It

[1] Du Cange, *ibid*: 'Infans qui ante nuptias natus sub actu consecrationis matrimonialis in
sinu et sub pallio collocatus legitimabatur.' Du Cange is alone, however, in suggesting
the father's cloak is used and is consequently baffled by the example from Mouskes. The
children must be under the mother's cloak in order to share with her in the legal ceremony linking her with her husband.

[2] *De monacho qui Ordinem Cisterciensem sub Mariae pallio vidit in Regno Caelorum*,
copied by Sussmann, p. 285f, from Caesarius Heisterbacensis, *Dialogus Miraculorum*, ed.
Strange, Bonn–Cologne 1851, vol. 2, p. 79 (*Capitulum* LIX).

has since been shown, however, that the same story was told of other orders.[1] In fact it is unlikely that this story could have been the beginning of the motif because it does not make sense to put saints and martyrs under the cloak: it is sinners whose souls are in danger that need protection (Künstle, pp. 635–7).

Perdrizet noted that other saints, notably Saint Ursula, are sometimes depicted with the cloak, but he believed the theme had been transferred to them from Mary. The cloak is associated generally with Mary, both in painting and literature; a 12th century Munich manuscript bears the prayer:[2]

> sante Marjen lîchemede,
> daz sî mîn fridhemede!

Nevertheless, representations with other saints are among the earliest. The oldest known picture of the kind shows Saint Ursula,[3] as do many 13th century pictures. One of these is painted on the side of a chest in Albi cathedral, while the lid shows the Madonna and child (Sussmann, p. 290). Another early picture shows Saint Odilia,[4] and a large number of different saints are shown in pictures of the 14th and 15th centuries.[5] It is unlikely that the gesture was originally associated with Mary, because the saint has to have both arms extended to achieve an effective spread of her cloak, even if she is assisted by angels or cherubs; this is an unusual position for Mary, who is usually portrayed with her child, and she is unable to hold the child while spreading her cloak. To overcome this difficulty the artist sometimes places the child in a mandorla (almond-shaped panel) on her breast; this produces the rather strange *Maria Platytera*, which was never popular outside the Byzantine Empire (cf. Künstle, p. 620f). It is therefore now generally believed that although the motif was most fruitful and popular when applied to Mary, it did not originate with her, but

---

[1] K. Künstle, *Ikonographie der christlichen Kunst*, Freiburg-im-Breisgau 1928, vol. 1, p. 637. Several orders depict Mary wearing their robes.

[2] *Münchner Ausfahrtsegen* 15f, see Müllenhoff-Scherer, *Denkmäler deutscher Poesie und Prosa*, Berlin 1864, p. 141, no. XLVII, 3.

[3] At Linz-am-Rhein, 1240–50, see Sussmann, p. 289.

[4] At Kierniel, Belgium, 1292, see Sussmann, p. 289.

[5] A table of the pictures, naming the saints concerned, is given by Perdrizet, pp. 220–36.

was transferred, probably in the 11th century, when she became the central figure of many legends which had been told of others before her special cult developed.[1]

The gesture cannot be dated earlier than 1240 in painting, but it can be traced back much further in literature, where apart from Wolfram there is the *Graf Rudolf*, the legend of Saint Francis of Assisi and the 12th century Munich prayer. Several tales involving the protective cloak are recorded by Caesarius of Heisterbach; these were known in Old French translation in the *Miracles* of Phillippe Gautier, written between 1214 and 1236.[2] Sussmann (p. 298f) found the motif of Mary's cloak in three legends older than Caesarius, the earliest of which is recorded in the *Itinerarium Bernardi*, written after 877, and concerns Mont Saint-Michel al Peril de la Mer (so called because it could only be reached on foot at low tide and pilgrims were often surprised by the sea before reaching safety). A woman going to the church of Saint Michael was suddenly overtaken by the sea and beyond hope of rescue. She and the crowd of onlookers called upon the archangel and the Virgin Mary, who came and led her to safety under her cloak, so that no part of her was touched by the sea.[3] It is possible that this story was told originally of Saint Michael and later transferred to Mary, but there is no evidence for this and it is improbable that this should happen so long before the cult of Mary developed. Mary had been particularly associated with the sea since the fifth century if not earlier, and was the supreme protectress from its dangers (Sussmann, p. 303); the name Maria was probably associated by popular or clerical etymology with Latin *maria*, 'the seas'. It is therefore probable that this sea rescue at Mont Saint-Michel was conceived as a miracle of Mary and so her cloak was known in

---

[1] Sussmann, p. 290; Schué, pp. 280, 577; Künstle, p. 635.

[2] Caesarius von Heisterbach, *Libri VIII Fragmenti Miraculorum*, ed. Aloys Meister, Rome 1901, pp. 166–8 (in *Römische Quartalschrift für christliche Alterthumskunde und für Kirchengeschichte*, 1901). One tells how Mary protected the city of Constantinople from the Muslims by spreading her mantle over it; the other tells how she rescued a shipwrecked traveller by taking him under the sea to land beneath her cloak. Cf. also Miracle no. 91 in A. Hilke, *Die Wundergeschichten des Caesarius von Heisterbach*, Bonn 1933, p. 101.

[3] Quoted by Sussmann, p. 298, after Vincent of Beauvais (see Vincentius Bellovacensis, *Speculum historiale*, Liber Septimus, cap. LXXXV, ed. Douai, 1664).

the ninth century. There is an earlier tale of Gregory of Tours about a Jewish boy who is saved from a fire beneath Mary's cloak, which confirms the great antiquity of the motif.[1] Nevertheless, the cloak does not seem to have been associated particularly with Mary at that early date; the gesture was available for anyone who could give protection. The oldest known legend of protection beneath a saint's cloak is told not of Mary but of Saint Columba. The night before the battle between the Saxons and the Britons in A.D. 635 Oswald of Northumbria dreamed that Saint Columba, who had died thirty-six years before, stood before him wearing a splendid cloak; the saint then spread out his cloak to cover all the Saxons and quoted the words of the Lord to Joshua: 'Have courage, for I am with thee.'[2]

Perdrizet concludes (p. 24) that the motif is of early Germanic or Celtic origin; the legal status of *filii mantellati* in England, Scandinavia and Germany certainly suggests knowledge of the cloak as a protection symbol among the Germanic peoples from the earliest times. As a token of very special favour and protective care on the part of a saint it probably dates from the translation of Christian doctrine into Germanic terms: it is as old as Germanic Christianity. Though at first applicable to any saint, it came to be associated particularly with Mary when she began to gain in importance, but it never became her private gesture, especially as it required Mary to be separated from her child.

Wolfram cannot have been ignorant of this motif. It was certainly current in his time and he had used it himself in *Parʒival*. He clearly expected his audience to understand the symbolic significance of Gyburg's gesture. He found it in *Aliscans*, where Guibourc wraps Rainouart in her cloak as soon as she realises he is her brother:

> Al. 4474　Et Guibors ouevre son mantel de porprine,
> 　　　　Si l'afubla, car li cuers li destine
> 　　　　Ke c'est ses freres, mais n'en fait nule sine.

[1] *De puero Judaeo valde memorandum miraculum*, Migne, *Patrologiae Cursus Completus*, vol. 71, saec. vi, cols. 713–15 (caput x).
[2] Text in *Acta Sanctorum*, 2 June, p. 199. Sussmann (p. 286) mistakenly quotes the saint as Columban and the enemy as the Bretons.

But there is nothing further in *Aliscans* that might suggest it had for the poet any significance other than as an emotional reaction on Guibourc's part. Wolfram, however, recognised it and knew its significance. He had used the gesture in *Parzival* as a sign of the respect shown to Kaylet by Herzeloyde, and it was there coupled with her personal attention to his wounds and his lifting her without a cushion. In that context the religious associations of the cloak could not be used. But in *Willehalm* the gesture can be more significant, as the context where it occurs is a crisis in the action and the scene is dominated by the religious problem which Gyburg has faced and which now confronts Rennewart and by the question of Gyburg's true relationship to Rennewart.

Rennewart has made it perfectly clear that he blames Willehalm for his cook's behaviour:

288, 1   Diss landes hêrre ist geschant,
          daz mich sîn koch sô hât verbrant.
          dar zuo an mir gehœnet sint
          des kreftegen Terramêres kint...
          ich pin doch Terramêres parn!

Rennewart's suspicion of Willehalm's lack of respect for the son of Terramer seems to be confirmed when he sends Gyburg into the kitchen rather than go himself. At a moment like this Rennewart might very well be lost to the Christians. Willehalm has roused his pride and resentment, as Loys had done and as, in Rennewart's mistaken view of his past, Terramer had done, by treating him disrespectfully and unkindly. Willehalm has not intended to offend him, but neither had Terramer or Loys, and the fault lies in every case very largely with Rennewart's own sensitivity; the man who earns Rennewart's devotion must be extraordinarily long-suffering and generous, but his *güete* will be well rewarded if he succeeds. When Gyburg comes, on Willehalm's behalf, her kindness and respect quickly arouse Rennewart's gratitude and modesty and he says he feels unworthy of the honour she has shown him. Her gesture with the cloak is no longer an instinctive reaction on discovering her brother, but an expression of her characteristic *güete*, which can conquer hatred and which here saves Willehalm and the Christians from losing Rennewart.

The gesture is first of all a token of respect; Rennewart's fear that to accept it would be *unvuoge* suggests that it is a very great honour. The gesture always does express honour, and it is here Gyburg's purpose to make him forget the humiliation that he has suffered through the consciousness of a greater honour. Rennewart's immediate reaction suggests that he can see nothing more than honour in it (291, 6ff). As a Saracen he may be incapable of understanding the religious sense of the gesture, as the heathen Feirefiz is unable to see the Grail, and he ignores the feudal motif of protection because he seeks respect, not protection. It is in any case no more than proper that he should pick out the lady's condescension in showing him so great an honour rather than seek the feudal or religious meaning: the modest interpretation is the most courteous.

The feudal interpretation may have been the first to suggest itself to Wolfram's audience, that is, Rennewart is taken from this moment under the special protection of the lady Gyburg, who henceforth exerts a civilising and ennobling influence upon him. In contradiction to his source Wolfram makes the special relationship of Gyburg and Rennewart begin with this episode: he has omitted Rainouart's earlier vow to help Orable (Al. 3818f), and while Guibourc had always addressed Rainouart as *frere* (cf. Al. 4448, 4467), Wolfram's Gyburg shows familiarity here for the first time.

The religious sense of the cloak symbol, though it is not accessible to Rennewart himself, appears significant in this context and seems to lead up to the representation of Gyburg as a saint at the beginning of Book IX. The cloak of a female saint is a common place of refuge from Satan and his devils in mediaeval painting; if Wolfram's prayer to Gyburg and the words '*Gyburg heilic vrouwe*' prove that Wolfram means us to see her as a saint, then beneath her cloak Rennewart may be protected from the very great danger that threatens his soul. He has persisted in his rejection of Christ and baptism and is about to enter a deadly battle; only a saint's intercession could save him. The context suggests that Wolfram intended the religious interpretation of the gesture, because Rennewart's speech ends with his invocation of Gyburg's god, not his own, and leads directly into a frank religious discussion in which Gyburg's understanding and tolerance are very marked, particularly if we compare her earlier unsympathetic and intolerant attitude when disputing with Terramer. Wolfram probably intended to refer again to the episode with Gyburg's cloak in the unfinished part of *Willehalm* as the motive for the final reconciliation between Willehalm and Rennewart; in *Aliscans* (7791–804) it is the memory of this meeting with Guibourc that finally causes Rainouart to forgive Guillaume for her sake, though he is angry at Guillaume's ingratitude (cf. p. 237). It would be consistent with Wolfram's method of expounding his source and bringing out its significance rather than altering the events if he were to preserve the later reference back to this episode.

The gesture has been interpreted at three levels – respect, feudal protection and divine protection. This was not possible with the comparable gesture at *Parzival* 88, 9, which would not support the religious interpretation, or *Willehalm* 274, 12, where Gyburg *güetlîch* extends the tablecloth to cover Rennewart, though the latter may well be a prefiguration of the episode with the cloak. Her gesture at the banquet can express respect and kindness, but nothing more: though the gesture is essentially the same, a tablecloth is not a lady's cloak and there is no tradition in religious symbolism about being wrapped under a tablecloth as a token of special favour. But when Gyburg repeats the gesture with her cloak at a moment of crisis, the symbol supports all three levels of interpretation at once: Gyburg is a feudal and a saintly protectress and to be her protégé is a great honour for Rennewart. The scene shows her *güete* and its immediate effect upon Rennewart, for it completely overcomes the worst effects that harsh treatment has had upon him and gives him cause for later gratitude.

IV · RENNEWART AND THE
CHRISTIAN EMPIRE

THE CHRISTIAN EMPIRE

The conflict in *Aliscans* is between Guillaume with his French supporters and Desramé with his Saracens. Guillaume's troops are constantly called *François* and France is the land they are defending, an attitude which was historically justifiable and perfectly natural to the French audience. Wolfram, himself loyal to the Hohenstaufen Empire of Frederick II, has introduced in *Willehalm* the concept of a 'Christian Empire', a powerful political union embracing all Christians, to which any Christian lord can turn when he is in danger from the infidels.[1] In this, Wolfram's interpretation of *Aliscans* has most probably been influenced by his knowledge of the *Rolandslied*. The background of the *Chanson de Roland* is *la dulce France* at war with Saracen Spain, and although the authority of Charlemagne and Baligant seems towards the end to transcend the national limits, this possibility of a wider view is not seized upon and made explicit. The famous rearguard is composed entirely of French warriors, and all twelve paladins are French. Charlemagne is usually called king of France,[2] and Baligant, champion of all the Saracens, plays a small part and does not live for long. The clerical writer of the German *Rolandslied* has changed this essentially French national background for a simple dichotomy between the realms of God and the Devil; his poem is inspired by the international crusading spirit and most of the references to France are omitted.[3] This is not merely a part of the process of adapting the poem for a

[1] Cf. Mergell, p. 160; Knorr and Fink, pp. 255–81; Bumke, pp. 126–52. H. Naumann, *Dichtung und Volkstum* 42 (1942), p. 124, traces this idea back to the Marburg *Rektoratsrede* of F. Vogt in 1908.

[2] This is not compromised by the use of *empereres*, cf. *Chanson de Roland* 16: *li empereres Carles de France dulce.*

[3] Cf. Wentzlaff-Eggebert, pp. 79–98; F. Ohly, 'Zum Reichsgedanken des deutschen Rolandsliedes', ZfdA 77 (1940), pp. 189ff.

German audience, for the 'Christian Empire' is far more extensive than the Holy Roman Empire of the Germans; it is the conceit of a cleric, for whom the whole Christian order is a far more worthy ideal than the glory of any single nation, and it stands in the tradition of the *Kaiserchronik*. The war is no longer a patriotic, but a religious duty, undertaken at the command of an angel and involving all Christendom. Charlemagne is not merely the king of France, but *der keiser Karl*, and the Christian soldiers are *Karlinge*.

Wolfram was at one with the spirit of his age in recognising and developing the concept of the Christian Empire which he found in the *Rolandslied* and making it an important part of his own poem. In his time there was a renewed interest in Charlemagne and in the ideal of a Christian Empire, as Bumke has fully demonstrated.[1] We also know Wolfram's own religious concern and his longing for a more immediate presence of the guidance and spirit of God in the institutions of this world, as expressed in his ideal of the Grail knight and in his insistence that a knight should serve God as well as *minne* and chivalry. If, as Schreiber suggests (p. 71), Wolfram actually fought in the service of the Hohenstaufen, this must have strengthened his allegiance to the imperial ideal still further.

The importance of the Christian Empire in *Willehalm* first becomes evident after Willehalm's crushing defeat in the first battle. The struggle is not over, but Willehalm can and must go to the Emperor for support: the *marcgrâve* defends the borders of the Empire and may expect its help in performing this duty. A generation earlier all the heathens under Baligan had fought against the Emperor Karl; now that Terramer, Baligan's cousin and successor, has come with still larger armies which represent the whole Saracen world,[2] his proper opponent is Karl's son and successor Loys, the new lord of all Christendom,[3] not his vassal

---

[1] Bumke, pp. 113–26. Cf. also F. Heer, *Die Tragödie des heiligen Reiches*, Stuttgart 1952.
[2] Wh. 108, 16: *für wâr nu ist mîn hervart/kreftiger und wîter brâht*; cf. 107, 16f; 398, 20.
[3] Wolfram never considers the claim of the Byzantine emperors to sovereignty over all Christendom, and mentions only Roman Catholic peoples when he speaks of the different nationalities represented in the Christian army (126, 8ff; 269, 24ff), cf. his frequent

Willehalm. As Willehalm rides to Munleun to secure imperial aid we gradually grow aware of the Empire as a great supranational authority which has not yet been clearly defined but must command far greater resources than Willehalm. From the episode at Orleans, where Willehalm refuses to pay customs duty, we discover that the highways are the emperor's property (115, 24: *des rœmschen küneges strâȝen*), and it is his duty to this emperor that forces Arnalt to pursue Willehalm:

> 116, 20   ich muoz in durch den künec jagen,
> bî dem mîn swester krône treit.

Customs duty may be required from a merchant, who needs protection in a strange country, but it is not due from a knight in the Emperor's service travelling within the Empire;[1] Wolfram makes this very clear, while his source had treated the episode differently.[2] As an imperial knight, Willehalm is not altogether a foreigner when he crosses the border from Provence to France (124, 1: *er ist uns doch niht gar ein gast*), particularly since he comes on imperial business and uses the imperial battle-cry.

When Willehalm arrives at Munleun and finds a festival in progress, Wolfram mentions that knights from the various lands

use of the term *Rômære* to describe Loys and the Empire's soldiers. He seems to have derived his view of Christian history from the *Kaiserchronik* (which he certainly knew) and probably Otte's *Eraclius*, which he seems to have known (cf. Parz. 773, 22). According to the view found in these works, the Christian emperors resided at Constantinople until the *translatio imperii*, when imperial authority was transferred to Charlemagne in the West, and his successors have been emperors ever since (*Eraclius* 4436ff; 4462ff; *Kaiserchronik* 14278ff), cf. E. Nellmann, *Die Reichsidee in deutschen Dichtungen der Salier- und frühen Stauferȝeit*, Berlin 1963, pp. 28–34, 116.

[1] Cf. Schultz, p. 507f; J. Falke, 'Das deutsche Zollwesen im Mittelalter', *Zeitschrift für deutsche Culturgeschichte* 4 (1859), p. 18f, 345f. Cf. also Parz. 531, 12; 544, 23; *Sachsenspiegel*, ed. Weiske, Leipzig 1929, p. 65, art. 27, para 2: *Phaffen und rittere und ir gesinde suln wesen ȝolles vrî* (quoted also by Singer, p. 46f). Despite this immunity to customs duty, Wolfram repeatedly states that he is carrying no goods (112, 30; 113, 22f) and so no levy on merchandise could be expected.

[2] Since Guillaume is wearing Aerofles' armour the townspeople suspect he may be a robber or a spy and apprehend him; Guillaume is enraged at being delayed and treated disrespectfully and in anger kills the *chastelain*, Al. 2081–120. There is no mention of the king's roads or knightly privilege; the latter may possibly have been prompted by Guillaume's line *Cevaliers sui, si faites vilonie* (Al. 2104), a protest against rude handling by the townspeople. The episode has lately been discussed in some detail by P. Csendes, 'Zur Orlensepisode in Wolframs *Willehalm*', ZfdA 97 (1968), pp. 196–206.

of the Empire are present (*Aliscans* does not mention them, but they may have been in Wolfram's version, cf. p. 58):

> 126, 8 manec Franzoys und Bertûn
> und vil der Engeloyse
> und der werden Burgunjoyse
> zer hôchgezît kômen dar.
> ichn mags iu niht benennen gar.
> dâ was von tiuschem lande
> Flæminge und Brâbande
> und der herzoge von Lohrein.

The constitution of the Christian army is referred to in a similar way later, when Rennewart appears before the soldiers at Orange:

> 269, 24 den Burgunjoys, den Bertûn,
> den Flæminc und den Engeloys,
> den Brâbant und den Franzoys
> nam wunder waz er wolde tuon.

Willehalm comes to Munleun as the emperor's vassal, as Loys recognises (148, 9). Loys is not called a *Franzoysære* but *der ræmesche künec* (95, 23; 143, 7; 146, 24; 156, 9): correspondingly Terramer's aim is not to capture Paris or Munleun, but Aachen and Rome (338, 22; 340, 4f; 396, 22. 28; 443, 29; 450, 24f). His invasion of Provence is an attack on the whole Christian Empire.

There is no heathen empire comparable to that of the Christians. There are many important similarities between the Christians and heathens which offered Wolfram an easy opportunity to represent the heathens' order as a simple counterpart to the Christian Empire; his resistance to that temptation reveals his firm grasp of the religious issue and his awareness in detail of the essential differences between the situation of the heathens and of the Christians. The heathens are equal to the Christians in chivalry and *minne*. They have a supreme temporal ruler, the *admirât*, who lives in Mekka, and a spiritual leader, the *bâruc*, who lives at Baldac, as the Christians have their emperor and their pope.[1] Although Terramer has no wish to go to war, the *bâruc* and his *êwarten* keep him to his duty to fight for the heathen *ê*. This *ê* might seem

---

[1] In *Parzival* the *bâruc* was the sole spiritual and temporal authority.

comparable to the Christian order, particularly when the battle of Alischanz is compared with that of Karl and Baligan in the *Rolandslied*, where dualism is explicit, and is ultimately traced back to the enmity of Caesar and Pompey. But there is one essential difference between the Christian and the heathen orders – the Christian Empire is holy. Its highest value is the true God, whom it serves, while the heathen gods are false and Terramer is the effective summit.[1] Their religion has a curiously negative quality, and they seem more concerned to dishonour Jesus and Christianity (e.g. 44, 25ff; 107, 28 – 108, 22) than to achieve any positive religious purpose of their own. The heathens are not the Devil's people, as in the *Rolandslied*, but creatures of the God whom the Christians worship and serve; there is no simple dichotomy that might be expressed politically in a kingdom of God and one of the Devil. The Devil never helps the heathens, while even the heathens have to admit that *der ʒouberære Jêsus* helps the Christians (357, 23f); Wolfram omits Al. 6814, where some heathens escape with the Devil's help. The heathens have no Trinity. *Willehalm* opens with a prayer to the God who is both three and one (*du drî und doch einer*) and Gyburg speaks to Terramer of *diu Trinitât* (218, 25ff), for this is one of the most common expressions for the Christian God in *Willehalm*, but Terramer is quite baffled by the concept of the Trinity (cf. 219, 2f). There is no comparable mystery about the Saracen gods, and there are four of them, not three (Apolle, Mahmet, Tervigant, Kahun).[2] Their gods are conceived as idols, which are brought to the battlefield on wagons and receive sacrificial offerings (cf. 9, 8ff).[3] When Wolfram speaks of the power of the Christian Empire, he contrasts Altissimus with Terramer, not the heathen gods (434, 16–23).

[1] Cf. Bumke, pp. 132–5; Bumke observes that Wolfram opposes *sîn rîche*, i.e. Terramer's Empire, to *daʒ rîche*, the Christian Empire.

[2] According to Türheim's *Rennewart* they have five gods (Mahmet Tervigant, Appolle, Kaun, Hamon).

[3] 352, 1ff; 358, 10; 383, 16; 398, 27; 404, 14f. The images of the Saracen gods appear quite frequently in the *chansons de geste* and they are sometimes mishandled in punishment when the Saracens suffer a disaster. The idea that they are brought to battle on wagons is implied in the *Rolandslied* (Rol. 2650, 3467f, 3816, 4684, cf. Palgen, p. 214f), which is doubtless Wolfram's source for this motif.

Wolfram does not oppose a heathen empire to the Christian one because he does not accept the dualism of the source. In this, as in other respects, Wolfram shows himself strikingly less inclined than most of his contemporaries to understand religious and moral differences in terms of simple opposites. The similarities between the Christian and Saracen political structures he owes largely to his source, which assumes that heathen practice must correspond to or be directly opposite to Christian behaviour (cf. the belief that the heathens, too, made images of their gods, see p. 132), and to his use of the *Rolandslied* for information about the heathens.

The Christian Empire is ruled by Loys, son of Charlemagne. It is part of the Old French epic tradition that Louis is an unworthy king and the power behind the throne is Guillaume, who first forces the barons to crown Louis and afterwards fights his battles for him.[1] Wolfram preserves this tradition. Loys owes his crown entirely to Willehalm's intervention:

> 145, 16   hêr künec, nu wænt ir kreftic sîn:
> gab ich iu rœmsche krône
> nâch alsô swachem lône
> als von iu gein mir ist bekant?
> daz rîche stuont in mîner hant:
> ir wart der selbe als ir noch sît,
> dô ich gein al den fürsten strît
> nam, die iuch bekanten
> und ungern ernanten
> daz si iuch ze hêrren in erkürn.
> si vorhten daz se an iu verlürn
> ir werdekeit unde ir prîs:
> ine gestatt in niht deheinen wîs,
> sine müesen iuch ze hêrren nemn.

Although Loys now holds supreme power, he is singularly ineffective. He has to be reminded of his imperial responsibilities

---

[1] In *Couronnement de Louis* (72–149) Louis hesitates when the crown is offered him at Aix by Charlemagne, and Charlemagne in anger insults his coward son in a colourful speech (e.g. lines 91f: *Deleȝ ma feme se colcha paltoniers/Qui engendra cest coart eritier*) and offers the crown to a traitor. In opposition to Charlemagne and all the barons Guillaume kills the traitor, seizes the crown and places it on Louis' head. Many *chansons* tell of Guillaume's subsequent battles for Louis.

and his authority by his vassal. He is extraordinarily vacillating: during the conflict with Willehalm he at first sides with the Queen and ignores Willehalm, but when confronted with Willehalm in anger he soon changes sides. Willehalm expects him to change his mind again after his wife's intervention, as he has done before:

> 158, 13 doch möhte mîn wol werden rât,
> wan daz si nu und dicke hât
> mir sküneges helfe erwendet.

The king's weakness gives his wife power and helps to account for Willehalm's extreme anger and concern at her unfavourable attitude to his request. When, without consulting Loys, the Queen has the gates closed against Willehalm, it becomes clear who really rules at Munleun, and Wolfram remarks:

> 130, 3 waz si gebôt, daz was getân.

In Charlemagne's day the political opinions of the emperor's wife had been of less account. Willehalm is justified in calling the emperor a coward (139, 1f: *disen ʒagen, den künec*). It is quite in character that even when Loys has been driven to summon an imperial army to fight Terramer, he will not lead it as his father had led the Empire's armies against Baligan.

Loys seems to have forgotten about the Empire of which he is ruler; he is interested only in France. When his imperial vassal comes to him at Munleun he treats him as a stranger (129, 4: *er ist der Franʒoyser gast*, contrast Arnalt, 124, 1: *er ist uns doch niht gar ein gast*). Accepting his wife's appraisal of the situation he decides that Willehalm's demand (i.e. the interests of the Empire) conflicts with the interests of France (129, 19–27), and his consequent behaviour shows that France must come first. When Willehalm angrily storms into the palace, Wolfram says that the knights at Munleun were so frightened that they wished themselves at Kanach or Assim, Alamansura or Scandinavia, Catus Ercules or Palaker (141, 11–21), but Loys when confronted thus with Willehalm wishes himself at Etampes or Paris or Orlens (148, 3–7): it seems that Loys only feels safe in France.[1] Hence his choice of

---

[1] In *Aliscans* only French names occur in both cases.

Munleun for his residence. Having at last raised an army, Loys leads it as far as Orlens, the last town in France, and then turns back. The attitude of Loys seems to have spread to his subordinates, for his men at Orlens treat an imperial knight only as a foreigner to France and at Munleun all the talk is of France and the French. Only Wimar the merchant welcomes Willehalm as a fellow Christian and not a foreigner.[1] Even when he is forced to face his responsibility Loys will not go to the war himself, as his father had done, but provides an army of French cowards without a leader (although he has stronger imperial forces in Germany, 210, 28–30); the cowardice of these soldiers is a reflection upon the emperor whom they serve (cf. Schwietering, p. 176.)

The attitude of Loys is determined by his Queen, who is the first to recognise Willehalm and declares at once that he is a danger to France (129, 19–24). She has the gates locked against him and she intervenes to stop Loys from offering him help. Her hostility is more serious than that of Loys, since it is more active – she gives the advice that guides her husband – and as sister to Willehalm she ought to be naturally sympathetic to his suit. Bumke observes that Loys is the only Germanic name which Wolfram has not translated from the French, possibly to avoid association with Ludwig von Thüringen.[2] It is equally significant that the Queen is the only important character with no name at all; all Willehalm's other relatives are named. In the source she is called Blancheflor. Wolfram suppresses her name because of her disgraceful *untriuwe* rather than because he dislikes that particular name;[3] comparably he omits to mention the names of the French

---

[1] E.g. 135, 28: *iuwer kumber sol mich riuwen/unz ir an vröuden habet gewin,/hân ich toufbæren sin.*

[2] Bumke, p. 193, note 59. If this is the reason, it is indicative of Wolfram's attitude to Loys.

[3] Cf. M. Gibbs, 'A Study of the Women Characters in the Works of Wolfram von Eschenbach', M.A. thesis, London 1965, p. 316, who remarks that Wolfram's apparent dislike for the name of Perceval's wife and Tristan's mother could not account for his avoiding it in the case of a woman he disliked as much as Loys' queen. Miss Gibbs also observes that the Queen is the only woman for whom Wolfram never employs descriptive epithets like *diu süeze, diu clâre*, presumably because he could find no word of praise for this woman. In both his epics it is the *person* called Blancheflor that he dislikes, not the name.

knights who speak at the army council expressly because they are to disgrace themselves at Pitît Punt (302, 1–7). Like her husband, the Queen changes her attitude for fear of Willehalm, and the reason which she finally gives for supporting him is not acceptance of her duty to the Empire but kinship with many of the men who died in the first battle of Alischanz (165, 14–16). This reason is natural for Willehalm's other kinsmen, who are not responsible for the Empire, but an Empress who even in a major crisis can find no reason to support the Empire apart from family loyalty seems to be quite unaware of her duty.

Neither the Emperor nor the Queen will defend the Empire's interests; consequently an open breach between them and Willehalm is inevitable. Willehalm knocks the Queen's crown off her head and breaks it (147, 16f), a gesture that shows very clearly that he no longer respects her authority, and he goes on to describe her publicly in extremely insulting terms (153, 1–25). Although they are later reconciled, with the help of Alyze's truly remarkable powers of persuasion, he never apologises for his behaviour and he never affirms his allegiance to her again.

Willehalm treats Loys similarly. He publicly calls him a coward and reminds him of his inglorious coronation (145, 6 – 146, 13). He bullies him into raising an army, taking full advantage of Loys' good mood following a good meal (177, 15–20). When Loys has led this army through France, he abdicates to Willehalm his authority as commander, together with the imperial banner and battle-cry (211, 20–2; 212, 17–24). After this Loys ceases to be the effective emperor; even in law his position becomes weak when he turns back, for it had been agreed at Munleun that all those who would not fight in support of Willehalm were deprived of all rights (185, 6–19). Loys' abdication of his imperial duty and authority to Willehalm; is comparable to the Queen's loss of her crown: from this time on they no longer function actively as the Empire's leaders. Loys and the Queen are never called *keiser* and *keiserinne*, although this is their proper rank and we often hear of *keiser Karl*;[1] instead they are always referred to

---

[1] 3, 30; 6, 9; 51, 12; 108, 13; 117, 3; 158, 24; 180, 28; 410, 26; 441, 7.

as *künec* and *küneginne*. They do contribute an army and some financial support to the Empire's cause, but this is no more than might be expected of the rulers of France, an important part of the Empire. Willehalm derives most of his support from his own kinsmen. The imperial throne is at Aachen[1] but it appears to be vacant; Loys and the Queen never leave France.

THE RISE OF RENNEWART

Independently of his source, Wolfram has established a strong association of Rennewart with the concept of a Christian Empire. It is present from the time when Willehalm comes to the imperial court and finds Rennewart there to the moment when he is rescued from certain defeat by the imperial army under Rennewart's command.

The Rennewart action begins properly with the introduction of Alyze. The passage devoted to this is very much longer than in *Aliscans*, occupying forty-eight lines instead of four (Al. 2812–15; Wh. 154, 1 – 155, 17), and Wolfram praises her in superlatives, using expressions with very strong moral and religious associations (*diu junge reine süeʒe clâr...Alyʒ diu sældenbære...diu gehiure...wunsch des gernden...von der meide kom ein glast... gróʒ sælde*; cf. later 157, 4; 174, 14; 180, 8f; 200, 12ff etc.). Such language at once places her on a much higher plane than any other character at Munleun and no comparable language is used elsewhere in *Willehalm* except for Gyburg and Rennewart. Wolfram praises Alyze more enthusiastically than any of his other heroines, either in *Willehalm* or in *Parʒival*.[2] Her *kiusche* is so perfect that

---

[1] Loys is called king of Rome (103, 13; 284, 9; 325, 29; 338, 19; 357, 21) and Rome is where emperors are crowned (394, 1; 396, 28; 434, 7; 443, 29), but at 450, 24 Aachen appears as an imperial capital with a throne and the relation between Rome and Aachen is not made clear. This does not affect the position of Loys.

[2] Cf. Gibbs, p. 235: 'For a long time Alyze stands without speaking, while Wolfram describes her tremendous beauty. The description is matched, in length and enthusiasm, by no other in all the praise which Wolfram gives of his heroines. He achieves by this means a unique impression of Alyze at her first appearance and succeeds in focussing complete attention on her for this period, as indeed must the attention of the whole court rest on her as she stands there.' Miss Gibbs suggests that Wolfram had the Virgin Mary in mind as he described Alyze.

it will heal a poisoned wound (154, 21–3) and the light that shines from her turns misery into bliss (155, 4–6); one word from her lips brings happiness for ever (155, 11f). The miracle of her healing presence is performed at once, for Willehalm's great anger, which until that moment held the whole court in terror, melts away as she enters the room (154, 1–5; contrast Al. 2916–47, where it takes the combined pleading of Aelis, Blancheflor, Aymeri and Louis to appease him). Unlike her parents, Alyze never mentions France but speaks at once of the Empire (148, 21), and she welcomes Willehalm and calls him uncle. Thus she shows at her entry her awareness both of the bonds of kinship linking her family with Willehalm and of their common allegiance to the Christian Empire.

Willehalm always treats Alyze with the greatest respect. He immediately recognises their kinship (*niftel*, 156, 6) and her superior rank as imperial princess (156, 9: *du bist des rœmeschen küneges kint*). He is embarrassed when she kneels before him and insists upon her standing because she is both by rank and by birth above him (156, 1–20). He offers his loyalty and his service:

> 156, 12 niftel, nu gestate mirs,
> daz ich in dîme gebote lebe:
> dîn güete mir den rât nu gebe.
> ob du mich niht spottes werst,
> sô stant ûf: swes du an mich gerst,
> des wil ich dir ze hulden pflegen.
> du hâst mir werdekeit durchlegen.

> 158, 1 der marcgrâve sprach 'liebez kint,
> in dîn gebot dich underwint
> mîns lîbes der hie vor dir stêt,
> der ninder rîtet noch engêt
> unz ich mit dînen hulden var. . . . '

These public speeches before the imperial court (156, 4–30; 158, 1 – 159, 30) are most important, for they are very long and solemn and the situation of Willehalm and of the Christian cause is extremely serious. The service which Willehalm offers is service from a vassal to his liege lady – it could not be *minne*-service, for his vow to Gyburg would not permit that – and we might have expected it to be addressed to the Queen, who is in fact his liege lady and yet receives no comparable pledge. It appears that since the Queen has betrayed both the Empire and her kinsmen and caused Willehalm to attack her and break her crown, he will no longer serve her; in her place he serves Alyze. Not prompted by his source, Wolfram says that Alyze's hair at that moment is so arranged that she seems to be wearing a crown:

> 154, 15   mit spæhen borten kleine,
> die verwiert wârn mit gesteine,
> het ieslich drümel sîn sunder bant,
> daz man niht ze vaste drumbe want,
> als ez ein krône wære.

This description of Alyze's hair is too detailed and unexpected to be without significance. It is deliberately indicative of her real function and perhaps prophetic of her future rank. Gottfried von Strassburg uses the same device when he describes the hair of Isolde, richly adorned with jewels, as resembling a crown shortly before she becomes queen of Cornwall and England (Tr. 10962ff, esp. 10980ff).[1] Alyze acts as her mother the Queen should have done and by her intervention for family and Empire makes possible the Empire's victory. By reconciling Willehalm and the court at Munleun she wins for Willehalm the imperial support and authority which he desperately needs, and gains for the Empire the service of the only man capable of inspiring confidence and leading an army against the Saracens. She heals the wound which her mother had poisoned. She serves the Empire's pressing need again when she secures against her father's will leave for Renne-wart, the only man able to defeat the strongest Saracens, to join Willehalm's army. Finally, by sending for Rennewart and kissing him she binds him to her in a *minne* relationship which not only guarantees his loyalty but also inspires manhood and courage in him.

[1] I am indebted to Professor Hatto for drawing my attention to this remarkable parallel.

Rennewart's own career also begins at the imperial court. Like Alyze, he is introduced at great length and Wolfram again uses superlatives and terms of very high moral and religious praise and suggestive power (188, 1 – 189, 28; cf. also 270, 12 – 271, 26). Before he is named we hear much of his extraordinary strength, high lineage and noble instincts (188, 1–19). From the beginning he is linked to the emperor's daughter. When he is brought to Munleun Loys gives him to her, and as children they play together; she is his only friend and only she knows the secret of his origin. She makes his career possible by securing his release from kitchen service and her *minne* sustains him in battle. Since she is the emperor's daughter and acts always loyally towards the Empire, Rennewart's bond with her brings him closer than any man to the leadership of the Empire. The idyllic scene where they kiss in the woods near Orlens shows at this very early stage the perfect courtesy, modesty and consideration that Rennewart is capable of in her presence. Here Rennewart and Alyze achieve for a moment a harmony between Christian and Saracen that does not depend on their obvious similar regard for honour and the chivalric code but on the more important and fundamental concern for religion which is the cause of their deadly conflict and yet might be their deepest bond. As they part, Rennewart says:

> 213, 27   der hœhste got behüete
> iuwer werdeclîchen güete.

In this moment of suprareligious understanding Rennewart anticipates the parting of Willehalm and Matribleiz, when Willehalm commends the noblest of his captured enemies to him who can count the stars and gave us the light of the moon.[1] Like Willehalm's reference to the creator's omniscience and power, Rennewart's expression *der hœhste got* is equally meaningful and emotionally suggestive by Saracen or by Christian interpretation (cf. also Willehalm's use of *der hœhste got* to Rennewart, 331, 5),

---

[1] Wolfram likes to think of the essential nature of divinity in terms of pure light (cf. St. John, 1, 4–10), a conception faithfully if misleadingly expressed by Herzeloyde (Parz. 119, 19–28) and confirmed in Trevrizent's description of God as an all-pervading light that never falters in his love (Parz. 446, 3: *der ist ein durchliuhtec lieht/und wenket sîner minne nieht*).

and it points to the common ground between Christians and
Saracens which lies precisely where they seem most tragically
divided. Spoken by the son of the *admirât* of all Saracens to the
princess of the Christian Empire these words bridge for a moment the gulf of intolerance and misunderstanding that separates
their parents, the masters of the present. Their kiss seals a union
that not only binds Rennewart to the Christian cause but also
hints at the possibility of a more sympathetic understanding in
a better future, when the union of Rennewart's strength and
Alyze's healing power may be fruitful for others.

During the brief sojourn at Orange Rennewart's determination
to help Willehalm is strengthened and the importance of his bond
with Alyze is brought out several times (271, 3; 284, 9–30; 285,
13–22; 287, 11–28). Just before reaching the battlefield Rennewart is obliged to return for his club, which he has forgotten
twice before, and this time he blames his own *tumpheit* for the disgrace of turning back:

> 317, 3   er sprach 'nu hât mir tumpheit
> alrêrst gefüeget herzenleit:
> diu scheidet selten sich von mir. . . .'

After turning back, however, he thinks, in another passage independent of *Aliscans*, that God may be testing him:

> 317, 28   waz ob mich versuochen wil
> der aller wunder hât gewalt,
> und ob mîn manheit sî balt?

Having conquered his pride by turning back for his weapon
despite the public shame, he has passed God's test: his loyalty
and obedience to God are greater than his concern for personal
honour. Soon we see Rennewart employed as God's chosen
instrument when, returning to Willehalm and battle, he meets the
French deserters at Pitît Punt and drives them back to their
proper place; at first they regard Rennewart's attack as sinful and
unfair (324, 16f), since Willehalm himself has given them leave to
go, but soon they recognise the hand of God acting through

Rennewart and saving them from the shame of turning back and the sin of neglecting their Christian duty:[1]

> 325, 1 Genuoge undr in begunden jehen,
> in wære al rehte geschehen:
> si slüege aldâ diu gotes hant,
> von der si flühtec wærn gewant.

The French no longer question Rennewart's authority, though he is contradicting Willehalm. Willehalm's decision was not proper, because the men were not fighting only in his service, but in the service of God and the Christian Empire; Willehalm could neither command their support nor release them from their duty. Their position is different from that of Willehalm's *sippe* who with their liege men are bound by filial duty to serve Heimrich and might be released by him from that service; neither he nor his son can release the imperial army from its obligation towards the Christian Empire. The soldiers at Munleun had been denied the normal right to decide for themselves whether they wished to earn Irmschart's *solt* by joining Willehalm: they are compelled by law to go to the war and are outlawed if they disobey, because it is their common duty as Christians to fight:

> 185, 6 die ze keiner helfe wârn gezalt,
> die sagete man gar rehtelôs,
> durch daz der touf die smæhe kôs
> von der heidenschefte,
> sine wertens mit ir krefte.

Rennewart's action in overruling Willehalm is comparable to Willehalm's earlier behaviour at Munleun, when with violence and with unfounded insults he had forced the Queen to reverse her earlier decision and support the Christian cause: the Empire's urgent need had justified his violent intervention on its behalf when its nominal head had failed to act. Rennewart's *tumpheit*, which had caused him to turn back, is now revealed as a divine quality, for through it God has been able to guide him.[2] When

---

[1] Bumke, p. 43: 'Gott selber greift durch Rennewart ein und hält die Abtrünnigen auf.' Cf. also Maurer, p. 191f.

[2] Cf. Willehalm's praise for Rennewart's *süeze einvaldekeit* (453, 3). For the religious significance of *einvaldekeit* see R. Gruenther, 'Parzivals *einvalt*', Euph 52 (1958), pp. 297–302, especially p. 300f.

Rennewart brings the imperial army back to Willehalm, Willehalm does not question Rennewart's authority or punish his insubordination, but guesses that Rennewart may be of higher rank than himself and offers, in that case, his service and that of all his kinsmen:

> 331, 1   Bistu von sölher art erkant,
> daz dich rîchen sol mîn hant
> (ich meine, under mir, niht obe),
> so bringe ich dich zuo sölhem lobe,
> gan der hœhste got des lebens mier,
> daz nie fürsten soldier
> für dich wart baz geêret:
> biste ab hôher dan ich bin,
> so trag ich dir dienstlîchen sin;
> und allez mîn geslehte:
> daz erteil ich in von rehte.[1]

He speaks similarly after the battle (453, 1ff), when he fears that Rennewart may have been killed and that he will never have the opportunity of serving him. Rennewart's achievement at Pitît Punt has made him leader of an army and has made Willehalm feel that he may be of very high rank; as a service to the Empire it is comparable with that of Alyze when she reconciles Willehalm and her parents: Rennewart has united the Empire's power with that of Willehalm in the battle against the Saracens.

From this point on, Rennewart is far more effective as leader of the Empire than either Loys or Willehalm. Loys has been so ineffective as emperor that his work has largely been done by Willehalm, who leads his army for him. But even Willehalm's position is weak. He is leader by nomination and election (214, 1f), not by right of birth; he is only a *marcgrâve*, and the imperial army contains many men who are his equals (214, 3f).[2] The

---

[1] Weber, p. 23, comments on the curiously dual nature of this speech, which caters first for the possibility of Rennewart's being Willehalm's inferior and then for his being superior to him, an indication of the importance of social rank for Wolfram.

[2] The leading men in the imperial army regard Willehalm as their equal (e.g. 212, 3ff). Bumke, attempting to show Willehalm as successor to Charlemagne, recognises that his relatively low rank is the principal difficulty: 'Willehalm ist kein Charismaträger, kein Gesalbter, entstammt keiner *regia stirps*' (p. 122). Willehalm compares himself in rank to an *amaẓûr* or *eskelîr* (207, 14f), but never to the *admirât*.

responsible task of dividing the army into its fighting units is undertaken not by Willehalm (as in the source), but by *die wîsen ime her*. Wolfram avoids referring to Willehalm's authority as commander of the army (328, 9–30; contrast Al. 4903: *Sa gent ordene Guillames li marchis*, 4932ff, 4938ff, etc.), while Terramer, though he has his advisers (222, 20), commands his army personally. Willehalm's instructions are generally expressed as requests (e.g. 278, 1–5), while Terramer commands, and Willehalm attends the conference as an equal rather than a superior (cf. 278, 8). He derives his authority from Loys, whose representative he is (211, 10–22), and he maintains it through his personal reputation and his powers of leadership. It is the Empire's war, but the proper leader of the Empire's forces is still in France. In the battle Willehalm is only co-leader of one of the six units, and Willehalm's unit is much less powerful than the imperial army. He never uses the imperial banner, but fights under the flag of Provence and is called *der fürste ûȥ Provenȥâlen lant* (422, 12; 452, 15). The army has chosen him as leader and their choice has been confirmed by Loys, but this authority is indirect and Willehalm cannot rely on the obedience of the imperial army as he relies on his kinsmen's loyalty because he has no natural bond with them and no natural authority over them.[1] To avoid the danger of their deserting during the battle and beginning a general flight he has to let them go before the battle begins.

Despite Rennewart's low standing at Munleun we have been

[1] Bumke, pp. 117–26, argues that Willehalm has inherited from Charlemagne the duty of defending Christendom against the Saracens and he derives his authority from his share in Charlemagne's office. Willehalm, however, explicitly rejects as false the thought that he has inherited the war from Charlemagne (455, 11–16; cf. Werner Schröder, *Euph* 55, p. 95). Willehalm's grief at Charlemagne's death does indeed suggest a personal loss (158, 28; cf. Bumke, p. 118) but it does not indicate any parallel between the two men; Willehalm's status as vassal to Charlemagne is never forgotten (6, 9; 91, 28; 182, 16; 455, 13). He has good cause to lament the loss of such a good lord in view of the weakness of his successor. In the French tradition Guillaume is always the emperor's loyal vassal and cannot be compared in status to Charlemagne; the historical relationship between them is consequently forgotten (William was grandson of Charles Martel and cousin to Charlemagne). Doubtless the cycles of Charlemagne and Guillaume developed separately because epics concerning Charlemagne would be favoured in royalist circles while the Guillaume cycle with the weak king pleased the more ambitious barons better: the close family link was therefore not mentioned by either side.

assured that he is the best man born in West or East since Charlemagne and Baligan (272, 14–17) and his father is the richest king
in the world (269, 28–30); this places him among the emperors
and suggests that he has a better natural right to lead the imperial
army than even Willehalm has, though he has not formally been
entrusted with authority. When he brings the imperial army to
Willehalm, Willehalm readily surrenders to him the imperial
banner, which bears the Cross, and formally puts him in command
of the men. The banner had been put into a sack by the men and
would not have been used at all but for their encounter with
Rennewart: Willehalm would then have had to fight simply as a
marcgráve defending his property and his wife and the Empire
would not have been involved in the battle. There is no question of
Willehalm's using the imperial banner himself, though it is in his
keeping and the imperial army in his charge. Wolfram probably
introduced the Cross banner here in support of Frederick II, who
had used it in place of the traditional eagle (see below, pp. 207ff);
the Cross symbolises the essentially Christian nature of the
Empire, which would have a natural attraction for Wolfram,
while the eagle had been the emblem of Rome and thus had a long
history as the symbol of imperial power. Rennewart is introduced in *Willehalm* with the image of a young eagle (189, 2–24);
there seems to be a parallel between the imperial eagle, which
gives way to the Cross as the Empire becomes the political
expression of Christian unity, and the young eagle as the image of
Rennewart giving way to the Cross when his strength is sanctified
by a new Christian purpose. When Rennewart with his fifteen
thousand men advances under this banner, Terramer believes
the Christian Emperor himself is coming against him:

> 340, 16 'der Karles sun da gein mir her
> rîtt: sît daz des rîches vane
> von den kristen ist gebunden ane,
> si bringnt ir rehten houbetman,
> des vater mir vil hât getân.'

Terramer's misunderstanding helps us to see that Rennewart,
not Loys, is *ir rehter houbetman*, and it is, by a profound

irony, *his* father who in his blind folly has done most harm to Terramer.[1]

Bumke has argued (pp. 43, 78, 84) that the Christian army is no bigger in the second battle than in the first, since it is described in either case as a *hant vol*:

> 13, 9   die hant vol als er mohte hân.

> 328, 29   waz touc diu hant vol genant
> gein dem her ûz al der heiden lant?

In the second case, however, the expression occurs after the desertion of the imperial army, when the faithful remnant have been formed into fighting units: these are a *hant vol* compared with the vast army of Saracens, and Willehalm's prospects of victory can at this point be no greater than before the earlier battle. But immediately after this Rennewart returns with the imperial army, which has fifteen thousand men (302, 12). The term *hant vol* cannot apply to these. They represent the support of the powerful Christian Empire which Willehalm must have if he is to win. Rennewart's army, *des rîches her*, is not only the biggest force by far on the Christian side; it also proves itself the most effective. In the course of the battle it quickly becomes evident that Willehalm could not have won without it. When the first six Saracen armies engage the six Christian units, Terramer still has four armies in reserve; only Rennewart's imperial army is able to engage several Saracen armies at the same time. It inflicts such damage on Terramer's second army, led by Ehmereiz and Tybalt, that Josweiz has to intervene with the seventh, and before long both armies prove inadequate against Rennewart and his men. Rennewart then attacks the first Saracen army, which is under Halzebier's command, and pursues it to the Saracen ships, where he frees the kinsmen of Willehalm who had been taken prisoner

---

[1] Bumke, p. 124, note 77, reads 340, 17–19 as a hint that Willehalm, not Loys, is really the Empire's *rehter houbetman*. This view is untenable, because the imperial flag is not used by Willehalm but by Rennewart; Terramer has known all along that Willehalm was present, as in the earlier battle, while the appearance of the imperial banner, which implies that *ir rehter houbetman* is present this time, comes as a great shock to him. Bumke's interpretation would also rob the line that follows of its significance – Willehalm's father has not, as far as we know, done great harm to Terramer.

in the earlier battle and they kill Halzebier. Wherever the fighting is hardest the imperial army and Rennewart appear, and they are always victorious. Leaderless, these men had put their banner into a sack and fled; under Rennewart's command they play the decisive part in saving Christendom from the Saracen invasion. After the battle Willehalm declares that he owes his victory to God and Rennewart:

> 452, 24 daz ich von im des siges pflac
> und von der hœhsten hende.

In giving credit for the victory to Rennewart rather than Willehalm himself, Wolfram is entirely in agreement with his source.[1] A fourteenth century chronicle of popes and emperors[2] follows Wolfram and names *got und daȝ rîche und Rennewart* as the victors in this battle. These three are interdependent, because the Empire is Christian and Rennewart, who commands the Empire's army, is God's instrument.

Rennewart's rapid rise in political importance – beginning as a kitchen boy and ending as a general – is matched by his gain of social esteem and public honour. At first he is unrespected and isolated (his rejection of baptism cuts him off even from Alyze), but later he wins respect and friendship first from Willehalm, then Gyburg, then the imperial soldiers, and finally from the whole Christian army. Willehalm's respect for Rennewart begins with sympathy (191, 22f) and admiration for his undaunted spirit (194, 1–4), grows to warm praise and gratitude when Rennewart brings him the imperial army (330, 27ff) and appears finally as immeasurable and inconsolable grief at the thought of

---

[1] Al. 4579g, 5689: *Se diex ne fust et Rainouars li ber*. Cf. Desramé's remark to his son, Al. 121c, 21: *Car par toi ont François le champ vaincu.*

[2] Quoted by Clarus, p. 364, from an Upper Rhine Chronicle published by F. Grieshaber, Rastatt 1850. On p. 20, under *Karolus der Groȝe*, we read: 'Ludewikus, sin sun, der des Markins swester hatte, der in der heidenschaft gefangen lag, dem got half under Arabel die künegin, die mit im fur, und sich lies toufen, darumbe ir fatter küning Terremer, und ir bruder und küning Tiebalt ir man, und vil andere küninge kamen uf Aleschantz und da striten, do er verlor Fifianz und Mile siner swester kint, und andere fillütz, und half ime got und daz riche und Rennewart, daz er Kilburg, die Künegin, und Oranz die burg und den sik behielt an den heiden.' The reference to Mile strongly suggests that the chronicler has derived his information from Wolfram's *Willehalm* and it reveals how Wolfram's epic was understood.

losing him, grief which cannot be compensated by Gyburg's *minne*, as his grief on Vivianz' death had been (456, 15–18; contrast 280, 2–13) and which drives him to blasphemy (456, 1f: *mîner flust mahtu dich schemn, der megede kint!*), while Christian faith had been an adequate consolation when Vivianz died. The respect which Rennewart commands at the end of the battle would seem absurd for the Rennewart of Munleun.

At Munleun no character seems more unlikely than Rennewart as leader of the Christian Empire. He is employed in the kitchen, he is a foreigner both to France and to the Empire, a Saracen who firmly resists Christianity, and he has the weakest of motives for going to war. While the Christian knights fight at one and the same time for *minne* and for their *sippe* and, like Vivianz, for the martyr's crown, Rennewart alone is outside their *sippe* and their religion and his motives are quite worldly (at first *êre* and resentment, later *minne*).[1] His hatred of the Saracens is quite unjust: his zeal to fight them is a consequence of his anger over the indignities he has suffered at the hands of Loys (285, 11–15), for which the Saracens are in no way responsible, and his bitter resentment at their failure to help him is based on an error (285, 4–10). But Rennewart's anger, however unjust, is vindicated by its employment in God's holy cause. Anger can be a major asset in battle; the cause for which it is employed is of the greatest importance, but it is not important how the anger was roused. A comparable case among the Saracens is Poydwiz, whose anger is roused by Terramer's disrespectful treatment of him and is vented on the Christians (390, 9–16).[2] Rennewart's anger is vindicated by his decision to trust the Christian God (193, 9–12). God answers that trust by directing his otherwise senseless anger into his own holy purpose and taking control of Rennewart's career;[3] this is precisely what the Saracen gods had failed to do, though he had trusted for so long in their aid. His simple *tumpheit* thus enables

---

[1] Cf. Schwietering, p. 179.

[2] Cf. Al. 91–3, where Vivien, horrified at having broken his vow, determines that Gorhant's men shall pay for his fault.

[3] Cf. Maurer, p. 192: 'Aus Irrtum also und ganz unbegründetem Hass siegt Rennewart für die Christen. Wieder offenbart sich Gottes Hand und Rennewart als sein Werkzeug.'

him to do God's will rather than his own, and his service to the Christian cause may be the more pure because it is not reasonably motivated, but natural and instinctive.[1] For all his *tumpheit* Rennewart is not taken in by the advice of the wise man (325, 23) who offers him a purely pleasurable life in France as an easier way of acquiring *êre*; thus he instinctively acts in accordance with the poet's ideal that one should not seek a life of *vröude* alone, but accept the interdependence of *vröude* and *trûren* (280, 13 – 281, 16).[2] In *Parzival* any one of the Christian knights at Munsalvæsche, whose lives are dedicated to the service of the Holy Grail, seems more worthy to become its king than the young inexperienced Parzival, who is interested in nothing so much as his own *êre*; similarly Rennewart at Munleun, anxious to earn *êre*, seems less worthy to lead the Christian Empire than any of the Christian knights in the Empire's service that surround him.[3] But although he sins at Munsalvæsche and renounces God, Parzival is by nature more deeply religious than any of the Grail knights and his natural *triuwe* warrants his promotion over them. So Rennewart, a declared Saracen, serving no God in battle but seeking only *êre* and *minne*, has natural *triuwe*; for him, as for Parzival, religion cannot be a simple unproblematic affair – even as a child he has shown conscientious firmness in religion despite the cost by suffering dishonour and separation from Alyze for the sake of a religious instinct: he is under heavy pressure to become a Christian but he will not yield (191, 1–18). It is possible for such a man to prove more deeply religious than any of the Empire's knights and worthy of promotion above them, even to the leadership of the Christian Empire.

In religion, the most perfect *triuwe* may be shown by a character

---

[1] Wentzlaff-Eggebert, p. 265, notes that Rennewart serves the Christian God instinctively, without reference to the *dienest-lôn* motivation which the other soldiers require. This seems, however, to overlook the secret reward which Rennewart says he desires, presumably the hand of Alyze.

[2] Cf. Mergell, p. 64.

[3] Wolff, p. 516, compares Rennewart's religious position at Munleun, where having received no help from Mahmet he turns to Christ, with that of Parzival in Book IX, when he considers the possibility that God may help and lets go his horse's reins so that God may guide him if he will.

who has first had to overcome *untriuwe*. It is Parzival, who has rebelled against God, that finds the Holy Grail and becomes its king, while Gawan, who is consistently pious, and in consequence has no religious struggle and development, seeks in vain. In Hartmann's *Gregorius* it is the greatest of sinners that ultimately becomes pope. In *Willehalm* it is the imperial army, which has deserted, that ultimately becomes the mainstay of the Christians and decides the battle. Wolfram's comparison with St. Peter is very apt: as Peter showed *zwîvel* and denied Christ, but later became Christ's firmest supporter, so they show *zwîvel* before the battle but later defeat the Saracens, where Vivianz had failed and Willehalm is inadequate. In the same way Rennewart, whose *tumpheit* causes him to turn back when battle is imminent, becomes the champion of the Christians; *tumpheit* is his *felix culpa*, for in Rennewart's case, as in the others, ultimate success depends upon initial failure.

Although our picture of Rennewart's rise must remain, like the epic, a fragment, its direction has become clear in the completed part of the poem: Rennewart has been associated more and more closely with the Christian Empire and has become its effective leader. If Wolfram intended to follow his source further, we might expect Rennewart to become a knight, accept baptism willingly, marry Alyze and become Christian king of Spain or some other land conquered from the Saracens.[1] By linking the new conception of the Christian Empire with the figure of Rennewart Wolfram has succeeded in making Rennewart's decisive

---

[1] There is a distinct possibility of his being elected Emperor one day, perhaps following the death or abdication of Loys. This is not ruled out by the source, as the *chansons* have nothing to say about Louis' successor or the Christian Empire. In the course of his quarrel with Guillaume Rainouart does twice declare his intention to be crowned at Aachen one day and to succeed Louis (Al. 7625f–i; 7778–78f), but the words are spoken in anger and, like his threat to destroy Orange, they lead nowhere in *Aliscans*. Rennewart's ultimate coronation as Emperor would make prophetic sense of Willehalm's promise (331, 8ff) that he and all his kinsmen will serve Rennewart in the future, and it would accord well with Rennewart's marriage to the present emperor's daughter (Loys has no son to succeed him) and his real assumption of the emperor's responsibilities. On the other hand, Wolfram's source did not go so far, and there may have been knowledge available at the Wartburg about the Empire's history which would have made this impossible. Rennewart as heir to the emperor can therefore be no more than an attractive speculation; his career can be brought to a satisfying climax without it.

part in the battle more feasible and more significant: in *Aliscans* the Christians owe their victory entirely to the incredible strength of one man; in *Willehalm* they owe victory not only to his personal strength, determination and initiative, but also in large measure to his leadership of a great army.[1] Rennewart's strength has been subordinated to a cause – the Christian Empire – and this cause, by virtue of its sanctity and its permanence lends sanctity and enduring significance to Rennewart's deeds.

EXCURSUS: *Rennewart and the imperial flag*

The passing of the leadership of the Christian Empire from Loys to Rennewart is illustrated in the history of the imperial banner, which is given by Loys to Willehalm and by Willehalm to Rennewart. Wolfram has introduced this banner independently of *Aliscans* and it is always described as bearing the Cross.

Bumke's explanation of the Cross, 'Das Kreuzbanner wurde von den deutschen Königen seit Heinrich VI als Reichsbanner geführt',[2] based on a quotation from Gritzner,[3] is not really satisfying: Gritzner traces the Cross as an imperial symbol back to Charlemagne[4] but his earliest reference to its use as the imperial standard is the one in Wolfram's *Willehalm* when Rennewart leads the Empire's army under the Cross:

> 332, 11 nu bindt die marter wider an:
> mit rehte sol des rîches van
> daz kriuze tragen, dar nâch gesniten
> dâ unser heil wart an erstriten.

---

[1] Bumke, p. 79, observes that the two decisive factors ensuring the Christian victory, i.e. Rennewart's strength and the unity of the Christian Empire, are linked through Rennewart's leadership of the Christian Empire. Harms, however (p. 106), believes that Rennewart's 'affektbestimmtes Handeln' and his killing of his brother Kanliun sever him from the Christian cause and end his career as a Christian leader. But the text never suggests that this career is ended. Most of the Christians are moved by passions more aggressive than Christian charity (cf. Willehalm's attempt to rouse them with tales of Saracen atrocities, 297, 14ff), and Rennewart's fratricide is the accidental result of his intervention to rescue Willehalm in a crisis; such a deed cannot divorce him from Willehalm and the Christians.   [2] Bumke, p. 130.

[3] E. Gritzner, 'Symbole und Wappen des alten deutschen Reiches', *Leipziger Studien aus dem Gebiete der Geschichte*, no. 8, Heft 3, Leipzig 1902, p. 65f.

[4] *Ibid*, p. 38. The eagle, emblem of the legions, represented Roman temporal power, the Cross stood for spiritual commitment; cf. p. 13: 'Diese zwei Richtungen in der erneuerten römischen Kaiserwürde von 800 finden in den ihrem Wesen entsprechenden Symbolen, dem alten römischen Reichsadler für die Weltherrschaft, dem Kreuz als Zeichen des Erlösers für die theokratische Auffassung der Würde ihren sichtbaren Ausdruck.'

Although Henry VI had used the Cross not only on his coins but also as his official banner at Cremona in 1195,[1] the imperial standard showed an eagle, both before and after Henry VI. Gritzner connects Henry's use of the Cross in 1195 with his incorporation of Sicily into the Empire (which took place in 1194): the Sicilian Normans had traditionally fought under the Cross, and that banner would remind people of the Sicilian background of the Hohenstaufens.[2] Henry's successor Philip von Schwaben regularly used the eagle (which also occurs frequently on his coins),[3] and the Welf Otto IV used both the eagle and the lion, and sometimes highly imaginative combinations of the two, but never the Cross.[4] Otto IV's banner is described by Walther von der Vogelweide (80, 32f) in the lines '*des aren tugent, des lêwen kraft/die sint des herezeichen an dem schilte*', and in more critical vein Thomasin von Zirclære describes his shield as showing '*drî lêwen und ein halber ar*' and concludes that the three lions signify *übermuot* and the halved eagle deficiency in *êre* (*Welscher Gast* 10479f; 12351–64). However that may be, it appears that the eagle remained the normal imperial device after Henry VI, and there is no evidence for the Cross as the imperial banner until Frederick II.

At Bouvines Frederick II used the Cross as his personal banner (while Otto had a mixture of dragons and eagles), and it appears that he continued to use it after his accession to the imperial throne, to judge by a papal letter just prior to his crusade in 1227.[5] Since at Bouvines he was fighting the established emperor, it is not likely that his Cross was meant as an imperial banner; it was rather the device of Hohenstaufen Sicily, recalling the strong Hohenstaufen emperors Frederick I and Henry VI, and challenging the imperial eagle. Only when the Hohenstaufens are again emperors can the Cross be a specifically imperial banner.

The passage in *Willehalm* has a strong polemical flavour; the force of such words as '*mit rehte sol...*' and the religious justification for using the flag would be out of place if it had been used regularly ever since Henry's time, that is, for twenty years or more. There is little to be said for Bumke's view that the Cross banner is a deliberate anachronism by Wolfram:[6] Wolfram is

---

[1] *Ibid*, p. 65.

[2] *Ibid*, p. 65f. The earliest reference to its use is in Muratori's account of Henry's investiture ceremony at Cremona on 6th June 1195: 'Confanonus, cum quo eos investivit, erat rubeus, habens crucem albam intus.'

[3] *Ibid*, p. 48. Cf. Philippes Mouskes: 'escut d'or a l'aigle de sable', quoted *ibid*, p. 57.

[4] *Ibid*, pp. 49–54. Otto's coins generally show both lion and eagle, as in Walther's description of the shield.

[5] A letter from Pope Gregory IX to Frederick II dated 22 July 1227 refers to 'vexillum, quod habes commune cum angelis', Gritzner, p. 66. Frederick also used the double-headed eagle, which apparently came into existence when he removed the Welf lions from the imperial shield and put a second halved eagle in their place – the two halves make up one eagle with two heads, *ibid*, p. 58.

[6] Bumke, p. 137: 'Wenn Wolfram das Reichsbanner des Königs Loys als Kreuzfahne stilisiert (s. oben S. 130), so hat er ebenso gut wie seine Hörer gewusst, dass dies die

not known to be fond of anachronisms, and such an anachronism would be dangerous twenty years after the introduction of the new flag, when the poet might be accused of simply being wrong and the allusion would no longer be topical. The polemical tone accords much better with the recent introduction of the banner by Frederick II than with an established tradition.

Since Wolfram has introduced the reference to the Cross independently, it seems likely that his intention is to support Frederick II's innovation. Frederick's use of the Cross at Bouvines and after doubtless caused controversy in aristocratic and military circles, since the eagle had a tradition going back to Rome and had been used by Welfs and Hohenstaufens alike, as well as by the Salian and Carolingian emperors before them. Wolfram is known to have favoured the Hohenstaufen party (cf. Schreiber, pp. 78ff; 120), and he can do them a service by describing the imperial banner in *Willehalm*, an authentic tale received on the best French authority, as definitely bearing the Cross. This takes the Cross back to the age of Loys, the son of Charlemagne, and gives it a tradition comparable with the eagle. The Cross is better suited than the eagle to Wolfram's conception of an essentially Christian Empire, as it is expressed in *Willehalm*, and he justifies the Cross by referring to its Christian significance, not its Sicilian political associations. Wolfram uses the eagle only as an image for the young Rennewart before his long development and his closer involvement with the Empire have begun; afterwards, he bears the Cross, indicating that his strength is now directed by Christianity. Rennewart's Cross is not an anachronism, but an argument for the Hohenstaufens and an expression of Wolfram's own conception of a *Christian* Empire.

This interpretation of Wh. 332, 11ff has a bearing on the dating of *Willehalm*. Wolfram's introduction of the Cross as the imperial banner and his defence of it in Book VII suggests that the controversy about Frederick II's use of that banner at Bouvines and after was still fresh when Book VII was being written. Interest in this affair is not likely to have been very lively at a date when Bouvines and the memory of the banner the Emperor had introduced there had receded into history. It consequently seems likely that Wolfram was near the end of *Willehalm* a year or two after Bouvines (i.e. about 1216–17) rather than ten years or so later, as Bumke suggests (p. 198).

Fahne des deutschen Königs ist; und man darf sogar vermuten, dass ihm nicht unbekannt war, dass das Kreuz erst seit wenigen Jahrzehnten vom deutschen König in der Reichsfahne geführt wurde.'

V · THE END OF WOLFRAM'S 'WILLEHALM'

IS 'WILLEHALM' A FRAGMENT?

Wolfram's *Willehalm* was first described as a fragment by Lach-mann;[1] his view has since been adopted by many scholars,[2] while many others have tried to prove the epic complete.[3] The principal grounds for regarding *Willehalm* as a fragment are these: Wolfram's text takes us little further than the end of the second battle, while its source went on to tell of the conversion of Baudins, Rainouart's quarrel with Guillaume and their reconcilia-tion, followed by Rainouart's baptism and investiture, his mar-riage to Aelis and Guillaume's gift to him of fiefs, possibly including the kingdom of Spain. There can be little doubt that Wolfram's version of *Aliscans* included these events.[4] Wolfram does not appear to have eliminated them in order to reach a dif-ferent conclusion, because his poem comes to an abrupt end be-

---

[1] Wolfram von Eschenbach, ed. K. Lachmann, 6th ed., 1926, *Vorrede*, p. xl. Lachmann may have been forestalled by the author of *Der jüngere Titurel*, however, since some lines quoted by San-Marte (p. 125) seem to mean that although Wolfram's source was complete (Jüng. Tit. ed. Hahn, 5883: *diu âventiure von Wilhalm habende vil ganʒe*), his own work is a fragment (5910ff: *Eʒ iehent die merkerîchen/daʒ mich an vreuden pfendet:/iʒ sî wunderlîchen/ein buoch geanevenget und daʒ ander gendet./Sant Wilhalmes anevanc si betoubet/und Parʒifâl ʒe letste/nâch ir beider werdicheit beroubet*).

[2] G. Gervinus, *Geschichte der deutschen Literatur*, 3rd ed., Leipzig 1846; Helm, p. 197f; Bernhardt, pp. 36–40; Schreiber, p. 161; Singer, p. 128 *et passim*; Wolff, *passim*; Knorr and Fink, p. 255; Ranke, p. 68; Kienast, p. 100; De Boor, p. 116; Maurer, p. 197; Ehrismann, p. 271; Mohr, p. 207f; Walshe, p. 170; Weber, 'Die Grundidee', p. 4.

[3] Clarus, p. 344; San-Marte, p. 75f; Rolin, p. v; Mergell, *passim*; Schwietering, p. 180; Bumke, *passim*.

[4] This is the climax of *Aliscans* and not omitted in any known redaction or ms (though the fragment M breaks off before the much-predicted marriage has actually taken place); we have no reason to suppose that the ms which Landgraf Hermann supplied for Wolf-ram was a fragment lacking the most important part of the story. On the other hand, Wolfram's forward references (cf. pp. 214ff) reveal his detailed knowledge of the end of *Aliscans* and lines from the end appear earlier in *Willehalm* (thus 282, 28ff, telling how Rennewart first came to France, is based on information mentioned only at the end of *Aliscans*; Wh. 444, 28–30 comes from Rainouart's battle with Baudins). Mergell, who believes Wolfram meant to omit all these episodes, concedes nevertheless that they must have been in his source (pp. 54, 94).

fore they are reached, leaving the Rennewart action unfinished. Wolfram generally finishes a book at the end of a 30-line block, but the last line of *Willehalm* (467, 8) is not at the end of such a block. Several predictions in Wolfram's text refer to events which in the source occur later than the point where Wolfram breaks off, which suggests very strongly that he intended to include these events in his own version of the tale; the most important of these are hints that Rennewart will marry Alyze (285, 15; 330, 27) and possess a horse (420, 22f). It has also been argued that the text as it stands is structurally asymmetrical, since Book VI, in which the most important ideas are developed, is not in a central position like Book IX of *Parʒival*, and the Prologue, with which the poem opens, needs an epilogue to balance it.[1]

Much of this has been challenged, particularly by Mergell and Bumke, who consider *Willehalm* complete. The counter-arguments are these:

1. Wolfram becomes so independent of his source towards the end of *Willehalm* that he cannot have felt bound to follow it to its conclusion.[2]

2. The Matribleiz episode, which Wolfram seems to have invented and which expresses his own ideal of humanity and respect between religions, has been introduced to replace the old continuation which he did not wish to follow.[3]

3. The last line (467, 8: *sus rûmt er Provenʒâlen lant*), which tells of the departure of the last Saracen from Willehalm's territory, brings to an end the main action, which began with the arrival of Tybalt and Terramer.[4]

4. The last lines of other books usually look forward to coming events (e.g. 57, 30; 105, 29f; 161, 28–30; 313, 30; 361, 26–30; cf. Ehrismann, p. 271, note 3); but this line is final.[5]

5. The end of a book does not always coincide with the end of

[1] Kienast, p. 112.
[2] Mergell, p. 178f; Bumke, pp. 39–55, especially p. 48f.
[3] Schwietering, p. 180; Werner Schröder, Euph 55 (1961), p. 93; Mergell, pp. 175–7.
[4] Maurer, p. 197; Bumke, *Wolfram von Eschenbach*, Stuttgart 1964, p. 85.
[5] Mergell, p. 175.

a block of 30 lines (e.g. *Parʒival*, books I, II, III, V, *Willehalm*, Book I, possibly Book VI).[1]

6. A subsidiary action must end before or with the main action. The victory in the second battle is the climax of the Willehalm action; any continuation of the Rennewart action after this would be an anticlimax. The structural principle employed by Wolfram, which may be termed 'Gothic' and leads to a climax at the end, excludes the possibility of following the source further than this climax; at most an epilogue might have been added to tie up the loose ends.[2]

7. The predictions do not necessarily refer to events that have not taken place at 467, 8. Some, such as Rennewart's acquisition of a horse, may have occurred without being specially mentioned in the text.[3]

The evidence supporting the view that *Willehalm* is a fragment is very considerable, and it is doubtful whether these counter-arguments are adequate to refute it. Each of them is open to objection. Thus:

1. We have seen in chapter two that Wolfram follows his source more closely than is generally supposed; Bumke's claim that Wolfram has all but abandoned his source in Books VIII and IX is based on his erroneous conception of Wolfram's source, which cannot have included the expanded Rainouart action. If his source resembled M, Wolfram has followed it closely with certain regular changes as outlined above (pp. 77ff).

2. The Matribleiz episode is not adequate as a conclusion for the whole epic, since it shows the new humanity only in a very limited way. Willehalm honours only Gyburg's relations for her sake, not all the Saracens. Though Matribleiz is freed, most of the Saracens are still in chains at the end of *Willehalm* (461, 16ff; 462, 13). Willehalm's token of respect in this scene is far less than a satisfying settlement between the opposing religions. We should like to see how the Saracens respond to Willehalm's

[1] Mergell, p. 127.
[2] Schwietering, p. 180; Mergell, pp. 175ff; Bumke, p. 40, note 80.
[3] Mergell, p. 86.

gesture and whether it will influence future relations between Christians and Saracens.

3. The departure of Matribleiz is not the departure of the last Saracen. Many have been left behind, unable to reach the last ship in time (436, 4ff). The action begins with the arrival of Terramer, not that of Matribleiz, and so, had Wolfram intended to conclude with the Saracens' departure, he would probably have chosen the departure of Terramer as the appropriate ending (443, 28f: *sus schiet von rœmscher erde/der dâ vor dicke ûf Rôme sprach/ê daʒ diu schumpfentiure geschach*). *Aliscans* ends with Guillaume's and Guibourc's resolution to rebuild Orange, which comes some time after the Saracens' departure; this returns to the place, persons and events of the beginning (the attack on Orange) far more effectively than the departure of Matribleiz could do.

4. There are several last lines in *Willehalm* which do not look forward (214, 30; 268, 30; 402, 28–30; i.e. three out of eight). If *Willehalm* is a fragment, then 467, 8 is not necessarily a last line and should not be expected to look forward.

5. The practice of ending a book at the end of a block of 30 lines is generally observed after *Parʒival* Book V, and the few cases of apparent irregularity have long been explained.[1] Nowhere is the last line nearly so far from the end of a block as 467, 8, although one would expect structural tidiness at the end of the whole epic even more than at the end of a single book.

6. The subsidiary action will not overlap the main action if we regard not the *victory* as the main action's climax, but the establishment of a peace firmly based on mutual respect and understanding. The honouring of Rennewart and his marriage to Alyze would make it possible for them to contribute very considerably to such a peace, and it could follow without disobedience to the rules of *Endgipfelstruktur* – the baptism and marriage of Feirefiz is possible at the end of *Parʒival*. It is in any case not yet conclusively proven that Wolfram wrote his epics according to 'Gothic' principles.[2] Schwietering's own hint (p. 180) that *Wille-*

---

[1] Lachmann, *Vorrede*, p. ix; A. Hatto, 'Zur Entstehung des Eingangs und der Bücher I und II des Parzival', ZfdA 84 (1952), pp. 232–40.

[2] Cf. Kienast, p. 100.

halm needs an epilogue to balance the Prologue suggests that he, too, is not completely satisfied with the ending as we have it. From the structural point of view, it is unlikely that a poet who, for the sake of completeness, begins his work with an account of events already well known to his audience (7, 23ff) would leave major problems unsolved at the end; the need for an epilogue, or at least a more formal conclusion, is increased by Wolfram's failure to name the patron who supported his work after the death of Hermann of Thuringia.

7. The predictions concerned are these:

> (a) 12, 2   etswenne ouch hôhen muotes tac
> und vröuden künfte sît erschein

This appears to look forward to a final Christian victory (cf. Wolff, p. 519f). Mergell's attempt to relate it to the brief idyll at Orange has been refuted most decisively by Wolff, AfdA 56 (1937), p. 32.

> (b) 285, 11   sîner hôhen mâge vil verlôs
> den lîp durh smæhe die er kôs.
> sîn hant vaht sige der kristenheit:
> sus rach er smæhlîchez leit
> des er vor Alyzen pflac:
> ir minne an prîse im gap bejac.
> sîn dinc sol iemer sus niht varn:
> Alyzen minne in sol bewarn.
> swaz man ie smæhe an im gesach,
> Alyzen minn die von im brach
> dar nâch in kurzen zîten
> in tôtlîchen strîten.

These lines, which all refer forward, definitely indicate a coming improvement in Rennewart's fortunes,[1] and that he will one day receive *êre* instead of *smæhe*. This has only begun to happen when the poem as we have it breaks off: Rennewart has fought for *minne* and deserved *êre*, but he has not received *minne's* reward or enjoyed public acclaim. Rolin argues that the glory to which Alyze's *minne* will lead him may be a glorious death rather

---

[1] Cf. Singer, p. 91.

than marriage, a death which may have occurred by 467, 8 and would justify Willehalm's lament,[1] but Wolfram never hints at such a death and the line *Aly\iota en minne in sol bewarn* does not give the impression that Wolfram intended him to die in battle.

> (c) 291, 21 der knappe dennoch vor ir stuont.
>   der vrouwen tet ir herze kuont
>   daz si niht ervuor wan lange sider.

These lines indicate a coming recognition scene between Gyburg and Rennewart, as the corresponding lines in the source (Al. 4475f) predict the recognition scene, Al. 184b, 1 – 184c, 93. In *Willehalm* we never find out what it is that Gyburg's intuition tells her. We expect Gyburg's uncertain presentiment as to Rennewart's identity to be proved beyond doubt, even if recognition were to be delayed until after Rennewart's death. The critics who consider *Willehalm* complete have not explained this apparent omission.

> (d) 331, 13 Rennewart sprach zem markîs
>   'hêrre, mac mîn hant dâ prîs
>   an den Sarrazîn bejagn,
>   den lôn wil ich von iu tragn;
>   und einen solt den ich noch hil:
>   mir ist halt gedanke dar ze vil.
>   nemt ir mich von herzesêre,
>   daz mac iu füegen êre.'

These lines, though not strictly a prediction, can only be significant if they refer to a desire which will later be expressed clearly and fulfilled. Since Rennewart is secretly *Aly\iota en soldier* (418, 15), we may safely assume that the secret reward he here refers to is Alyze's hand in marriage, which in *Aliscans* he does thus win.

> (e) 420, 22 ez wart ouch Rennewarte sider
>   ein ors, hiez Lignmaredî.

This Lignmaredi appears to be the horse Li Margaris which is given to Rainouart at his investiture, Al. 8027–38. Mergell

---

[1] Rolin, p. xxvi; cf. Vogt, *Geschichte der mittelhochdeutschen Literatur*, 3rd ed., Berlin and Leipzig 1922, p. 301; Mergell, p. 177f. We need not consider the extraordinary suggestion of Weber ('Die Grundidee', p. 5) that Rennewart is killed by his own men; for this there is not a shred of evidence and it would be in blatant contradiction to the source.

(pp. 86–8 and vol. II, *Parzival*, p. 357f) argues that the word *sider* might refer to the past and that Willehalm would not give Rennewart 'ein versprengtes und offenbar verwundetes (412, 24ff) Schlachtross' but mentions the horse here because the investiture scene, where it appears in *Aliscans*, was not to be included in *Willehalm*. Each part of the argument is unconvincing. Mergell's idea that the capture of Lignmaredi takes place but is not narrated ('eine im einzelnen nicht ausgeführte Kampfszene... die aber aus der vorhergehenden Entwicklung mit Leichtigkeit erschlossen werden kann', p. 86) has naturally met with scepticism, since the episode occurs neither in Wolfram's account of the battle nor its source, and a scholar should not base his argument on a scene he has himself supplied. It is doubtful whether the horse has been wounded at all;[1] in any case, a minor wound does not much affect a horse's value,[2] and a horse that has been captured is perfectly respectable (thus Willehalm's horse, Volatin, was captured from Arofel). There is no textual support for Mergell's quite arbitrary notion (p. 87) that Rennewart has captured the horse and lost it again by 420, 22f,[3] and Wolff and Ranke had no difficulty in showing that *sider* must here refer to the future.[4] We have noted Wolfram's practice of introducing a brief reference

---

[1] The relevant lines are 412, 24ff: *dâ was im durch daz tehtier/dez houbetstiudel ab geslagen:/ez mohte des zoumes niht getragen./des wart er umbe gewant/von des schêtîses hant,/daz er den rücke kêrte/dem der in sterben lêrte*. The meaning of *houbetstiudel* is not certain, but Lexer suggests it is a kind of *gugerel* (vol. I, col. 1354, under *houbetstiudel*), i.e. 'Kopfschmuck eines Pferdes, vielleicht eine Art Federbusch' (*ibid*, col. 1114, under *gugerel*). The passage suggests that the *houbetstiudel* was attached to the bridle straps. Heimrich der Schetis cuts through the horse's *tehtier* (a piece of head armour, see Schultz, vol. 2, p. 103f), so that the *houbetstiudel* falls, bringing the bridle with it. Poydwiz loses control of the horse because the reins are no longer secured, and so Heimrich can turn the horse and kill him, but the horse is not necessarily wounded at all.

[2] Willehalm attempts to save Puzzat despite far more serious injuries, 82, 9–14; 88, 22f.

[3] If anyone has captured the horse it is most likely to be Heimrich der Schetis (cf. 412, 22ff), but it is running free later (420, 24f: *daz lief mit lærem satel bî/dem künege Oukîne*), perhaps because the reins are severed.

[4] Wolff (review of Mergell), AfdA 56 (1937), p. 32; Ranke (review of Mergell on *Parzival*), AfdA 64 (1948), p. 26. In fact the problematic word is not *sider* but *wart*; Mergell's reading is possible if *wart* is read as a pluperfect (thus in Kartschoke's very free rendering: 'Auch Rennewart hatte kurz darauf ein Pferd...erbeutet'), but since this *wart* occurs among other verbs in the simple past, Wolfram's normal narrative tense, we cannot legitimately assume it is meant as a pluperfect; *wart* is modified only by *sider*, which gives it a forward, not a backward reference.

in anticipation of an important coming scene (pp. 8off), and this mention of Lignmaredi appears to be such an anticipation of the important investiture scene; it therefore indicates that the scene will be included, not omitted.

The key to the problem of the end of *Willehalm* is the uncompleted Rennewart action: this is fully recognised by most recent scholars.[1] It was also recognised by Wolfram's contemporaries, hence the need for Ulrich von Türheim's *Rennewart*, undertaken to 'complete' Wolfram's work as the same poet's *Tristan* 'completed' Gottfried's fragment. Türheim's introduction shows his awareness that the completeness of the Rennewart action is the epic's most urgent need:

> *Rennewart* 176   dem markîse tet vil wê
> dô er Rennewartes vermiste
> und nit die wârheit wiste
> ob er was lebendic oder tôt.

The history of Rennewart has ended with neither his vindication nor his death, but simply no news about him, but he has become far too important to be forgotten so easily. The battle with Poydjus, which plays such an important part in *Aliscans* (Al. 6857–7254), has been motivated (see p. 234) but has not taken place. Rennewart's development towards true chivalry is incomplete: he has learnt to use the sword instead of the club, and he has been promised a horse, but he has not become a knight. His constant striving after *êre* and *werdekeit* has raised him to leadership of a great army and a very high place in Willehalm's respect, but he has not received recognition of his true rank and the general respect for which he had hoped. His efforts to become worthy of Alyze have not led to her reappearance, her recognition of his deeds and the supreme glory of marriage to the highest Christian lady. Gyburg's and Willehalm's growing awareness of Rennewart's true rank and identity has not become explicit in a recognition scene such as seems to be predicted at 291, 1–3. The religious

---

[1] De Boor, p. 116; Bumke, p. 40; Johnson, p. 371; Werner Schröder, Euph 55 (1961), p. 92; Vogt, p. 301f; Wolff, p. 519.

development, which began with Rennewart's willingness to trust in the Christian God and led to God's acceptance of that trust and his employment of Rennewart for a divine purpose, is incomplete without Rennewart's willing acceptance of Christian baptism. The Rennewart action thus provides proof by itself that *Willehalm* is a fragment; no complete court epic could leave such important motifs unresolved.

A theory advanced by Bernhardt and Leitzmann and developed by Bumke sets out to reconcile the apparent finality of the Matribleiz scene with the incompleteness of the Rennewart action: the Matribleiz scene is a *Notdach*, a makeshift conclusion introduced because *Willehalm* could not be finished according to the original plan.[1] Such a change of plan might be motivated by the poet's awareness of his approaching death, by loss of interest in his poem or by inability to follow the source to its end. The strongest evidence for a *Notdach* is the absence of the Matribleiz scene from the continuations in *Aliscans* and in Türheim's *Rennewart*.[2]

The weakness of the *Notdach* theory is the inadequacy of the last lines of *Willehalm* as a conclusion. We do not expect a specially invented conclusion to end on the eighth line of a 30-line block; we expect, if not an epilogue, at least some general remarks referring to the main themes of the whole poem and a word of gratitude to the patron. The Matribleiz scene brings the Rennewart action no nearer to a conclusion, ties up none of the loose ends and fulfils none of the predictions. If we forget Rennewart, as Bumke suggests (p. 54), then there are not many riddles

[1] Bernhardt, p. 40; A. Leitzmann, 'Untersuchungen über Wolframs Titurel', PBB 26 (1901), p. 150f; cf. Bumke, pp. 34–55; M. Richey, 'Wolfram von Eschenbach and the Paradox of the Chivalrous Life', *German Studies Presented to Leonard Ashley Willoughby*, Oxford 1952, p. 170: 'Though more remained to tell, it may well be that Wolfram himself recognised the poetic fitness of such an ending, and, regardless of what posterity might think, chose to carry the tale no further.' The term *Notdach* is taken from Bernhardt's image of a Gothic cathedral which could not be completed and was given an improvised flat roof ('ein flaches Notdach') instead of the fine spire that had originally been planned.

[2] There is something similar in *Storie Nerbonesi*, however, when the Saracen kings related to Rainouart are put into rich sepulchres in his honour. Singer (p. 126) suggests that Matribleiz has taken the place of Baudins, who in the corresponding part of *Aliscans* (immediately after the plundering of the Saracen camp) is freely allowed to return to his own country.

left unsolved, but it is not easy to forget an action that has lately been so very important. A *Notdach* invented for the purpose might easily have indicated what has happened to Rennewart, what kind of peace is to be made with the Saracens and how the prisoners can be exchanged.[1] A *Notdach* would be a definite conclusion, if an unsatisfactory one; but the problem with *Willehalm* is not that the conclusion is unsatisfactory, but that there is no sign of a conclusion at all. It is scarcely possible that Wolfram imagined the Matribleiz scene would do as a conclusion, even as an emergency conclusion, to a work of the dimensions and the seriousness of his *Willehalm*, and Türheim in his introduction shows that contemporaries certainly did not consider *Willehalm* completed. *Willehalm* is a fragment, and it is unlikely that the Matribleiz scene was ever meant to disguise that fact; that scene cannot be an improvisation if Gyburg's early praise of Matribleiz and Terramer's proposal that he should supervise a similar peace settlement after the first battle (257, 1–10, independent of *Aliscans*) were introduced in preparation for his important rôle later (cf. p. 80). But however we view the *Notdach* theory, the important fact that the epic was never completed as Wolfram planned it compels us to consider such problems as why it remained a fragment and how Wolfram originally had intended to complete it.

Wolfram's failure to finish *Willehalm* is usually explained in one of three ways:

(*a*) Wolfram died before it could be finished.

(*b*) Wolfram's patron died before it could be finished.

(*c*) Wolfram found the continuation offered by his source unacceptable.

The first of these hypotheses presupposes that Book IX of *Willehalm* must be later than *Titurel* or contemporary with it; this is quite feasible, though the relative dating of *Titurel* and *Willehalm* is a very complicated problem.[2] Wolfram's awareness of approaching

---

[1] Cf. K. Helm, 'Die Entstehungszeit von Wolframs Titurel', ZfdP 35 (1903), p. 198.

[2] For the dating of *Titurel* see: Helm, *op. cit.*; Wolff, 'Wolframs Schionatulander und Sigune', *Festschrift für Friedrich Panzer*, Heidelberg 1950, p. 117; Richey, 'The "Titurel" of Wolfram von Eschenbach', MLR 56 (1961), p. 93. Barbara Könneker,

death would fit in well with his hint at the end of Book VIII that he would agree to someone else taking on his work (402, 28–30); it is possible, however, to interpret that remark quite differently.[1] Bernhardt quotes as evidence that Wolfram's death interrupted his work the lines from Türheim's continuation:

Rennewart 21711   Hey, künsterîcher Wolfram!
                    daz nit dem sûzen got gezam,
                    do er nit langer solte leben,
                    daz mir wær sin kunst gegeben,
                    sô wær ich âne angest gar.

But since these lines express only Türheim's wish that he had inherited Wolfram's skill, they prove only that Wolfram was dead when Türheim wrote them, a fact which is beyond doubt.[2] Türheim writes elsewhere:

Rennewart 160   ich von Türheim Ůlrîch
                  mit vorhten mich dar binde
                  daz ich mich underwinde
                  dar er gestecket hât sîn zil.
                  dar umme ich doch nit lâzen wil,
                  es enwerde volle tihtet.
                  er hât uns dar berihtet
                  (daz ist gnugen wol bekant)
                  'sus rûmt er Provenzâlen lant.'

Rennewart 10255   swer hât daz vorder leit[3] gelesen
                    diss bûches, der müste wesen
                    in clage, als er ez gelas.
                    als sîn danne niht mêre was,
                    so begunde er sprechen: 'âwê!
                    daz er uns niht des bûches mê

'Die Stellung der Titurelfragmente im Gesamtwerk Wolframs von Eschenbach', *Literaturwissenschaftliches Jahrbuch* 6 (1965), pp. 23–35, assumes *Titurel* is later than *Willehalm* but does not argue the case at all.

[1] Helm, p. 197, considers that the line '*deste holder ich dem wære*' (402, 30) implies that Wolfram foresaw completion in his lifetime. Mergell, p. 80, says the lines are not to be taken seriously. Wolfram may have wished to draw attention to the fact that nobody could pick up his threads at the end of Book VIII, where the action has become very complicated; in this case it is a proud challenge from a man who feels himself at the height of his powers.

[2] *Rennewart* 21720: *ich von Türheim Ůlrîch/wölte niht er sîn gewesen./er ist tôt und ich genesen.*

[3] For *leit* read *teil*.

in tütsche hât gesprochen!
er hât ez abe gebrochen
da ez was aller beste.'

The words *gestecket hât sîn ʒil, uns* [=*unʒ*] *dar*, and *er hât eʒ abe gebrochen* seem to suggest that Wolfram freely laid the work aside, and so Türheim's testimony, which is all we have to go on, does not favour the hypothesis of Wolfram's death before *Willehalm* could be completed.[1] The evidence is far too scant and ambiguous, however, to allow a clear conclusion and so we must reckon with the possibility of Wolfram's death.

The theory that Wolfram had difficulty in continuing his poem after the death of his patron, Landgraf Hermann of Thuringia,[2] who died on 25 April 1217, is made particularly attractive by references to Hermann at 417, 22–6 and *Titurel* 61, 1M, which imply that he is dead.[3] Schreiber elaborates this possibility, arguing that Hermann's death is the reason for Wolfram's desire to be relieved of the work at the end of Book VIII and that Book IX was written when a new patron was found, William of Baux, who as governor of the Arelate had a particular interest in *Willehalm*. The death of William of Baux in 1219 caused Wolfram to abandon the work completely.

---

[1] Cf. Richey, p. 170: '*er hât eʒ abe gebrochen*: those words indicate plainly, that Wolfram, whatever his reason, left off where he did of his own free will.'

[2] Wh. 3, 8f: *lantgráf von Dürngen Herman/tet mir diʒ mær von im bekant.* Cf. Reinbot's *Georg* (ed. Kraus, 1907) 34–43: *von Dürngen lantgráf Herman/in franʒois geschriben vant/ daʒ er in tiutsche tet bekant/von Wilhalm von Naribôn./des hât er hiut ʒe himel lôn./er was des buoches urhap,/wan er die matêrje gap/hêrn Wolfram von Eschenbach:/daʒ er von Wilhalme sprach,/daʒ ist vom lantgráven komen.*

[3] Tit. 61, 1M: Si müezen in erkennen: er mac et niht veralten.
  von Dürngen der genende,   Herman pflac êrn, der wunsches prîs kund walten:
  swâ man hœrt von sînen gnôsen sprechen,
  die vor im hin gescheiden sint,   wie kund sîn lop für die sô verre brechen!
Leitzmann, PBB 26 (1901), pp. 103, 146, has shown that this verse is genuine and quotes further literature. Cf. Wh. 417, 22ff: *lantgráf von Dürngen Herman/het in ouch lîhte ein ors gegebn./daʒ kunder wol al sîn lebn/halt an sô grôʒem strîte,/swâ der gernde kom beʒîte.* Palgen, p. 241, argues that these lines do not imply Hermann's death since *al sîn lebn* might refer to the present (cf. 'ich habe mein Leben nichts so schönes gesehen'), and one would expect a more elaborate obituary for so famous a patron (cf. Singer, p. 7; Ehrismann, p. 271, note 4). This is countered by Bumke, p. 184, note 15, who does not regard the lines as an obituary. Furthermore, the use of the preterite tense (*kunder*) indicates that *al sîn lebn* must refer to the past.

Bumke believes that most of *Willehalm* was written after Hermann's death for his son, Ludwig der Heilige, since its Franciscan piety and the concept of a Christian Empire agree better with the mood at the Wartburg under Ludwig, who consistently supported Frederick II and the Empire, than in the time of his more worldly father. Frederick II's planned crusade, in which Ludwig vowed to participate, would be a good motive for stylising the battle at Alischanz as a crusade, and Gyburg may be modelled on Ludwig's wife, Saint Elisabeth. In this case most of *Willehalm* was composed during Ludwig's reign, i.e. after 1217. This view has received some support,[1] but its opponents have shown that Ludwig was no less worldly than his father and owes his reputation largely to his wife and to his death on the crusade of 1227.[2] Even Hermann, for all his worldliness, commissioned *Willehalm* and founded the Katharinenkloster at Eisenach for the good of his soul and the souls of his father and brother, and there are religious works among those executed under his patronage; a contrast between the religious piety of father and son cannot have been marked in Wolfram's time.[3] The possibility of Ludwig's joining Frederick II's crusade was not discussed until 1221 and no decision was made until 1224 (Wentzlaff-Eggebert, p. 247); since *Willehalm* was begun under Hermann, it is impossible to derive the crusading motif from events that occurred so late. Elisabeth derived her holiness mainly from events which occurred much later[4] and she was only ten years old

---

[1] Johnson, p. 372; Walshe, p. 175; Wentzlaff-Eggebert, p. 247, accepts Bumke's dating but does not believe that Elisabeth was the model for Gyburg.

[2] Werner Schröder, Euph 55 (1961), p. 97.

[3] Cf. J. Mendels and L. Spuler, 'Landgraf Hermann von Thüringen und seine Dichterschule', DVJS 33 (1959), p. 372. They regard Wolfram's remark about Otto IV, which occurs late in *Willehalm* (340, 4–11), as typical of Hermann, p. 376, and they compare Rennewart's appearing for a meal in battle harness to the practice of Hermann and his father, Ludwig der Eiserne, p. 374.

[4] For example, her association with the Franciscans after 1225, her munificence to the people during the famine and plague of 1226 while Ludwig was away, her refusal to marry again when Ludwig died in 1227 and her gift of five hundred marks to the poor that year, her endowment of a hospital at Marburg in 1228 and her admission to the Franciscan order, her early death in 1231 and the miracles that occurred at her grave, leading to her canonisation in 1235. See *Catholic Encyclopaedia* under *Elizabeth of Hungary*.

in 1217, when at least the first book of *Willehalm* had been written; it is therefore extremely unlikely that she influenced the portrait of Gyburg, a mature woman in Book I, or contributed anything significant to the religious atmosphere of Wolfram's book. The *religiöse Laienbewegung* was widely active before Ludwig's reign, and a change of government would not be necessary to bring its ideas to Wolfram.[1] Hermann is mentioned twice in *Willehalm* and once in *Titurel*; Ludwig is never mentioned. Ludwig was not a great patron of the arts like his father, as Bumke himself recognises;[2] it is not likely that a man uninterested in the arts would be sufficiently discriminating in his taste and interests to have made an exception in the case of one particular poet and given his poem the support it wanted. Ludwig's meanness as a patron might explain both Wolfram's threat to abandon the work altogether at the end of Book VIII and the praise of Hermann's generosity in Book IX, which may imply a contrast with the new Landgraf.[3] For these reasons it seems extremely unlikely that Wolfram enjoyed the patronage of Hermann's successor, and the death of Landgraf Hermann in 1217 with the consequent withdrawal of patronage from Wolfram may well be the reason why his poem was not completed; it is also tempting to follow Schreiber in attributing Book IX, which seems to have been written after a pause, to the generosity of William of Baux.[4]

---

[1] Werner Schröder, Euph 55 (1961), p. 96.

[2] Bumke, p. 185; cf. Schreiber, p. 155; Leitzmann, p. 151. Of the works on patronage, Linzel, 'Die Mäzene...' does not mention Ludwig at all, and Mendels and Spuler think it very unlikely that Wolfram, or Hermann's other great poets, received any support from Ludwig, cf. p. 388: 'Mit dem Landgrafen Hermann starb auch die blühende Dichterschule von Thüringen.'

[3] It would be odd for Wolfram to praise the Landgraf's predecessor without ever mentioning Ludwig himself, particularly if Ludwig was now Wolfram's patron, unless relations between them were sadly strained. There also seems to be a veiled expression of resentment against Ludwig in the strange remark, which seems uncalled for in its context (how the fallen kings are mourned for after the battle), that if Wolfram himself had a bad lord and were to accompany him into battle it would be hypocrisy for the poet to lament over that lord's death (445, 24ff). The *Titurel* verse quoted above (p. 221, note 3), which rather emphatically makes the point that Hermann was able to outshine his predecessors, may be significant as a hint that Ludwig cannot.

[4] Mendels and Spuler (p. 376) agree that Wolfram enjoyed the favour of William of Baux and gave Willehalm the device of Baux (a golden star on a blue field) as a compliment to him. As regards the genesis of *Willehalm*, a more attractive theory than Bumke's

The view that *Willehalm* was not completed because Wolfram could not accept the conclusion of the Rainouart action which he found in *Aliscans* is favoured particularly by Bumke,[1] despite the large measure of freedom which he generally attributes to Wolfram in his treatment of his source. Walshe emphasises the dangers of speculation on this issue but suggests that Rennewart's baptism and marriage might trivialise the serious main action and the theme of holy war might clash with Wolfram's own belief in God's love for all his creatures: 'it seems not unlikely that Wolfram's lofty mind had inwardly transcended his theme'.[2] Bumke argues that the continuation of the Rennewart action would destroy the poem's balance: after the battle Rennewart has made his full contribution to the main action and is no longer required;[3] to follow the source further would be damaging to Willehalm. In the source Guillaume forgets Rainouart and celebrates victory without him; Rainouart in great anger kills some of the French knights who are sent to placate him, rejects Christianity and swears to conquer Orange for the Saracens, and he will not make peace until he has thoroughly humiliated Guillaume. Wolfram is not able to motivate such events, in Bumke's view, because he has made the main characters more noble and their behaviour after

was proposed by Singer, pp. 4ff, who links the epic with Frederick II's visit to Hermann in January 1215. Hermann had led the rebellion against Otto and did not feel adequately rewarded by the new emperor, who came to the Wartburg to appease him. It is likely that Frederick discussed his plan to go on the Crusade, which became official a few months later, and which Hermann must have supported both as an old crusader himself and because it was to his political advantage to have the emperor away. At such a time it would suit Hermann's interest to have a public reading of *Aliscans*, where a strong, faithful vassal urges an emperor to join the holy war, and Wolfram (Wh. 7, 23ff) seems to refer to *Aliscans* as a poem his audience have already heard. Since Hermann could not identify himself with so rough a hero as Guillaume or accept such a humiliating portrait of the emperor, he set Wolfram to adapt the tale for a more courtly society. Though not entirely satisfactory (e.g. Wolfram's Loys and Willehalm do not much resemble Frederick II and Hermann), the dating this requires is much more likely than that proposed by Bumke, and it is possible that Hermann's original motive was soon forgotten when Wolfram began the work.

[1] Bumke, p. 41; cf. W. J. Schröder, p. 177.

[2] Walshe, p. 174. Cf. *ibid*: 'It is conceivable that Wolfram found it impossible to discover a satisfying solution to the problems posed, though he had been equal to the task of concluding *Parzival*.'

[3] Bumke, p. 45: 'Er könnte hier für immer abtreten, denn er wird fortan nicht mehr gebraucht.' Cf. Clarus, p. 346.

the battle would contradict his characterisation of them. Bumke (pp. 46ff) illustrates in detail Wolfram's inability to follow the source in Book IX. Wolfram has motivated Rennewart's battle against Poydjus by having Tedalun, a vassal to Poydjus and his standard-bearer, kill Gandaluz, one of Rennewart's men, but realising that he will not be able to accept Poydjus' conversion to Christianity by force, as told by the source, Wolfram then avoids the battle and has Poydjus escape, ignoring Rennewart's challenge. He has brought Rennewart and Terramer face to face and is reminded of Hildebrand, but he then compares Terramer instead to *Hildebrants vrouw Uote* and says no more of the encounter; the reference to Hildebrand shows that Wolfram had intended to narrate the battle, but he had suddenly changed his mind:

> Wolfram vertraute seiner Quelle, liess Rennewart sich Terramer auf Sichtweite nähern und bog plötzlich ab. Sollte ihm auf einmal bewusst geworden sein, dass er seine eigene Konzeption durchkreuzte, wenn er jetzt der Quelle folgte? Jedenfalls ist er an dieser Stelle gründlich zurückgeschreckt und hat gleich mehr als 40 Laissen übersprungen.[1]

Wolfram could not let Rennewart die at his father's hands and thus be rid of him because he had led the audience to expect him to marry Alyze and earn glory, and so he introduces the possibility of his having been taken prisoner, but this will not solve his problem convincingly because Rennewart was free after the battle was over and Terramer would not be able to return his own son to Willehalm in an exchange of prisoners. His predictive references to the later part of the Rennewart action have committed him to following the source, and so he breaks off just before Rennewart's quarrel with Willehalm, where the source could no longer be followed.

The weakness of Bumke's explanation is its implication that Wolfram *suddenly* found the poem unfinishable ('plötzlich...auf einmal...an dieser Stelle gründlich zurückgeschreckt'). Wolfram

---

[1] Bumke, p. 46. Cf. Singer, p. 124: 'Aber diese Art, den Wagen plötzlich auf ein totes Geleise zu schieben, lässt sich kaum anders als aus Improvisation erklären. Der Dichter ist eben im Begriff, den Zweikampf zu schildern; auf einmal kommt ihm in den Sinn, "ich will es lieber doch nicht tun", und er ändert mit blitzschneller Wendung Vers und Reim, auf die Gefahr hin sogar, etwas Unsinniges oder Plattes zu sagen.'

certainly knew the end of *Aliscans* before he started work on the beginning; if, in Book IX, he found his plan unfinishable, then the plan was faulty from the start.[1] Wolfram never follows his source slavishly, but plans for coming events well ahead and reorganises his material (cf. pp. 77ff), and so he could scarcely fail to see a difficulty before reaching it.[2] The predictions which commit him to following his source have been introduced by Wolfram himself, independently of *Aliscans*.[3] The horse Lignmaredi is not mentioned until 420, 23 (well into Book IX), and at 418, 15 we are reminded that Rennewart is *Alyzen soldier*. Neither of these lines is essential and both are independent of *Aliscans*; they clearly indicate that Wolfram had not considered abandoning his plan for the Rennewart action in the early part of Book IX, and he could hardly begin so confidently if he had not planned ahead, at least as far as the end of the book. Particularly strange is Bumke's notion that the mention of Hildebrand, with its suggestion of a father–son duel, was *suddenly* twisted into an image of patient waiting. There is plenty of evidence that Wolfram planned more than half a line ahead, in which case Uote was introduced deliberately. The image may appear bizarre, but we know that Wolfram is fond of bizarre images and not above a joke at the expense of his audience;[4] it is simpler to catalogue this one with the others than to invent a special hypothesis for it. Wolfram's possible difficulties in following the source at the end of Book IX seem to have been greatly exaggerated. *Willehalm* is a very different poem from *Aliscans*; Wolfram has had to alter important matters, such as characterisation and motivation, throughout the work, and to judge by the predictions he foresaw no particular difficulties with Book IX while he was working on it. Had the epic broken off at

---

[1] Cf. Meissburger, p. 312.

[2] Johnson, p. 372.

[3] Cf. Werner Schröder, Euph 55 (1961), p. 93.

[4] He lets his audience expect a moving comparison to the tragic Hildebrand only to disillusion them by comparing Terramer with Uote. There are similar examples of this kind of humour, e.g. in his description of Belakane, Parz. 24, 6f: *ist iht liehters denne der tac,/dem glichet niht diu künegîn*; cf. also Parz. 238, 8ff; 397, 7f; Wh. 208, 28ff. The twist from the expected tragic comparison to bizarre humour at the expense of the audience favours the view that the outcome of the encounter will not be tragic.

any other point, the motivation of the next events might have seemed equally difficult to modern critics looking at the continuation in the source. It is easy to imagine how scholars might have demonstrated the impossibility of following the source further if Wolfram's poem had broken off in Books VII or VIII, where the battle narrative had to be completely reorganised and so many *laisses*, including the fantastic deeds of Rainouart in the second battle, seem to have been omitted, or in Book VI just before Rainouart roasts Guillaume's cook over his own fire, or in Book III, before Guillaume attacks his sister and calls her Tiebaut's whore, or in Book II before the killing of Aerofles. Since Wolfram has motivated both Willehalm's victory feast without Rennewart and Rennewart's battle against Poydjus in Book IX shortly before the epic breaks off, it seems that Wolfram himself did not feel unable to cope with his source.

Of these several possibilities, the most likely explanations of Wolfram's failure to complete *Willehalm* are the death of his patron just before Book VIII was finished (in which case we might see *Titurel* as the expression of his new freedom to try out a new poetic experiment of his own choosing) or the rather less attractive possibility that Wolfram himself fell ill and died before he could finish his task. In either case Wolfram must have had plans for the whole of *Willehalm*, and so we must consider how he intended the epic to finish. There has been considerable speculation on this point – even the unwritten tenth book has been supplied[1] – for a picture of the end of the epic, although it is incomplete and uncertain, may help us interpret the work as a whole.

THE CONTINUATION OF THE RENNEWART ACTION

Although a number of scholars have believed that Rennewart was never to be mentioned again,[2] we have seen that the predictions, which continue in Book IX, rule out the possibility of Wolfram's having intended to abandon the Rennewart action shortly before

---

[1] Bernhardt, p. 39f; Wolff, p. 521f.
[2] Clarus, p. 347; San-Marte, p. 126f; Rolin, p. x; Bumke, p. 53f; K. Borck, *Archiv* 198 (1962), p. 263.

its climax. Others have argued that Rennewart's history was
to finish with his death in battle: in this way he could be
honourably dropped without being forgotten.[1] The account
of his glorious deeds in that battle might then be regarded
as his aristeia. The main evidence for this view is Wolfram's
description of his tale as a *klage*:

> 4, 25   gan mir got sô vil der tage
> sô sage ich mîne und ander klage
> der mit triuwen pflac wîp und man
> sît Jêsus in den Jordân
> durch toufe wart gestôzen.

Ehrismann concludes: 'mit *klage* bezeichnet Wolfram selbst den
inhalt seines werkes 4, 26'.[2] De Boor explains that *Willehalm* is
necessarily a 'Klage' because the hostility between Christians and
heathens is unalterable and must always cause suffering.[3] Schwietering believes that the 'Endgipfel' must be tragic.[4] Mergell
(p. 177) finds the same view confirmed by Willehalm's lament for
Rennewart, after which he must be dead. More recently, Werner
Schröder, using Schanze's dissertation on the manuscript tradition,[5] has amended Lachmann's edition of the line to read '*sô sage
ich minne und ander klage*';[6] the word *minne*, which Wolfram uses
elsewhere to refer to the suffering that love causes (e.g. 163, 9:
minne und ander nôt), strengthens the effect of *klage* and makes its
reference more general: it points not specifically to a tragic end
but rather to all the suffering caused by the clash of religions,
which is present as a major theme throughout the work. As he
had announced in the Prologue to *Parzival* a tale of great *triuwe*,

[1] Meissburger, p. 111, note 5, notes that Willehalm's lament and Bernart's speech show
that Rennewart is not forgotten. Mergell interprets Gyburg's words 272, 24f: '*mir sol
freude odr ungemach/vil schier von sîner kumft geschehen.*' thus: 'Will Wolfram bereits
hier den tragischen Ausgang der Rennewarthandlung andeuten?' (p. 52).

[2] Ehrismann, 'Über Wolframs Ethik', ZfdA 49 (1908), p. 462.

[3] De Boor, p. 121; cf. Ehrismann, p. 285.

[4] Schwietering, p. 173. Schwietering does not insist, however, that the tragic ending
must be Rennewart's death, cf. p. 179: 'Der grösste Schmerz, den der Sieg in seinem
[Willehalm's] Herzen zu einer Niederlage macht, ist sein "Freund" Rennewart, der
nicht unter den Toten gefunden, vielleicht als Gefangener fortgeschleppt wurde.'

[5] H. Schanze, *Die Überlieferung von Wolframs Willehalm*, Munich 1966.

[6] W. Schröder, 'Minne und ander klage', ZfdA 93 (1964), pp. 300–13.

describing the whole work rather than merely its ending, so here in the Prologue to *Willehalm* he promises a tale of love and grief. As early as 1923 Wallner had understood the word *klage* in this line not as 'lament' but as an expression of deeply felt grief and sympathy for the sufferings of others;[1] Schröder's revision of the line makes such an interpretation far more probable. There is plenty of *klage* in this sense in *Willehalm*: the death of so many noble men and the consequent grief of many ladies, the grief that overwhelms Willehalm in the hour of victory no less than in defeat, and the grief that surely must come when Rennewart learns how completely unfounded his fatal resentment against his nearest relations has been, how his uncle Arofel was killed, and how he has killed his own brother, thus realising the tragic potential of Willehalm's encounter with Arnalt or of Parzival's with Feirefiz.[2] Of the main characters, only Rennewart appears unaware that the conflict is tragic and unmoved by the plight of the heathens; he cannot remain so foolish and unsympathetic when he learns the truth and knows his kinsmen better. We know that Rennewart is sensitive and capable of deep emotion; the moment when he fully understands what he has done must surely be more painful for him than all his past humiliations. Mohr (p. 208) has remarked that whereas the heroes of courtly romances are generally glad of a fight and see no tragic possibilities (at least until afterwards), the warriors in *Willehalm*, like those of heroic literature, fight reluctantly because they must, and they are always fully aware of the grim reality of their situation. It is this realistic grasp of the battle's tragic implications, coupled with the sad but brave acceptance of the duty to fight, that gives this epic its tragic tone, which is akin to that of the *Nibelungenlied*. Thus understood, *klage* is always present in *Willehalm*, and Rennewart, too, must become aware of it when his *tumpheit* is overcome and his vision clear. But this *klage* does not depress or inhibit the characters; it is a sorrow with a positive

---

[1] A. Wallner, 'Der Eingang des Willehalm', PBB 47 (1923), pp. 221–5.
[2] This comparison is particularly close because Kanliun, like Feirefiz, is an elder brother by the father's first wife (358, 16f).

quality which functions constantly as a stimulus to the action.[1] And there is not only sorrow in *Willehalm*: there is joy as well, and the joy is not less important than the sorrow. Wolfram states centrally and with emphasis his conviction that joy and sorrow are involved in each other (280, 13 – 281, 16), and against the ever-present grief may be set the *vröude* which Willehalm and Gyburg derive from their *minne* and the *vröude* of the banquets at Munleun and Orange, not to mention the coming celebration of victory. Life always gives joy together with sorrow (cf. Parz. 103, 24f: *alsus vert diu mennescheit,/hiute freude, morgen leit*). The reference to *klage* in the Prologue seems to be balanced by 12, 1: *etswenne ouch hôhes muotes tac/mit freuden künfte sît erschein*; taken together these early predictions of *klage* and *vröude* refer to the inter-dependent joy and grief which is present everywhere in the epic, and the word *klage* in the Prologue does not indicate Rennewart's death at the end any more than the word *vröude* refers specifically to his glory. His death is not required as an 'Endgipfel'; indeed, Wolfram would have failed to subordinate the Rennewart action if the epic ended with his death rather than with Willehalm and Gyburg.[2] If the events are leading up to a climax, then we should expect the second battle to be significantly different from the first, bringing us nearer that climax, not a copy of the earlier battle with Rennewart's death parallel to that of Vivianz. The argument that Rennewart must be dead because Willehalm laments for him is particularly weak because Willehalm himself is tormented precisely by his uncertainty; one might as well argue that Erec must be dead after Enite's lament. Had Rennewart's death been intended, we might expect his father to be the Saracen best able to defeat him and death at his father's hands to be the most

---

[1] Cf. Schwietering, p. 175: 'ein *genendeclîchez klagen*, ein *klagen mit ekken* (Schwertern), eine Trauer, die nicht lähmt und verzweifelt, sondern im Vertrauen auf Gottes Hilfe zu weiteren ritterlichen Taten antreibt.' Cf. Maurer, p. 168: 'Nicht nur eine "Klage" würde ich das Werk nennen; sein Thema ist das Leid in der Welt, aber auch die Überwindung dieses Leides.'

[2] A more fitting conclusion is offered by a scene in the very last part of *Aliscans*, when Rainouart's marriage and investiture are over and Guillaume's kinsmen and Baudins have gone away. Guillaume and Guibourc survey the ruins of their home and Guibourc urges him to rebuild at once. Her last words, 'Refai Orenge!',. give noble expression to her indomitable spirit.

moving and appropriate of the possible tragic ends for him. Wolfram is evasive about the battle between Rennewart and Terramer, but its outcome appears to be that Terramer is injured, certainly by Willehalm and perhaps also by his son, but he is rescued, thanks to Kanliun's intervention, and carried to his ship (443, 3–15). This is followed by the general flight of the Saracens (443, 21ff). Rennewart's battle with Tedalun (444, 22–5) and his inconsequential encounter with Poydjus (444, 28ff) are later than this, and he is mentioned alive once again shortly afterwards (445, 1–5); he is not found among the dead when the Christians search the battlefield later (446, 10ff). No injury to Rennewart is mentioned, either by Wolfram or the source, and when he meets Poydjus, who had been left behind when Terramer escaped (see p. 91), we know that Rennewart has not been killed by his father.[1] When Poydjus flees from him there is no other Saracen left who might conceivably kill him: Rennewart is alive with the battle over and the enemy gone.

The alternative possibility that Rennewart has been taken prisoner is suggested by Bernart von Brubant:

> 458, 22 waz ob uns ûf dem nâhjagt
> Rennwart ist ab gevangen?
> ist ez im sus ergangen,
> da engegen hab wir gæbez pfant.
> gevangen ist in Larkant
> der künec von Skandinâvîâ...
> gein dem wirt Rennewart wol quît.

Several scholars have argued that Terramer will be bound by chivalric honour to answer Willehalm's gesture in releasing Matribleiz and show similar generosity in setting Rennewart free.[2] It is scarcely possible, however, that Rennewart, who was

---

[1] Harms, who assumes (p. 105) that Rennewart must have been killed by his father in retribution for his fratricidal killing of Kanliun ('Der Kampf zwischen Vater und Sohn ist Folge von des Sohnes Brudermord; der zu erschliessende Tod des Sohnes in diesem Kampf bringt die Sühne für jenen Verwandtenmord'), has ignored Rennewart's later battles with Tedalun and Poydjus. He also assumes a parallel between Willehalm's laments for Vivianz and for Rennewart, although real correspondences are hard to find (see p. 98), and draws from this assumption the conclusion that Rennewart, like Vivianz, must by this time be dead.

[2] Helm, p. 198; Wolff, p. 521; Ranke, p. 68.

still free when the Saracen leaders took to their ships, could later be taken prisoner,[1] and it is most unlikely that an enlightened Rennewart would wish to leave his family again or that Terramer would willingly surrender his own son to the Christians. When Willehalm honours Terramer through Matribleiz he states very plainly that he will not for any cause surrender Gyburg (466, 10–15; cf. the failure of Halzibier's similar plan to exchange the eight captured Christian counts for Gyburg, 47, 1–14); he must understand that Terramer will be equally firm in a similar case. Bumke (p. 51f) considers that the possibility of an exchange of prisoners has been abandoned when Willehalm sets Matribleiz free without mentioning Rennewart. Thoughts of an exchange for Rennewart certainly do not seem uppermost in his mind when he wishes Matribleiz a safe journey to Gaheviez, not to Baldac or Tenabri, where he might expect to find Terramer. It therefore seems unlikely that Rennewart has been captured or killed.[2]

In *Aliscans* the tale of Rainouart continues with his battle against Baudins (Wolfram's Poydjus von Frîende and von Griffâne), who has become the leader of those Saracens who were left behind after the general flight. Rainouart forces Baudins to become a Christian and then allows him to go to Spain to recover from his wounds, after which he returns and becomes Rainouart's companion. Several scholars believe that Wolfram has deliberately omitted all this. Rolin argues (p. x) that Wolfram did so in

---

[1] This has been observed by Werner Schröder, 'Der Markgraf und die gefallenen Heidenkönige', p. 136f.

[2] G. Weber, 'Die Grundidee in Wolframs Willehalm', interprets *Willehalm* as a tragic poem in accordance with his own view that the prevailing mood of the late courtly period was tragic, and argues 'dass Rennewart von vornherein als eine tragische Gestalt angelegt war' (p. 6). Similarly, Alyze, Gyburg, Willehalm and Terramer are tragic figures. He makes no attempt to answer the objections to this view (e.g. he does not discuss the predictions Wolfram has introduced or consider Wolfram's source) but promises to produce the evidence which will justify his view in a forthcoming book, which has not yet appeared. As it now stands, each stage of Weber's argument is open to serious objection, and it is a pity he has condemned Wolff's interpretation energetically ('gänzlich abwegig', 'vollends unhaltbar', etc., p. 4) before producing evidence that might justify his own. Weber's starting point is not a study of the text but his own assumption that *Willehalm* must, like *Tristan* and the *Nibelungenlied*, be tragic, from which it follows that the Rennewart action must end tragically, and so must the careers of the other major characters; consequently Weber is obliged to force the facts to fit a simple preconceived theory.

order to avoid resurrecting a dead man to fight again: this is what happens if one ignores M's distinction between Baudus and Baudins; only Baudus (= Poydwiz) is dead (cf. p. 53). Mergell makes the same mistake (p. 94). San-Marte believes these events were omitted because they were not to Wolfram's taste. Bumke (p. 47f) believes Wolfram had no intention of following his source here because he contradicts it when Poydjus turns and flees instead of accepting Rennewart's challenge (444, 28–30).

Bearing in mind the great courage and nobility of all the Saracens in *Willehalm*, we ought not to expect Wolfram to have brought an important Saracen king face to face with Rennewart in order to take flight and never be heard of again. This is especially unlikely in the case of Poydjus, who is far more prominent in Wolfram's poem than in *Aliscans*. Wolfram has promoted him to be leader of the fifth Saracen army (including within it the men of Tesereiz, whom Terramer bids him avenge) and introduces a description of his wealth and valour at unusually great length (375, 14 – 380, 1 !); the magnificence of Poydjus is beyond belief (e.g. 376, 19ff), and Wolfram strains his imagination for grandiose images that might convey some impression of it to a German audience. He is king over the golden Kaukasas mountains, where the streams are lined with precious stones, and his helmet is carved from an *antrax*.[1] Long before the battle, at 36, 5ff and 282, 19ff, we are told that he brings Tesereiz with him and is extremely wealthy, being king over the Kaukasas, and that he is maternal nephew (*swestersun*) to both Rennewart and Gyburg (267, 25; 282, 19). The purpose of these early references is to prepare Poydjus for the great rôle that is still to come, and they bear witness to Wolfram's careful planning as well as to the special importance of Poydjus among the Saracens. Only the very greatest Saracens have a heraldic device of any kind, and those of the other leaders are of no great significance (a ship, a chess castle, a swan); Poydjus has *ecidemôn* (379, 24ff), the device of Feirefiz. Since Rennewart has been compared with Parzival, it is tempting to see in this the promise of a parallel between Poydjus and

[1] 376, 29ff. Cf. the helmet of Gahmuret, which is an *adamas* (Parz. 53, 3–6 *et al.*).

Feirefiz, which might be brought out more fully in his coming battle with Rennewart. This battle is followed in the source by the reconciliation and friendship of Rainouart and his nephew, the baptism and marriage of Rainouart and the conversion of Baudins; these events bear a marked similarity to the conclusion of *Parzival*. Wolfram is more likely to have noted and responded to such similarities at the end of his two great poems than to have got rid of them.

The career of a man like Poydjus cannot end in flight. Willehalm has fled from the enemy to return and conquer, and Rennewart after his involuntary retreat at the start of the battle has come back at the head of an army. The tragedy of Vivianz is caused by his failure to do the same (*Vivianz ungerne vlôch*). Poydjus surely has fled to return later and become Rennewart's most formidable opponent (as he most certainly is in *Aliscans.*) Their battle is motivated when Rennewart, in vengeance for Gandaluz, Count of Schampâne (already mentioned honourably at 366, 16ff), kills Tedalun, the standard-bearer of Poydjus:

> 444, 22 daz selbe gelt hin wider bôt
> Rennwart der unverzagete
> ze fuoz snellîchen jagete,
> Tedalûnen er resluoc,
> der ime sturm manlîche truoc
> sînes swestersunes vanen.
> dô begunde er Poydjusen manen
> daz er wider kêrte an in.
> des tet er niht: daz lêrt in sin.

Poydjus, then, is *swestersun* to Tedalun as well as to Rennewart. There is always a particularly close bond between a man and his sister's son (e.g. Charlemagne and Roland, Arthur and Gawein, Guillaume and Vivien, Tedbalt de Beürges and Esturmi, Anfortas and Parzival, Trevrizent and Parzival). This is a survival of the avunculate and it is commonly associated with matrilineal kinship, whereby a man's progenitor was necessarily outside the family and his nearest male kinsman was his mother's brother. The marriage bond being loose, the bond of brother and sister was correspondingly close. The avunculate does not need to be derived from matriarchy, however, and since it is most marked in patrilineal systems of kinship anthropologists are nowadays inclined to explain it differently.[1] It is very important in the *chansons de geste*, where there is often hostility between father and son (e.g. Aymeri disowning his sons, to the embarrassment of Wolfram, 7, 16ff; Charlemagne's repudiation of Louis as his heir; Desramé arming his nephew Baudins to kill his son Rainouart), while affection is regularly shown to the nephew.[2] This bond is also important in *Willehalm*: Halzibier is *swestersun* to Terramer and Arofel, hence his staunch support for them and his command of Terramer's first army, and it may be for the same reason that Arofel can be cold-bloodedly killed to avenge a deed of Halzibier (the killing of Vivianz); Vivianz and Mile are both *swestersun* to Willehalm, hence their importance on the Christian side and the intensity of Willehalm's grief when they die.[3] Poydjus cannot leave the death of Tedalun unavenged, since they are linked by this close personal bond. Although he flees, it appears that he does not board a ship and escape.[4] Many of the Saracens fail to reach their ships and flee to the *muor* and *muntâne*, where many of them are still to be slain (436, 6). These are the very men whom Baudins in *Aliscans* defends and leads, and so it is very likely that

[1] A man's relationship to his sister's son is not one of authority, as one might expect in a matriarchy, but of special indulgence and responsibility. It may be that since senior men of the father's line had patriarchal authority over him, a man normally looked for indulgence to his closest blood relation *outside* of formal kinship. In matrilineal systems the father's sister holds a position similar to that of the mother's brother in a patriarchy. See R. Fox, *Kinship and Marriage* (Pelican, Harmondsworth 1967), p. 231.

[2] See W. O. Farnsworth, *Uncle and Nephew in the Old French Chansons de Geste. A Study in the Survival of Matriarchy*, New York 1966. The importance of the avunculate among the early Germans is mentioned by Tacitus (*Germania* 20: *sororum filiis idem apud avunculum qui apud patrem honor. quidam sanctiorem artioremque hunc nexum sanguinis arbitrantur et in accipiendis obsidibus magis exigunt, tamquam et animum firmius et domum latius teneant*).

[3] We are constantly reminded that Vivianz is Willehalm's *swestersun* (48, 5; 49, 19, 26; 60, 16; 62, 1; 65, 7, 22; 66, 21, 22; 67, 4; 69, 1; 70, 7, 29; 71, 21; 89, 3). This relationship on the Saracen side also explains why Halzibier needs to avenge Pinel (45, 30; 46, 18).

[4] The ships are defended (438, 27–30) until Terramer and a few others are safe (443, 13–19), and then they leave without waiting any longer (443, 24: *dâ wart niht langer dô gebiten*). Poydjus is still fighting after this (444, 28ff), and so he must have missed the boat.

Rennewart, who is missing, is engaged in battle with these men and Poydjus is defending them against him. We have seen that Wolfram generally avoids contradicting his source and follows it more closely than he has been given credit for in recent years. This continuation not only follows the source faithfully, but also accords well with the new nobility of the Saracens, which Wolfram has supplied, and rescues Poydjus from the charge of cowardice. In Ulrich von Türheim's continuation Baldewin (= Poydjus) does in fact return to fight with Rennewart. The battle is likely to end, as in the source, with Rennewart's victory. Although such encounters in *Willehalm* (as in *Aliscans*) usually end in death, it would not be out of character for Rennewart to spare a defeated enemy (as he has spared the Nubian guards, in contradiction to the source), particularly in the one instance where even the Rainouart of *Aliscans* had done so. Poydjus, particularly if he can be converted to Christianity, is a worthy man to be Rennewart's comrade and must be about the same age.[1] Wolfram's enthusiastic portrait of Poydjus has led us to expect great things of him; if he intended never to mention him again after his flight from Rennewart, then his action would be as incomplete as the Rennewart action and therefore unsatisfactory. The continuation which the source offers makes Wolfram's praise for Poydjus intelligible and gives his flight from Rennewart significance.

A scene of *Aliscans* which we might expect Wolfram to avoid is the quarrel between Rainouart and Guillaume. Nevertheless, he begins to motivate it. We are told at length (457, 3 – 460, 26) how Willehalm is persuaded by Bernart to conceal his extreme grief at the loss of Rennewart and how the Christian soldiers celebrate their victory with carousal (447, 1 – 449, 30). We know very well how extremely sensitive Rennewart is when he feels he is not being treated with proper respect and how he had longed to earn glory in the battle, and so we can imagine how offended he will be when he returns from his strenuous duel with Poydjus to find Willehalm and the whole army celebrating victory without

[1] He cannot be much older, since Rennewart is his uncle, but he cannot be much younger, since Rennewart himself is barely old enough to go to war.

him, apparently not caring what has become of him. Wolfram has solved the problem of motivating this embarrassing quarrel without offence to Willehalm, because Willehalm's behaviour, which in the source had been the consequence of inexcusable ingratitude, is in his poem very proper and prompted by Bernart's advice:

> 460, 18 ez ist des houbetmannes sin,
> daz er genendeclîche lebe
> und sîme volke trœsten gebe.

As Bernart says, it is Willehalm's duty to celebrate victory with his men; at this moment he is not free to withdraw and lament. To give way to sorrow would be unmanly (457, 1ff; cf. 268, 3ff, Heimrich tells Gyburg that she may not weep while her guests are at their pleasure; cf. Hardiz to Gahmuret, Parz. 93, 3f: *ob ir manheit kunnet tragn,/so sult ir leit ʒe mâʒen klagn*); but though he is bound to rejoice with his men, Willehalm's sorrow is so overwhelming that he admits his rejoicing in victory is a mere pretence (460, 16: *ich muoʒ gebáren als ich vrô/sî, des ich leider niht enbin*). His immoderate expressions of grief at the possibility of having lost Rennewart, which go as far as blasphemy when he blames Jesus for the disaster (456, 1: *mîner flust maht du dich schamn,/der meide kint*), show us how concerned Wolfram is to clear him of the charge of ingratitude when he celebrates without Rennewart. Furthermore, he acts as he does through Bernart's prompting, not his own inclination, which helps to relieve him of personal responsibility (cf. p. 161, note 1). It appears that, far from abandoning his source, Wolfram is here preparing to relate one of its most distasteful scenes, a scene he could hardly approve of himself and which, unless handled with the greatest care, threatened to become highly damaging for both Rennewart and Willehalm. In *Aliscans* Rainouart finally abandons the quarrel at the entreaty of Guibourc, who reminds him of the occasion at Orange when she had taken him into her room and given him fine clothes and arms (corresponding to the scene 'Gyburg's cloak' in *Willehalm*, cf. pp. 173ff); since Wolfram has emphasised

Gyburg's especial kindness to Rennewart and in that connection has paid particular attention to that particular scene, it seems that he was reckoning with her intervention at the end to restore peace and goodwill, showing again the power over Rennewart which her *güete* gives her.

When Rainouart and Guillaume have been reconciled, Rainouart is baptised. On account of the religious point of view of *Aliscans* this scene is absolutely essential – Rainouart cannot remain unbaptised – but it contributes little to the action and the poet treats it with good humour. It seems as though the greater part of Guillaume's *lignage*, doughty and numerous though they are, are needed to lift Rainouart out of the water:

> Al. 184e, 1   Baptisiés fu et levés Rainouars
> Si le leva Guillaumes et Bernars
> Et Aimeris, et Bertrans et Guichars
> Et Aïmers, qui est fiers et gaillars,
> De Commarcis Bueves, ses fils Gerars,
> Hernaus li Rous et Guibert d'Andernas.

Although Wolfram has overcome the religious dualism of his source and allows his Rennewart to resist baptism instead of being denied it, it is not likely that he intended Rennewart to persist in his denial of the true faith. When Rennewart loses faith in his Saracen gods and trusts in Christ, he expresses the hope that Christ will help him in his efforts to find a worthier way of life (193, 9ff). After Christ has justified that trust, Rennewart will have no cause to resist baptism any longer: what he had refused as an imposition he might now accept willingly. Although baptism is foreign to him by birth (193, 19: *nu ist mir der touf niht geslaht*), he has no god but Christ, and when he sees that his trust in Christ has been rewarded, then he must accept baptism as the essential symbol of his becoming a Christian; his situation is not significantly different from that of Gyburg, who has been baptised, and in baptism he will be more closely united with her.[1] If,

---

[1] Rennewart's words to Willehalm on the subject of his baptism, 193, 2–30, are grotesquely distorted in Weber's interpretation, 'Die Grundidee', p. 9: 'Rennewart bekannte sich zu der Meinung, für eine Konversion sei er nicht geschaffen; Christ werden sei seine Sache nicht; er wolle es nicht und er tue es nicht.'

as the predictions indicate (285, 15; 331, 13), Rennewart is to marry the daughter of the Christian emperor, then baptism will almost certainly be necessary as a preliminary condition, as when Feirefiz marries the bearer of the Grail. Nowadays we do not like to see a man lightly throw aside his religion, though that religion may not be our own; but for Wolfram the religion of Christians and that of Saracens are two quite different things. He respects the Saracens for their chivalrous qualities, but their religion is quite worthless, and no heathen can be praised for his loyalty to such deceivers as Mahmet and Tervigant – in this case infidelity is more commendable, as when Kanliun abandons his gods to follow his father. Wolfram certainly approves the same infidelity in Feirefiz, who abandons his gods at once to win a lady's hand. If a heathen deserves salvation, then it is not for his devotion to false gods, but for such genuine values as *triuwe* (Belakane), courage (Razalic) or exemplary *minne* (Tesereiz), and it is through *minne* that Gyburg and Feirefiz come to the true religion and will be saved. The religious depth of Gyburg is beyond dispute, but she plainly puts *minne* above the Saracen religion when she tells her father she would stay with Willehalm and remain a Christian even if the heathen gods were superior (220, 1ff).[1] Wolfram has set Rennewart upon the path that Gyburg followed, in full agreement with his source, and he has already revealed Rennewart's lack of faith in the Saracen gods and his deep concern to win Alyze's *minne*. Such preparation indicates that Wolfram intended to save Rennewart in the same way as Feirefiz and Gyburg. Mergell proposes (p. 179) that the difference between 'Frauenethik' and 'Mannesethik' might make this kind of conversion possible for Gyburg but not for Rennewart, and that Gyburg's conversion was unavoidable because it was so firmly established in the source; both these ideas may be ruled out in view of the example of Feirefiz, who is not hindered by 'Mannesethik', and the fact that Rainouart's baptism is just as

[1] At 298, 21 Willehalm implies that religion was her more important motive, but that is more modest than true; he says this in a political speech which contains at least one dreadful political lie (297, 14–19). Gyburg also stresses the religious motive on the same occasion (310, 17ff).

firmly established in the French tradition as Guibourc's conversion. Mergell also argues (p. 56) that Rennewart's marriage will not take place because Wolfram has not translated the early references to this event which occur in *Aliscans*, and he complains 'diese Tatsache wird meist nicht genügend gewürdigt'. The reason why it may safely be discounted is that *Aliscans* is packed with such allusions to coming events and it is regularly Wolfram's practice to ignore them (thus he ignores the many allusions to Rainouart in the early part of the *chanson*, cf. p. 94); the occasional predictive lines in *Willehalm* are Wolfram's own. But though he omits such references, he generally preserves the events when he comes to them. The argument of Rolin and Clarus that Rennewart is too low in rank and manners to marry a princess[1] is indefensible in view of Wolfram's very frequent references to Rennewart's high rank and his *ʒuht*; Alyze's kiss suggests that she does not consider him beneath her love. His baptism and his marriage are required for the satisfactory completion of the Rennewart action.

The prediction that Rennewart will receive the horse Lignmaredi is introduced very late (420, 22) and indicates that Wolfram still expected to finish his poem whilst working on Book IX. Rennewart has acquired other horses by killing their riders, but Lignmaredi belonged to Poydwiz, who is killed by Heimrich der Schetis, and so Wolfram may have intended the horse to be presented by Heimrich. In *Aliscans* Li Margaris is presented at Rainouart's investiture (we are not told by whom), and the theme of Rennewart's development which Wolfram has introduced suggests the episode will still be required. It will fulfil the expectation that Rennewart will eventually exchange the unworthy kitchen environment for true chivalry and it will make appropriate the sword that Gyburg gave him. Given a sword and a horse, and with the secret of his birth at last revealed, there can be no further doubt as to his worthiness to be accepted by knights as a knight. His investiture can thus be his public vindication and the proper climax to his career.

---

[1] Rolin, p. ix–x; cf. Clarus, p. 291.

A major reason for regarding *Willehalm* as a fragment has been the absence of a final settlement between Christians and Saracens.[1] This need might be satisfied through the marriage of Rennewart and Alyze, as Meissburger observes (p. 112): 'Wolfram lässt ahnen, dass Rennewarts Liebe zu Alyze in christlicher Ehe hätte erfüllt werden sollen – keine politische, aber eine poetisch-symbolische Überwindung der grossen Gegensätze, wie sie auch vom Parzival her bekannt ist.' This marriage can make Renne-wart's bonds to Christendom unbreakable while he remains linked by family and race to the Saracens. The marriage bond need not lack political value, because Rennewart's rank and power could enable him to express in deeds the sympathy which he and Alyze had achieved despite their religious differences before the battle (cf. p. 196). If reconciliation is at all possible, they are best able to bring it about; since only Rennewart is not moved by the desire to avenge Vivianz he alone may be able to break the vicious circle of revenge that has made tragedy inevitable (cf. 305, 30: *sus râch widr râche wart gegebn*). Alyze's ability to reconcile enemies is always her most striking feature.[2] By willingly giving his daughter, Loys might now atone for his earlier humiliating treatment of Rennewart, and if Terramer could approve the match with a message or gifts, as he might well do after Willehalm's generous show of respect for him (466, 19ff), then he would have overcome that *unvuoge* which Wolfram so sternly censures (11, 19–30) when he refuses to accept as a friend the husband whom his daughter has freely chosen. Together with Rennewart's investi-ture and baptism, this marriage can make an adequate conclusion to the Rennewart action, leaving no problems unsolved. The main action need not suffer from Rennewart's prominence, because his investiture and marriage contribute to the main action and Renne-wart will accept these honours from Willehalm. Willehalm himself must therefore be very prominent at this point and his magna-nimity will be equal to Rennewart's reward. Gyburg, too, will be

---

[1] Kienast, p. 114; Ranke, p. 68; Wolff, p. 521.

[2] Cf. p. 194. It is possible that Willehalm's strange remark, 156, 7, that it would be more fitting for Alyze to kneel before Terramer than himself, might be a prefigurative pre-diction of such a reconciliation.

prominent if her premonition that Rennewart may be her brother is to be proved correct and end in recognition, as at the end of *Aliscans*. Rennewart has been subordinated to Willehalm already, through the Matribleiz scene in which he has no part, and he will be subordinated again if Poydjus is to receive honours from Willehalm; Willehalm's generosity dominates all these scenes, while Rennewart appears only in some of them.

We have seen that the function of the Matribleiz scene is not, as has often been supposed, to facilitate an exchange of prisoners. The nature of the Saracen retreat suggests that Terramer has no prisoners. The scene may instead be regarded as the preparation for a final reconciliation which will translate Gyburg's *güete* (as expressed in her speech, 306, 1ff) into reality; such a reconciliation has been made possible by Gyburg's and Willehalm's kindness to the Saracen Rennewart: if this Saracen is acceptable, unbaptised, among Christians, then Saracen and Christian peoples might live side by side in mutual respect. It only remains for the Saracens themselves to accept this point of view; in particular, Terramer must abandon his claim to universal sovereignty. Such a change in the Saracen attitude has become possible because the catastrophe they have suffered may overcome their earlier stubbornness: their pride, which had made peace impossible, has now been humbled in defeat, and their suffering may make them earnestly desire peace.[1] It is the more probable because Willehalm has taken care not to humiliate the Saracens in defeat but to honour them. That is the meaning of the Matribleiz scene. Willehalm ignores Bernart's proposal that Matribleiz might be exchanged for Rennewart; to put pressure on the heathens at such a time by offering the noblest of the prisoners for barter could only humiliate them and arouse Terramer's defiance. Instead, Willehalm honours Terramer and sets the prisoners free without

---

[1] Cf. Knorr and Fink, p. 267. Bumke, pp. 36–9, regards Terramer as incapable of change. This discounts the effect of overwhelming defeat, of Gyburg's teaching and Willehalm's generosity in the Matribleiz scene, and it makes the poem unfinishable by bringing it back to a position very similar to its beginning. There seems to be a hint that defeat might cause the Saracens to modify their attitude when Oukin, shattered by the death of his son Poydwiz, expresses the wish that the Christians could respect a noble Saracen enemy and take his surety instead of killing him (421, 10–14).

imposing conditions or asking for reciprocation; this magnani-
mous gesture expresses Willehalm's *güete*, a quality that plays an
important rôle throughout the poem and a power to be reckoned
with. It enables Terramer to respond without compromising his
pride, and it may win for Willehalm the respect of the father as it
has won that of the son. Matribleiz faces his conqueror with
dignity and pride, speaking defiantly of his own honour and of the
battle so regrettably lost, yet he responds immediately to Willehalm's gesture, falling on his knees before him and praising his
triuwe and his *unverswigeniu güete* (463, 2–10). If this most honour-
able of Saracens can recognise Willehalm's *güete* and be thus
moved by it, despite the humiliation of capture and defeat, then
Terramer is not likely to respond otherwise. Terramer had been
urged to fight by the *bâruc unt de êwarten sîn* (217, 23): by expressing his respect not only for Terramer's *art* but also for the Saracen
ê (465, 19), Willehalm enables these authorities to recognise an
independent Christendom without loss of face (Terramer himself will be personally bound to the Christians through his son's
marriage to Alyze) and makes possible a final settlement in mutual
respect. In *Parʒival* the *bâruc* was able to set a Christian cross
upon Gahmuret's grave; the Saracens in *Willehalm* need show no
more respect than this.[1]

Rennewart's death offers no solution to the problems of the
main action; his baptism and marriage can contribute to a con-
ciliatory conclusion in which hostility is replaced by mutual
respect and goodwill. Rennewart does not usurp Willehalm's
rôle, but the poem ends as it began, with Willehalm and Terramer.
The function of Rennewart is to link the families of Willehalm,
Terramer and Loys through a marriage which seals and symbolises
the understanding between East and West which has been announced earlier in the poem, through Rennewart and Alyze and
through Gyburg, and which must reappear at its close.

[1] Parz. 107, 7–15. Cf. Mergell, p. 175.

SELECT BIBLIOGRAPHY

* Where several works by one scholar are listed, the asterisk marks the one to which I refer in the text by citation of the author's name alone.

EDITIONS OF TEXTS

Aliscans, ed. E. Wienbeck, W. Hartnacke and P. Rasch, Halle a.d.S., 1903.

Bataille Loquifer, ed. M. Barnett, Ph.D. thesis, London, 1959.

Chançun de Willame, ed. D. McMillan, *La Chanson de Guillaume*, SATF, Paris, 1949–50 (2 vols).

Chanson d'Antioche, ed. P. Paris, Paris, 1848 (2 vols).

Chanson de Roland, ed. F. Whitehead, Oxford, 1947.

Charroi de Nîmes, ed. J.-L. Perrier, Paris, 1931.

Chevalerie Vivien, ed. A. Terracher, Paris, 1909.

Couronnement de Louis, ed. E. Langlois, *Classiques Français du Moyen Âge*, col. 22, Paris, 1920.

Enfances Vivien, ed. C. Wahlund and H. von Feilitzen, Uppsala and Paris, 1895.

Kitzinger Bruchstücke, Die Schlacht von Alischanz, Kitzinger Bruchstücke, niederdeutsches Heldengedicht vom Anfange des 14. Jahrhunderts. Paderborn, 1874.

Prose Aliscans, ed. F. Reuter, *Die Bataille d'Arleschant des altfranzösischen Prosaromans Guillaume d'Orange*. Halle a.d.S., 1911.

Storie Nerbonesi, ed. I. Isola. Bologna, 1887 (4 vols).

Ulrich von Türheim, *Rennewart*, ed. A. Hübner, *Deutsche Texte des Mittelalters*, vol. 39. Berlin, 1938.

Wolfram von Eschenbach, ed. K. Lachmann, 6th edition. Berlin and Leipzig, 1926.

SECONDARY LITERATURE

Adler, A. 'Rainouart and the Composition of the Chanson de Guillaume,' Mod. Phil. 49 (1951–2), pp. 160–71.

Bacon, S. *The Source of Wolfram's Willehalm* (*Sprache und Dichtung*, Heft 4). Tübingen, 1910.

Barnett, M. La Bataille Loquifer, Ph.D. thesis, London, 1959.

Becker, P. 'Das Werden der Wilhelm- und der Aimerigeste,' *Abhandlungen der phil.-hist. Klasse der Sächsischen Akademie der Wissenschaften*, vol. 44, no. 1, Leipzig, 1939.*

Die altfranzösische Wilhelmsage und ihre Beziehung zu Wilhelm dem Heiligen. Halle a.d.S., 1896.

Review of Rolin, ZfrP 19 (1895), pp. 108–18.

Bédier, J. *Les Légendes Épiques*, vol. 1, *Le Cycle de Guillaume d'Orange.* Paris, 1926³.

Bernhardt, E. 'Zum Willehalm Wolframs von Eschenbach,' ZfdP 32 (1900), pp. 36–57.*

Review of Nassau Noordewier, ZfdP 34 (1902), pp. 542–9.

de Boor, H. *Die höfische Literatur.* (De Boor/Newald, *Geschichte der deutschen Literatur von den Anfängen bis zur Gegenwart*, vol. 2.) Munich, 1960⁴.

Buhr, W. *Studien zur Stellung des Wilhelmsliedes innerhalb der ältesten altfranzösischen Epen*, diss. Hamburg, 1963.

Bumke, J. *Wolframs Willehalm, Studien zur Epenstruktur und zum Heiligkeitsbegriff der ausgehenden Blütezeit.* Heidelberg, 1959.*

'König Galopp', MLN 76 (1961), pp. 261–3.

Wolfram von Eschenbach (Sammlung Metzler, no. 36). Stuttgart, 1964.

Chadwick, H. and N. *The Growth of Literature.* 3 vols, Cambridge, 1932.

Clarus, L. (pseudonym of W. G. W. Volk), *Herzog Wilhelm von Aquitanien, ein Grosser der Welt, ein Heiliger der Kirche, und ein Held der Sage und Dichtung.* Münster, 1865.

Csendes, P. 'Zur Orlensepisode in Wolframs *Willehalm*,' ZfdA 97 (1968), pp. 196–206.

Ehrismann, G. *Die mittelhochdeutsche Literatur, 1. Teil, Die Blütezeit (Geschichte der deutschen Literatur bis zum Ausgang des Mittelalters, vol. 2, 2).* Munich, 1935.*

'Über Wolframs Ethik,' ZfdA 49 (1908), pp. 405–65.

Frappier, J. *Les Chansons de geste du cycle de Guillaume d'Orange.* Paris, 1955.

Gibbs, M. A Study of the Women Characters in the Works of Wolfram von Eschenbach. M.A. thesis, London, 1965.

Gritzner, E. 'Symbole und Wappen des alten deutschen Reiches,' *Leipziger Studien aus dem Gebiete der Geschichte*, vol. 8, Heft 3. Leipzig 1902.

Guessard, F. and Montaiglon, A. de. *Aliscans (Les Anciens Poètes de la France*, vol. 10). Paris, 1870.

Harms, W. *Der Kampf mit dem Freund oder Verwandten in der deutschen Literatur bis um 1300 (Medium Aevum* 1). Munich, 1963.

Hatim, A. *Les Poèmes Épiques des Croisades.* Paris, 1932.

Helm, K. 'Die Entstehungszeit von Wolframs Titurel,' ZfdP 35 (1903), pp. 196–203.

Histoire Littéraire de la France, par les Réligieux Bénédictins de la Congrégation de S. Maur. Paris, 1733–1949 (revised by P. Paris, 1865).

Hitti, P. *A History of the Arabs.* London, 1958⁶.

Johnson, S. Review of Bumke, JEGP 60 (1961), pp. 371–3.*

A Commentary to Wolfram von Eschenbach's Willehalm, diss. Yale, 1953.

'Wolfram's *Willehalm*: 1952–1962,' JEGP 63 (1964) pp. 72–85 (a clear account of *Willehalm* research during the period under review).

Jonckbloet, J. *Guillaume d'Orange, Chanson de Geste des XIe et XIIe Siècles.* The Hague, 1854 (2 vols).

Kartschoke, D. *Willehalm. Urtext und Übersetzung* (including a useful commentary). Berlin, 1968.

Kienast, R. 'Zur Tektonik von Wolframs "Willehalm",' *Festschrift für Friedrich Panzer.* Heidelberg, 1950, pp. 96–115.

Knorr, F. and Fink, R. *Willehalm* (translation into modern German). Jena, 1944.

Koppitz, H. *Wolframs Religiosität. Beobachtungen über das Verhältnis Wolframs von Eschenbach zur religiösen Tradition des Mittelalters.* Bonn, 1958.

Krappe, A. 'The Origin of the Geste Rainouart,' *Neuphilologische Mitteilungen* 24 (1923), pp. 1–10.

Künstle, K. *Ikonographie der christlichen Kunst.* Freiburg im Breisgau, 1928 (2 vols).

Lorenz, P. 'Das Handschriftenverhältnis der Chanson der geste "Aliscans",' *ZfrP* 31 (1907), pp. 385–431.

Lot, F. 'Études sur les Légendes Épiques Françaises,' IV: 'Le Cycle de Guillaume d'Orange,' *Romania* 53 (1927), pp. 449–73.

Maurer, F. *Leid. Studien zur Bedeutungs- und Problemgeschichte, besonders in den grossen Epen der staufischen Zeit.* (*Bibliotheca Germanica* 1), Bern and Munich, 1951.

McMillan, D. *La Chanson de Guillaume*, SATF. Paris, 1949–50 (2 vols).*
Review of Riquer, *Romania* 75 (1954), pp. 255–62.

Meissburger, G. 'Willehalmprobleme', *Archiv* 198 (1961), pp. 310–14.*
Review of Bumke, ZfdP 81 (1962), pp. 109–17.
'Gyburg,' ZfdP 83 (1964), pp. 64–99.
'"Güete" bei Wolfram von Eschenbach,' *Festgabe für Friedrich Maurer zum 70. Geburtstag.* Freiburg im Breisgau, 1968, pp. 158–77.

Mendels, J. and Spuler, L. 'Landgraf Hermann von Thüringen und seine Dichterschule,' DVJS 33 (1959), pp. 361–88.

Mergell, B. *Wolfram von Eschenbach und seine französischen Quellen*, 1. Teil: *Wolframs Willehalm.* Münster, 1936.*
Wolfram von Eschenbach und seine französischen Quellen, 2. Teil: *Wolframs Parzival.* Münster, 1943.

Mohr, W. 'Parzivals ritterliche Schuld,' *Wirkendes Wort* 2 (1952), pp. 148–60 (reprinted in *Wirkendes Wort, 2. Sammelband: Ältere deutsche Sprache und Literatur*). Düsseldorf, 1962, pp. 196–208.

Nassau Noordewier, J. *Bijdrage tot de Beoordeeling van den Willehalm*, diss. Groningen, publ. Delft 1901.

Nellmann, E. *Die Reichsidee in deutschen Dichtungen der Salier- und frühen Stauferzeit* (PSQ 16). Berlin, 1963.

Palgen, R. 'Willehalm, Rolandslied und Eneide,' PBB 44 (1920), pp. 191–241.

Panzer, F. *Studien ȝur germanischen Sagengeschichte.* (2 vols.); vol. 1: *Beowulf.* Munich, 1910.*
Italische Normannen in deutscher Heldensage (Deutsche Forschungen, Heft 1). Frankfurt-am-Main, 1925.

Perdrizet, P. *La Vièrge de Miséricorde, étude d'un thème iconographique.* Paris, 1908.

Rajna, P. *Le Origini dell'epopea francese.* Florence, 1956².

Ranke, F. *Gott, Welt und Humanität in der deutschen Dichtung des Mittelalters.* Basle, 1953.

Richey, M. 'Wolfram von Eschenbach and the Paradox of the Chivalrous Life,' *German Studies presented to Leonard Ashley Willoughby.* Oxford, 1952, pp. 159–70.

de Riquer, M. *Los Cantares de Gesta Franceses, sus problemas, su relación con España.* Madrid, 1952 (there is a translation into French by I. Cluzel, *Les Chansons de Geste Françaises,* Paris, 1957).

Rolin, G. *Aliscans, mit Berücksichtigung von Wolframs von Eschenbach Willehalm (Altfranȝösische Bibliothek* 15). Leipzig, 1897.

Runeberg, J. *Études sur la Geste Rainouart,* diss. Helsinki, 1905.

Rychner, J. 'Sur la Chanson de Guillaume,' *Romania* 76 (1955), pp. 28–38.

San-Marte (pseudonym of A. Schultz), *Über Wolframs von Eschenbach Rittergedicht Wilhelm von Orange und sein Verhältnis ȝu den altfranȝösischen Dichtungen gleichen Inhalts.* Quedlinburg and Leipzig, 1871.

Scherer, W. *Geschichte der deutschen Literatur.* Berlin, 1883.

Schreiber, A. *Neue Bausteine ȝu einer Lebensgeschichte Wolframs von Eschenbach (Deutsche Forschungen* 7). Frankfurt-am-Main, 1922.

Schröder, W. J. Review of Bumke, PBB 82 (1960), pp. 411–21.

Schröder, Werner. 'Armuot,' DVJS 34 (1960), pp. 501–26.
'Süeziu Gyburg,' Euph 54 (1960), pp. 39–69.
Review of Bumke, Euph 55 (1961), pp. 91–7.
'Christliche Paradoxa in Wolframs *Willehalm,*' Euph 55 (1961), pp. 85–90.
'Zur Entwicklung des Helden in Wolframs "Willehalm",' *Festschrift für Ludwig Wolff ȝum 70. Geburtstag.* Neumünster, 1962, pp. 265–76.
'Minne und ander klage,' ZfdA 93 (1964), pp. 300–13.
'Zum gegenwärtigen Stande der Wolfram-Kritik,' ZfdA 96 (1967), pp. 1–28.
'Der Markgraf und die gefallenen Heidenkönige in Wolframs "Willehalm",' *Festschrift für Konstantin Reichardt.* Bern and Munich, 1969, pp. 135–67.

Schué, K. 'Das Gnadenbitten in Recht, Sage und Kunst,' *Zeitschrift des Aachener Geschichtsvereins* 40 (1918).

Schultz, A. *Das höfische Leben zur Zeit der Minnesinger.* Leipzig, 1889[2] (2 vols).

Schuwerack, J. *Charakteristik der Personen in der altfranzösischen Chançun de Guillelme (Romanistische Arbeiten 1).* Halle a.d.S., 1913.

Schwietering, J. *Die deutsche Dichtung des Mittelalters.* Darmstadt, 1957.

Singer, S. *Wolframs Willehalm.* Bern, 1918.

Steinhoff, H. *Die Darstellung gleichzeitiger Geschehnisse im mittelhochdeutschen Epos (Medium Aevum 4).* Munich, 1964.

Suchier, H. *La Chançun de Guillelme.* Halle a.d.S., 1911.*
'Über das niederrheinische Bruchstück der Schlacht von Aleschans,' *Germanistische Studien* 1 (1872), pp. 134–58.
'Vivien,' ZfrP 29 (1905), pp. 641–82.

Sumberg, L. 'The "Tafurs" and the First Crusade,' *Mediaeval Studies* (Toronto) 21 (1959), pp. 224–46.

Sussmann, V. 'Maria mit dem Schutzmantel,' *Marburger Jahrbuch für Kunstwissenschaft* 5 (1929), pp. 285–331.

Vogt, F. *Geschichte der mittelhochdeutschen Literatur.* Berlin and Leipzig, 1922[3].

Walshe, M. O'C. *Mediaeval German Literature. A Survey.* London, 1962.

Wathelet-Willem, J. 'La Chançun de Willame, Le Problème de l'unité du ms. British add. 38663,' *Le Moyen Âge* 58 (1952), pp. 363–77.
'Quelle est l'origine du tinel de Rainouart?,' *BRABLB* 31 (1965–6), pp. 355–64.

Weber, G. *Wolfram von Eschenbach, seine dichterische und geistesgeschichtliche Bedeutung,* vol. 1: *Stoff und Form (Deutsche Forschungen* 18). Frankfurt-am-Main, 1928.*
'Die Grundidee in Wolframs "Willehalm",' *Literaturwissenschaftliches Jahrbuch* 6 (1965), pp. 1–21.

Weeks, R. 'The Newly Discovered Chançun de Willame,' Mod Phil 2 (1904), pp. 1–16, and Mod Phil 3 (1905), pp. 211–34.

Wentzlaff-Eggebert, F. *Kreuzzugsdichtung des Mittelalters. Studien zu ihrer geschichtlichen und dichterischen Wirklichkeit.* Berlin, 1960.

Willson, B. 'Einheit in der Vielheit in Wolframs Willehalm,' ZfdP 80 (1961), pp. 40–62.
'Bernard Willson zu Werner Schröder,' Euph 56 (1962), p. 208f.

Wolff, L. 'Der Willehalm Wolframs von Eschenbach,' DVJS 12 (1934), pp. 504–39.

INDEX